Unless otherwise credited, photographs, charts, tables and images were taken or created by the author.

Copyright 2016 by Fred L. McGhee, Ph.D.

Original copyright 2000, by Fred L. McGhee, Ph.D.

All rights reserved. No part of this publication may be reproduced, stored in a retrieval system, or transmitted, in any form or by any means, electronic, mechanical, photocopying, recording or otherwise without prior written permission of the publisher.

Published by Fidelitas Publishing
2316 Thrasher Lane
Austin, TX 78741-6622

Cover: The "Moral Map of the United States" by Julius Rubens Ames was first published in 1837 before the annexation of Texas and was republished several times in the years leading up the Civil War. Public domain image stored at the Cornell University Library and furnished under the GNU Free Documentation License.

Library of Congress Control Number: 2016900997

ISBN 978-0-9972218-0-0

Printed in the United States of America

THE BLACK CROP: SLAVERY AND SLAVE TRADING IN NINETEENTH CENTURY TEXAS

by

Fred Lee McGhee, B.S., M.A.

Dissertation

Presented to the Faculty of the Graduate School of

the University of Texas at Austin

in Partial Fulfillment

of the Requirements

for the Degree of

Doctor of Philosophy

The University of Texas at Austin

May 2000

I am...of those who believe that the work of the American Anti-Slavery Society will not have been completed until the black men of the South and the black men of the North, shall have been admitted, fully and completely, into the body politic of America.....A mightier work than the abolition of slavery now looms up before the Abolitionists. This society was organized, if I remember rightly, for two distinct objects: one was the emancipation of the slave, and the other the elevation of colored people. When we have taken the chains off the slave, as I believe we shall do, we shall find a harder resistance to the second purpose of this great association than we have found even upon slavery itself.
Frederick Douglass, 1863

Every artist, every scientist, must decide NOW where he stands. He has no alternative. There is no standing above the conflict on Olympian heights. There are no impartial observers. Through the destruction—in certain countries—of the greatest of man's literary heritages, through the propagation of false ideas of racial and national superiority, the artist, the scientist, the writer is challenged. The battlefront is everywhere. There is no sheltered rear.
Paul Robeson, 1937

The mere imparting of information is not education.
Carter G. Woodson, *The Mis-Education of the Negro*, p. xxx

....just because you have colleges and universities, doesn't mean you have education. The colleges and universities in the American educational system are skillfully used to miseducate.
Malcom X, interview in *Young Socialist*, March-April, 1965

What we want is the right to be right, and the right to be wrong.
Bob Marley, 1976

My feelings about myself have been terrible. The whole of where I came from, the Brazos Valley in Texas, picking cotton in my early life, being with my mother and not with my father, living through the 1930's, the lack of a real father, not having enough food sometimes, going around to those churches and the Dew Drop Inns, all left an enormous stain and a sense of inferiority that lasted for many years. I felt that no matter what I did, what ballet I made, how beautifully I danced, it was not good enough. Even now I doubt whether the new ballet is going to be what it really should be—even though I've made 150 ballets. That's one of the worst things about racism, what it does to young people. It tears down your insides so that no matter what you achieve, no matter what you write or choreograph, you feel it's not quite enough. You're not quite up to snuff.
Alvin Ailey, 1988

Great musicians are like great fighters. They have a higher sense of theory going on in their heads. I feel strong creatively now, and I feel I'm getting even stronger.
Miles Davis, 1989

THE BLACK CROP: SLAVERY AND SLAVE TRADING IN

NINETEENTH CENTURY TEXAS

Publication No._____

Fred Lee McGhee, Ph.D.
The University of Texas at Austin, 2000

Supervisor: Samuel M. Wilson

This dissertation is an interdisciplinary investigation of the origins, development and effects of nineteenth century African and African-American slave trading in Texas. The research is mainly archival in nature and relies theoretically on material from several humanities disciplines and social sciences, including ethnohistory, anthropology, geography, and archaeology.

The project is the first investigation to focus on both African and African-American slave trading into and/or through Texas and is thus significant as a baseline study. The main history of Texas slavery, Randolph Campbell's (1989) *An Empire for Slavery*, discounts the role of the internal slave trade, as does a 1972 Master's Thesis on the subject (Robbins 1972), but Tadman's (1989) more exhaustive inquiry of antebellum Negro speculation reveals that fully <u>up to 70 percent</u> of Blacks in Texas in 1860 had been traded into the state. This stunning statistic has obvious implications for the social and economic development of Texas, as contemporary race relations in the Lone Star State attest. My investigation is a follow-up to projects such as Du Bois's 1896 landmark study on the African slave trade *The Suppression of the African Slave Trade to the United States* (Du Bois estimated that 75,000 Africans were smuggled into or through Texas in the nineteenth century), and situates the role of the trade in its proper historical perspective as being fundamental to Texas' economic and social development.

The study also situates the role of the internal and

external slave trade into ongoing discussions concerning the development of nineteenth century American westward expansion and imperialism, as well as into the development of nineteenth century American capitalism. Slave trading was a basic and underappreciated component of the economic development of Texas, and also enriched many northern business elites such as Charles Morgan, who provided the first regular steamship service into Texas, as well as William Marsh Rice, for whom Rice University is named.

In addition to discussing some of the economic and historical effects of the trade, the dissertation uses ethnohistory—primary source material includes personal correspondence and the WPA slave narratives—to uncover the attitudes and passions exhibited by masters and traders in Texas, and emphasizes how the trade felt from the slaves' point of view.

TABLE OF CONTENTS

INTRODUCTION	1
CHAPTER 1: A BRIEF WORD ON THEORY	17
Noam Chomsky and Edward W. Said	21
The Du Boisians: Herbert Aptheker, Manning Marable and Ronald Bailey	35
Paul Gilroy's Black Atlantic	42
Michel-Rolph Trouillot's Silencing the Past	45
Michael Tadman's Speculators and Slaves	49
CHAPTER 2: ASSESSMENT OF SOME OF THE LITERATURE	54
Abigail Curlee Holbrook	58
Richard Francaviglia's From Sail to Steam	68
Randolph B. Campbell's An Empire for Slavery	73
Edward T. Cotham Jr.'s Battle on the Bay	84
Stephen R. Wise's Lifeline of the Confederacy	89
CHAPTER 3: THE GEOGRAPHY OF THE TEXAS GULF COAST AND AN OVERVIEW OF THE TEXAS SLAVE TRADE	96
Physiography	96

Climate 100

Human Habitation And Adaption Along The Gulf
Coast 102

European Impressions Of Texas 104

Rivers In Texas 108

Disease 110

A Smuggler's Haven 114

Characterizing and Estimating the Extent of the
Slave Trade 117

CHAPTER 4: PIRATES, PRIVATEERS, AND ANGLO
SETTLERS; THE FIRST SLAVES COME TO TEXAS 134

The Beginning of the African-American Slave Trade:
Anglo Settlement 151

Anglo African Slave Trading 157

The Role of Slavery and the Slave Trade in the
Texas Revolution 162

CHAPTER 5: THE INCREASE OF SLAVERY AND SLAVE
TRADING DURING THE REPUBLIC PERIOD AND THE

FLOWERING OF MANIFEST DESTINY 179
Other Evidence of African and African-American
Slave Trading 190
Texas: A Place to Make One's Fortune 195
The Slave Trade and the Annexation of Texas 197

CHAPTER 6: THE GOLDEN AGE OF THE TEXAS "SUGAR
BOWL" AND KING COTTON 208
A Brief Snapshot of Antebellum Texas 212
Foxes Minding the Henhouse: The Misadventures of
Being a Free Sailor in Texas 219
Texas African Slave Trading in the 1850's 231
The Lone Star Yankee: Two Case Studies 240
The Texas Planter Class 266

CHAPTER 7: "SOLD FROM THEIR MAMA'S BREAST"; THE
FOLKTALES AND ORAL HISTORY OF ENSLAVED
TEXANS 283
The WPA Narratives 287
Reeves Tucker 292

Mary Gaffney	293
Mariah Robinson	294
Betty Simmons	295
William Hamilton	296
Walter Rimm	296
Mintie Maria Miller	297
James Brown	298
Tom Holland	299
Henry Lewis	299
Wes Brady	300
Uncle Cinto Lewis	300
Annie Hawkins	300
Lewis Jenkins	301
Allen V. Manning	302
Phyllis Petite	303
Harriet Robinson	304
Andrew Simms	305
Liza Smith	307

Lou Smith	307
Mollie Watson	309
John White	310
The Peculiar Experiences of Female Enslavement	312
Rose Williams	317
Betty Powers	319
Lizzie Jones	319
Lewis Jones	320
Katie Darling	320
Mary Gaffney	321
Fannie Norman	322
Ida Henry	323
Harriet Robinson	324
Lou Smith	325
CHAPTER 8: THE USE AND ABUSE OF TEXAS HISTORY	327
"Means Testing" Historical Significance	336
Military Sites and What Else?	344

APPENDIX A: A NEW DIRECTION FOR HISTORY AND

ARCHAEOLOGY IN TEXAS (AND ELSEWHERE)	352
REFERENCES	358
VITA	385

INTRODUCTION

Texas is more than a place. It is a frame of mind. A Texan believes that the individual is powerful. Texas has that rugged individualism. It may not be polished, may not be smooth, and it may not be silky, but it is there. I believe that I get from the soil and the spirit of Texas the feeling that I, as an individual, can accomplish whatever I want to and that there are no limits, that you can just keep going, just keep soaring. I like that spirit.
—Barbara Jordan (cited in Lanker 1989)

This dissertation constitutes my interpretation of central aspects of Texas history. More specifically, it is a revisionist view of African American history in Texas, and places specific empirical emphasis on the impact of the practice of slave speculation between about 1816 and 1870. The study also comments extensively on the legacy of racism and historical silencing that still exist as a result of the processes of the "manufacture of consent" in Texas and the United States at large.

Any scholar attempting a revisionist retelling of Texas history is inviting criticism and controversy, and I might as well begin by stating up front that this dissertation is by no means the final word on slavery and slave trading in Texas. It really isn't the beginning word either; much of the information

I present here is familiar to Texas historians. What is different is my interpretation of the information. My hope is that this study will launch a prolonged and fruitful discussion about contemporary race relations in Texas and can serve as an empowerment tool for activists in the ongoing "culture wars" being waged not only in educational institutions but in other public policy arenas as well. Since I am also actively and explicitly committed to advancing the cause of race, class, and gender justice and am attempting a historical reformulation that in many circles would be considered "radical," or "Marxist," I also here provide a brief reflexive discussion and positioning about my political and personal feelings regarding this topic.

I first came to Texas in September of 1993 (other than a brief stay at the Dallas/Ft. Worth airport four years earlier) while serving onboard a U.S. Navy mine warfare vessel, USS GLADIATOR (MCM-11). During my two year tour of duty onboard this ship I had ample opportunity to familiarize myself with the peculiarities of life and culture along the Texas gulf coast. I grew to appreciate the coast's unique and often strange geographical features and learned much about the people inhabiting the coastal bend region, from shrimpers and fishermen/women to surfers. After leaving active duty in April of 1995, I came to the University of Texas to study Polynesian seafaring but eventually realized that my experiences as an African-American sailor, an increasing interface with students and faculty affiliated with UT Austin's well regarded and dynamic African Diaspora program (the jointly sponsored UT Austin/UNESCO African Diaspora conference that took place in January of 1996 was particularly influential on my thinking in this regard), and a developing political commitment to first study "locally" instead of in a far removed place, led me to focus my scholarly and activist energies on the Lone Star State.

During the spring of 1996 I began working for the Housing Authority of the City of Austin (HACA), first as a "learning center" teacher at a public housing site, and later as the agency's communications specialist. I resigned in protest from the agency in August of that year and have since worked as an affordable housing and public housing activist. As I would eventually find out, there is considerable overlap between the public housing world and archaeological practice, particularly the practices of CRM (cultural resource management). Since April 1997 I have been involved in community attempts to preserve the well known neighborhood of Fourth Ward in Houston. In Austin I have worked on an individual basis as well as with various educational, advocacy, and social service institutions in addressing Austin's large wealth and wage inequalities. In addition to my academic interests and pursuits, I am also serving as an unpaid housing policy analyst and consultant/advisor to the Chalmers Courts Resident Council in Austin, and serve as a "special advisor" regarding archaeological, historical, and anthropological matters to the Resident Council of Allen Parkway Village in Houston. Working with these groups has been a great honor and privilege, and have been professionally and personally very enriching experiences.

As a result of these connections and experiences I grew to understand some of the unique racisms that exist in Texas and decided that the situation merited further study. The more I learned, the more fascinated I became. I came to realize that the settlement of the state, particularly by nineteenth century Anglos, involved interesting and particularly disturbing variants of American racism and imperialism. It also seemed to me that the role of African-Americans in the "making of Texas" (Montejano 1987) was underappreciated and understudied, at least when compared with the more numerous studies of Mexican and Mexican-American life in the Lone Star State.[1] There is an urgent need

---

[1] My investigation of Black Texas is in many ways an extension of the work of Black anthropology pioneer (and Native Texan) William S. Willis Jr., whose ethnohistories of the American Southeast consistently stressed the need to study the experiences and roles of African-Americans in addition to Native Americans (Willis 1970). In much of Texas, particularly in Austin, the study of Texas history and culture has been explained largely from the standpoint of Mexican-Americans. While this is certainly understandable, the narrative is in significant need of modification.

to set the record straight about the African-American experience in Texas; schoolbooks and studies are still perpetuating the myth that slavery in Texas was less oppressive and easier than in other states (Willoughby 1993), despite overwhelming evidence that this was hardly the case. As I hope to show in this dissertation, the central role of speculation—the buying, shipping, and selling of enslaved people with the intention of making a profit on these transactions—could lead one to argue that slavery in Texas was <u>worse</u> than in other states.[2] The nineteenth century demographic and economic "development" of Texas demand a focus on the institution of slavery and the most ribald component of the institution of slavery, slave trading.

I have chosen to begin this introduction with a quote by Barbara Jordan because the former congressperson and

---

[2] Although one could develop such an argument, I will not do so. The attempt would be an exercise in moral doublethink. However the seeming need by Curlee (1932) and others since to perpetuate the notion of "easy" slavery in Texas is a peculiar and all too familiar remnant of the paternalistic and hypocritical justifications put forth by mid-nineteenth century slavery apologists who believed that the institution was "necessary" and "civilizing" for the slaves. I will discuss Curlee's role in the perpetuation of Texas slavery myth in chapter two.

educator is a highly regarded, even worshipped, member of the late twentieth century African-American elite in Texas. I have also enclosed a photograph of her grave at the Texas state cemetery (Figure 1) to illustrate some of the race and class irony that was and remains a significant part of Texas culture, an irony which Limón (1994) characterizes as "dancing with the devil."[3] I am not particularly concerned here with whether the "rugged individualism" Jordan lauds infuses Texans with a special, perhaps even unique, spirit or toughness. The folklore and tall tales Texans have spun over the years about such matters are well known and widespread; it should not come as a surprise that elites such as Jordan should also engage in such pompous bantering.[4] What I find fascinating is that elitist and unremarkable individuals such as Jordan are celebrated in

---

[3] As figure 1 shows, Barbara Jordan is buried next to a grave marked "Fannin." The Fannin in question is Minerva Fannin, daughter of James W. Fannin, "hero" of the battle of Goliad during the Texas revolution, and a notorious slave trader.

[4] That Jordan should now be lauded across a wide spectrum of political opinion in the Lone Star State despite her rather mediocre legislative record (i.e. very pro-corporate) bespeaks a recurring trend in Texas culture and sociopolitics to glorify style over substance and to emphasize personalities instead of realities in the contemporary discourse and historical record.

Texas and nationally as <u>progressive</u> forces in American race relations, despite the fact that even a cursory examination of the evidence (e.g. their voting record) indicates that these individuals are thoroughly mainstream ideologically, and are held up as examples as much as for what they <u>do not</u> question as for what they do manage to accomplish.[5]

In his recent book on late nineteenth and early twentieth century racial and ethnic relations in Texas, Foley (1997: 2) captures the dominant sentiment well: "tourists flock to San Antonio more than any other Texas city because it alone captures the image that Texans most like to project of themselves—defenders of the Alamo, victors in the war against Mexico, pioneers in the western wilderness, manly cowboys and rich cattle barons." Regarding slavery, Campbell (1989: 1) notes that "there is a widespread popular misconception,

---

[5] Another contemporary example of this phenomenon would be Mary Frances Berry, current controversial chair of the Pacifica Board.

Figure 1: Barbara Jordan's headstone next to Minerva Fannin's headstone at the Texas State Cemetery in Austin
Photo by the Author

particularly in Texas, that somehow the institution of Negro slavery was not very important in the Lone Star State. This is not really surprising in that many historians, writers, and creators of popular culture have preferred to see Texas as essentially western rather than southern." It is a cornerstone of my argument that Texas, in the nineteenth century at least, is best viewed as the western end of the south instead of as distinctively "southwestern."

The time has now come to take the next step in the rewriting of Texas and the west. Not only was slavery a fundamental and intrinsic aspect of nineteenth century Texas, but slave trading—or "negro speculation" as it was technically known—was an integral aspect of the peculiar institution as it was practiced in the Lone Star State. Recent scholarship (e.g. Tadman 1996[1989]) is pointing out the degree to which both African and African-American slave trading were indispensable components of not only the plantation system, but also a way for eager entrepreneurs to earn quick and easy returns on a relatively small investment. A significant (and the most speculative) portion of this activity was conducted via the sea and enriched both northern merchant shippers as well as southern planters, and is thus a proper topic of investigation for maritime history.

When George W. Featherstonhaugh who visited Texas between 1834 and 1835 noted that the "*black crop* will produce more money to the proprietors than any other crop they can cultivate" (Featherstonhaugh 1844: 189) he recognized, as the Texans themselves did, that the institution of slavery and the "Texas Dream" advertised by Stephen F. Austin and his successors were inextricably bound. Slavery and slave trading were not an aberration in the history of Texas, and the story of the slaves themselves should not be considered "bumps in the road" of a Texas storybook otherwise filled with wisdom, progress, and enlightenment. Furthermore, the ideology of "free enterprise" and of mid-nineteenth century "Manifest Destiny" and imperialist expansion were also inseparably intertwined with slavery and slave trading.

This dissertation begins with a discussion of the theoretical underpinnings underlying the discussion that follows in the later chapters. Throughout, the approach is an interdisciplinary, sometimes eclectic one, but the arguments raised are basically anthropological and sociological ones. Chapter two contains a brief assessment of some of the literature on Texas slavery and slave trading and critiques much of the scholarly and quasi-scholarly literature on the subject as being little more than racist, sexist, and classist Texas propaganda.[6] Chapter three is a brief description of the geography of the Texas gulf coast, and briefly discusses the environmental adaptions of the aboriginal inhabitants of the area based on a study by Ricklis (1996). These environmental adaptions remain a fundamental part of the geography of the

---

[6] I will also make some brief observations about how the "history" of slavery and slave trading is presented (or not presented) in Texas schools. As might be imagined, this history is woefully misrepresentful, blissfully ignorant, and in spots outright racist.

Texas gulf coast.[7] I also provide a summation of the character and degree of the nineteenth century slave trade; figures and charts are produced to provide a rough outline of how the slave trade grew in the fifty or so years between 1815 and 1865. Chapter four begins with a general description of the early nineteenth century Texas slave trade (1815-1836) as it was conducted by pirates and privateers, and ends with a brief discussion of some of the politics underlying the Texas revolution and the justifications put forth by Texans for secession.

Chapter five assesses the role of slave trading during the republic period and attempts to situate the role of slavery and slave trading in the agitation for statehood by Texanized northerners and southerners.

---

[7] I do not wish to be perceived as an environmental determinist, however. My position on prehistoric adaption is similar to Clive Gamble's: instead of arguing that "human colonization [was] driven by chance, hunger, population pressure, the wind or that lucky technological breakthrough" as is often the case in archaeology, I prefer a more agentive interpretation that emphasizes "....a human prehistory where choice and contingency played a dominant part in exploration and colonization although tempered by the forces of the environment" (1997: 144-145).

Chapter six examines the period between 1845 and 1865, a period when slave trading was flourishing along the gulf coast and when many Texas elites were propagandizing for the decriminalization of the African slave trade into Texas. This period also saw the introduction of a remarkable number of slaves into Texas and can be utilized to make some general observations about the prospects for continued expansion of the institution had the civil war not resulted in gradual abolition of the traffic. Emphasis is based on the maritime component of the trade, particularly the trading of the Morgan steamship line and the activities of smugglers and bootleggers active on the Texas frontier.

Chapter seven is based almost exclusively on the Texas slave narratives and attempts to "ethnographize" slavery and slave trading. By letting the oral history speak for itself, I hope to show that the narratives have the potential for extensive use by scholars interested in emphasizing historical agency in addition to or in place of facts and figures. The slave narratives are an essential component of any attempt to produce an ethnohistory of the institution and in my view have been unfairly maligned as being inaccurate or as being source material of questionable value. I hope to show that the narratives are as good a source of information as any source, and are for the slave trade scholar one of the best sources available. In addition to citing a representative sample of the WPA narratives, I also briefly examine African-American folktales from Texas and make some comments on the light they shed on the slavery and slave trading experience in the Lone Star State.

Chapter eight assesses the evidence introduced in the previous chapters and argues that contemporary Texas sociopolitics have been profoundly influenced by what Michel-Rolph Trouillot (1995) terms the attempts by elites to "silence the past" of the historically disenfranchised and exploited. I briefly describe a contemporary example of political misuse of history in Houston, compare the justifications given by elites for marginalizing and manipulating African-Americans and other minority groups, and draw correlations between these contemporary attitudes and their antecedents.

I show that deliberate and unconscious propaganda is utilized by various actors in the Texas history and historic preservation community to keep the public misled and misinformed about the true nature and legacy of slavery and slave trading in Texas; I also show that much of the factual information regarding the institution is readily available if one chooses to look; many of the studies, however, are in obscure or old regional journals, are out of print, or are studiously ignored by scholars and public/private officials. The lessons to be learned from this are instructive and not surprising.

CHAPTER 1: A BRIEF WORD ON THEORY

The African American experience holds a different lens up to an old tale. The wide angles reveal heroes standing in the shadows. Its close-ups either challenge or add new dimensions to ancient myths, and ask scholars and citizens to scrutinize afresh treasured events and figures that have been placed on pedestals.
—William Loren Katz (1996: xviii)

The primary theoretical perspective utilized in this study is "postcolonialism," a sometimes messy but by now reasonably well understood term. Within disciplines such as anthropology and literary criticism, postcolonial theory has been influenced by, among other things, Marxist-influenced critical theory, poststructuralism, and hermeneutics, as well as by native intellectuals writing "against" colonialism and imperialist domination. Within history and historiography the perspective which most closely approximates this approach is the "new historicist" school, embodied by historians such as Eric Foner, Ronald Bailey, Maggie Montesinos Sale and others.[8] The "new" historians have been more prone to write about domestic

---

8   Foner is best known for his monumental "new" historical treatment of reconstruction (Foner 1988). Sale's recent work *The Slumbering Volcano* is an excellent analysis of nineteenth century slave ship revolts and the manner in which these were portrayed in the press. I cover Bailey's work later in this chapter.

subject matter such as the Civil War or Reconstruction, whereas postcolonial anthropologists have largely confined themselves to the study of culture and politics outside of the U.S. One of my theoretical goals in this study is to utilize anthropological insights usually applied in the study of "exotic" cultures in an examination of "empire" and nation-building within the mainland United States. One of the more powerful and insightful criticisms made by some of the writers discussed in this chapter is the idea that loci of power (and in the contemporary world, this means the United States and its satellites) should be vigorously scrutinized, denormalized, and situated within a socioeconomic context that never loses sight of the imbalanced and historically constituted power relations that drive modern domestic and international relations. The nineteenth-century subjugation of much of North America by the United States is not only a fascinating and very important historical phenomenon, but is also far too infrequently studied by anthropologists. The primary reason why this is so is not that difficult to ascertain: anthropology facilitated the process of conquest, colonization, genocide, and enslavement. In his important study of "European Mythmaking in the Pacific", for instance, (1997: xiii) Gananath Obeyesekere makes clear the degree to which "science" and empire colluded to justify imperial rule, and also skillfully fleshes out some of the "serious methodological and ethical problems pertaining to the writing and construction of ethnography and the ways in which the native has been represented" within anthropology.[9] There is considerable and exciting room to expand upon the arguments Obeyesekere makes. The rationale (and methods) utilized by the United States in the annexation of Hawai'i were

---

[9] The problems are well understood by the Natives themselves. Native Hawaiian intellectual Haunani-Kay Trask observes: "At some time in their professional lives, anthropologists live with Natives who are in struggle, dispossessed, and in some cases endangered. But in the interests of knowledge or science or some other abstraction, the anthropologist has no obligation to aid the people he or she studies, to withhold information that threatens the people or is considered sacred or privileged to them, or to be a part of their struggles, whatever they may be. *In other words, the anthropologist is a taker and a user.* And if people who are taken suffer from the anthropologist's work, too bad. No moral or ethical responsibility attaches to the anthropologist or the archaeologist" (Trask 1999: 127).

well rehearsed and applied in Texas about fifty years before.[10]

---

[10] Interestingly, political deliberation in Congress and southern propaganda in the press regarding the annexation of Texas was already envisioning the eventual colonization and annexation of Hawai'i and other territories in the Pacific. For further illuminating discussion regarding the imperial ambitions of Presidents Tyler and Polk (who mentioned "the need to protect U.S. shipping interests in Hawai'i" in the early 1840's while the Texas and Oregon questions were being debated), see Hietala (1985), *Manifest Design*.

Noam Chomsky and Edward W. Said

I have chosen to discuss these theorists together because they are the most direct influence on this study and because their work (as well as their activism) overlaps to a considerable degree.[11]

Chomsky is well known as a linguist and critic of U.S. foreign policy; what often gets overlooked is the fact that he is also a first rate social theorist and a tenacious sociologist and historian, although Chomsky would eschew the label of "theory" for his historical approach.[12] In his introduction to *The Chomsky Reader*, James Peck writes that "Chomsky's achievement lies in the extraordinary and illuminating

---

[11] Said, for instance, thanks Chomsky in his introduction to *Orientalism*, and wrote the introduction for the latest edition of *Fateful Triangle*, Chomsky's well known study of the Mideast.

[12] For Chomsky "theoretical understanding" refers to mathematically specific and verifiable methods of comprehension, and thus he has never claimed the status of "theory" for any of his historical writings; in fact, he has often claimed that very little theoretical understanding exists at all outside of the natural sciences. It is for this reason that Chomsky has strongly negative feelings about postmodernism and its practitioners whom he considers to be taking truistic observations, couching them in vague terminology, and elevating this arcane rhetoric to the status of "theory" (Barsky 1997: 197).

consistency with which he uses his rational intensity on any problem he analyzes" and that "his use of science and reason is essentially the same everywhere" (1987: ix). Indeed Chomsky has consistently maintained that he considers himself to be a "child of the enlightenment" and that his approach to the study of language is deeply grounded in (his interpretation of) Cartesian rationalism. In linguistics, Chomsky's method of "methodological naturalism" (Chomsky 1993: 42) seeks to develop a scientific understanding of the manner in which universal grammar— "the basic design underlying the grammars of all human language" (Pinker 1994: 483)—operates. Curiously, when leaving the realm of what he considers "science," which would include his historical studies, Chomsky becomes surprisingly modest:

> Plainly such an approach [methodological naturalism] does not exclude other ways of trying to comprehend the world. Someone committed to it (as I am) can consistently believe (as I do) that we learn much more of human interest about how people think and feel and act by reading novels or studying history than from all of

naturalistic psychology, and perhaps always will; similarly, the arts may offer appreciation of the heavens to which astrophysics cannot aspire. *We are speaking here of theoretical understanding, a particular mode of comprehension. In this domain, any departure from a naturalistic approach carries a burden of justification.* (emphasis added, Chomksy 1993: 42).

Peck goes on to note:

Chomsky's persistent application of reason exposes the inconsistency of others—and their often active propagation of ideology under the guise of rational analysis and science. His laserlike rationality is so radical, as others' thinking is not, because of its intense anti-ideological ethos. Ideology and science are veritable opposites in Chomsky's thought (Peck: x).

While it may be true that Chomsky's "laserlike" use of reason and science is remarkably consistent, it is not accurate to state that he is "a spokesman for no ideology" or that "no intellectual tradition quite captures his voice" as Peck does on the opening page of his generally flattering introduction to *The Chomsky Reader.* As Barsky (1997) and others have noted—indeed Chomsky has repeatedly stressed the point himself—Chomsky's philosophy and methodology are firmly rooted in left-Marxist and anarchist traditions and are in many ways a continuation of that late nineteenth and early twentieth century legacy.[13]

A detailed description of the work of left-libertarians such as Pannekoek, Rocker, Luxemburg, Bakunin, Kropotkin, and others is beyond the scope of this study although over the years Chomsky has become somewhat of a pop culture hero for popularizing the works of these and other thinkers, and introductions to his work and thought are readily available.[14] Without going into too much detail I now list what for me are some of the more salient advantages and insights (in no particular order) of a "Chomskyan" social science and humanities approach:

1. A commitment to humanistic rationality and reason. What

---

[13] There is also considerable overlap between Chomsky's politics and the work of Frankfurt School critical theory (Barsky 1997), although Frankfurt School theorists have been relatively silent on questions of empire. Chomsky and Michel Foucault debated one another on Dutch television in the early 1970's and the two see eye-to-eye on many issues (Achbar 1994: 31-33) as well.

[14] *Chomsky for Beginners* is available from Writers and Readers Publishing, Inc. And the award winning documentary film *Manufacturing Consent* is available from Necessary Illusions in Montreal.

this translates to in practice is this: a dedication to fixing the nature of historical truth to the greatest extent possible, given the limitations. Chomsky is aware of the arguments put forth by postmodernists and others about the subjective nature of "truth" and my discussion later in this chapter (in the Trouillot section) of the role of power in historical production delves more deeply into how the process works and why. The point is that the fact that power and history are inseparably intertwined and that the distinction between "what happened and what is said to have happened" (Trouillot 1995: 106) don't invalidate the honest attempt to search for what actually occurred—and to act accordingly based upon what is found.

The point is perhaps best illustrated by a quote. Another take on the search for "truth" in history is provided by noted *Annales* historian Fernand Braudel. In his classic history of the Mediterranean, he (1972[1966]: 18) writes:

> Perhaps the day will come when we shall no longer be working on the great sites of history with the methods of small craftsmen. Perhaps on that day it will become

> possible to write general history from original documents and not from more or less secondary works. Need I confess that I have not been able to examine all the documents available to me in the archives, no matter how hard I tried. This book is the result of a necessarily incomplete study. I know in advance that its conclusions will be examined, discussed, and replaced by others and I am glad of it. *That is how history progresses and must progress.* (emphasis mine).

Clearly Braudel views history as a discipline engaged in a continuous and shifting process of neo-positivistic "falsification." Understanding is advanced by the consistent search and reinterpretation of what came before. While such an approach is not without problems, especially if questions of power are left unaddressed, its basic assumptions and goals form the basis for the furtherance of knowledge, and are a fundamental aspect of Chomsky's approach and method.

2. Two aspects central to Chomksy's historical analytical technique are the following: a. concrete, easy to understand examples that span both time and place, and b. brilliant comparisons between these examples. In *Year 501: The*

Conquest Continues, for instance, Chomsky begins chapter 10 ("Murdering History") by examining contemporary rhetoric surrounding the 500th anniversary of Columbus's arrival in the New World and compares this rhetoric with another anniversary that shortly pre-dated the event: the fiftieth anniversary of the bombing of Pearl Harbor by Japanese forces. Chomsky sees a connection between celebrations of the Columbus landing and the pressures generated by the American political class[15] on the government of Japan to "properly atone" for its mortal sin of having sneak attacked the American colony of Hawai'i on December 7, 1941. His masterful scrutiny and interrogation of *The New York Times* and other newspapers, as well as his incredibly extensive command of the professional policy and planning literature, demystifies the inflated rhetoric used by politicians and their

---

[15] "The political class, which is roughly the 20 percent of the population that is educated, articulate, and is expected to play some role in decision making. Essentially they function as social managers, so this group must be deeply indoctrinated. Their consent is important" (Cogswell 1996: 78)

associates to keep the people they supposedly represent at a comfortable distance, and suggests that "proliferating numbers of experts and specialists do not breed greater insight into the innermost workings of our society, but obfuscate it, making people feel passive and less able to effectively participate" (Peck 1987: xiii).

Chomsky also interrogates the logic of "Manifest Destiny" and makes a skillful comparison between U.S. arguments behind the annexation of Texas and the arguments put forth by Iraq in its annexation of Kuwait:

> The logic of annexation of Texas was essentially that attributed to Saddam Hussein by US propaganda after his conquest of Kuwait. But the comparisons should not be pressed too far. Unlike his 19th century American precursors, Saddam Hussein is not known to have feared that slavery in Iraq would be threatened by independent states nearby, or to have publicly called for their "imbecile" inhabitants to "become extinct" so that the "great mission of peopling the Middle East with a noble race" of Iraqis might be carried forward, placing the "destinies of the human race in the hands" of the conquerors. And even the wildest fantasies did not accord Saddam potential control over oil of the kind the American expansionists of the 1840's sought over the

major resources of the day. There are many interesting lessons to learn from the history so extolled by enraptured intellectuals (Chomsky 1993: 27).

3. Chomsky's historical inquiries operate within a fairly long and established tradition of socially responsible and activist oriented scholarship. Accordingly, Chomsky does not target his writing toward academics or intellectuals but at "those considered to be 'riff-raff'—the kind of people that I like and take seriously" (Barsky 1997: 215). The conscious choice on Chomsky's part to avoid addressing the intellectual establishment flows from his belief (based on his interpretation of Gramsci and others) that this group for the most part acts as a "secular priesthood" whose job is to generate (historical and contemporary) justifications for wealth and power.[16] Chomsky

---

[16] "The professional guild structure in the social sciences, I think, has often served as a marvelous device for protecting them from insight and understanding, for filtering out people who raise unacceptable questions, for limiting research—not by force, but by all sorts of more subtle means—to questions that are not threatening. Take a look at any society, I'm convinced, and you'll find that where there is a more or less professionalized guild of people who inquire into the social process, there will be certain topics that they will be very reluctant to investigate. There will be striking taboos on what they will study. *In particular, one of the things that they are very unlikely to study is the way power is actually exercised in their own society, or their own relationship to that power. These are topics that won't be understood, won't be studied*" (emphasis added, Chomsky 1987: 30).

thus sees much of his work as a "primer in intellectual self-defense" (Achbar 1994) and as part of a larger effort to help ordinary citizens see the contemporary world in an unromanticized fashion and as an attempt to assist people to penetrate the increasingly intricate layers of propagandized distortion perpetuated by the mass media (Chomsky and Herman 1988). "The responsibility of the writer as a *moral agent* " according to Chomsky, "is to try to bring the truth about *matters of human significance* to an *audience that can do something about them*" (emphasis in original, Chomsky 1996: 56). His historical studies are meant to show that contrary to popular opinion, much of foreign and domestic policy is neither complicated nor unknowable; it is in fact the case that the moral and political principles behind elite decision making under scrutiny reveal themselves to be quite simple and understandable.

Furthermore, Chomsky's scholarship is meant to stir readers into action. Like much of the left wing literature that has influenced him, Chomsky's writing style is ironic—at times even dramatic— and always powerful. In keeping with his anarchistic principles (which emphasize concrete revolutionary action[17], not Marxist "iron laws" of history), Chomsky does not tell people <u>how</u> to act; he consistently emphasizes, however, that if people want to see a change in their circumstances that they <u>have to act</u> to implement that change.

Like his friend Howard Zinn, Chomsky usually writes from a "people's" perspective (Zinn 1980), and in his political activities has "usually been on the side of the losers" (Cogswell 1996: 13) whether it was the anarchists in Spain or other oppressed groups such as the East Timorese. But his honesty, conviction, moral courage, and commitment not only do a great job of advancing historical and sociological insight and understanding, but serve as an outstanding example of scholar activism.

---

[17] Which theory is meant to serve, not the other way around.

Unlike Chomsky, who sees himself as being a scientist (concerning linguistics, at any rate), Edward Said considers himself to be a professional humanist. Professionally, he is known as a literary and cultural critic. His two most famous books, *Orientalism* and *Culture and Imperialism* have been very influential, and because Said over the years has had more interaction with anthropologists, his work has been accorded more consideration within the field than Chomsky's work.

Like Chomsky, Said sees the influence of imperialism almost everywhere within the cultural products of the west. Unlike Chomsky who tends to focus on macro-processes and power within political institutions, Said does a better job of describing and discussing micro-processes of power, particularly within artistic production.

Said has been explicit in remarking that two of his biggest influences have been the works of Michel Foucault and of Raymond Williams. From Foucault, Said developed the understanding that colonialism and imperialism, particularly at micro to middle levels of complexity, need to be analyzed as a discourse. In his introduction to *Orientalism,* he notes:

> My contention is that without examining Orientalism as a discourse one cannot possibly understand the enormously systematic discipline by which European culture was able to manage—and even produce—the Orient politically, sociologically, militarily, ideologically, scientifically, and imaginatively during the post-Enlightenment period (Said 1978: 3).

Like Chomsky, however, Said recognizes that colonialism and empire were more than simply cultural or intellectual enterprises:

> ....any wisdom of ideas that can remain unchanged as teachable wisdom (in academies, books, congresses, universities, foreign-service institutions) from the period of Ernest Renan in the 1840's until the present in the United States must be something more formidable than a mere collection of lies. Orientalism, therefore, is not an airy European fantasy about the Orient, but a created body of theory and practice in which, for many generations, there has been a considerable material investment (p. 6).

From the work of Raymond Williams[18] and Foucault Said has also adapted the idea that orientalist discourse has not been

---

18   Particularly Williams' *The Long Revolution.*

"unilaterally inhibiting" but that its "internal constraints upon writers and thinkers [has been] *productive*" as well (Said 1978: 14). By focusing on the productivity of power, Said is able to unlock the passions and motivations behind much of nineteenth century European and Euro-American literature and artistic production in general. Said mostly focuses on overseas empire in his work,[19] but his technical and cultural analysis applies domestically and especially in Texas. In this dissertation I intend to focus on the shifting ways in which power intersect with interest (something in which Chomsky excels) as well as demonstrate how the power to name, identify, and vilify were used by nineteenth century Anglo-Texans to dehumanize and enslave Africans and African-Americans.

---

[19] The last chapter of Culture and Imperialism, however, contains a devastating critique of U.S. imperialism and the 1991 Persian Gulf War, as well as a sober assessment of leading intellectual justifications for the war and for U.S. exceptionalism generally. Regarding more recent (late twentieth century) forms of imperialism, Said observes: "Earlier rationales—the Monroe Doctrine, Manifest Destiny, and so forth—lead to 'word responsibility,' which exactly corresponds to the growth in the United States' global interests after World War Two and to the conception of its enormous power as formulated by the foreign policy and intellectual elite" (Said 1993: 285).

The Du Boisians: Herbert Aptheker, Manning Marable and Ronald Bailey

It's impossible for a white person to believe in capitalism and not believe in racism. You can't have capitalism without racism. And if you find one and you happen to get that person into a conversation and they have a philosophy that makes you sure they don't have this racism in their outlook, usually they're socialists or their political philosophy is socialism.
-*Malcolm X (cited in Breitman 1990: 69)*

It is difficult to not be in awe of the sheer range and extent of Du Bois's scholarship and activist example. I have made extensive use of Du Bois's first book (which is based on his dissertation), *The Suppression of the African Slave Trade to the United States*, which in many ways remains the best book on the topic, as writers such as Mannix (1962: 295), Hugh Thomas (1997: 819) and Du Bois's most recent biographer (Lewis 1995) have noted.[20] As in many areas, Du Bois was in many ways ahead of his time and was not only an early critic

---

[20] In his outstanding biography of Du Bois, David Levering Lewis observes that the main argument put forth in *Suppression* (the fact that "vast profits [were] coming not from the maritime slave trade but from the total slave-economy universe") was "pathfinding" although he also notes that Du Bois' estimate of 250,000 illegal African slave importations has since been lowered considerably. Lewis cites Philip Curtin's figure of 54,000 illegal African slave importations as the "now prevailing" estimate. In *Suppression* Du Bois estimated that approximately 75,000 Africans had been smuggled into or through Texas. This is certainly a rather high figure but as I show in this dissertation it is not as unreasonable an estimate as might be thought at first glance.

of what he termed "the propaganda of history,"[21] but was also in the unique position of being able to observe the construction of the propaganda as it was taking place during the worst years of early twentieth century Jim Crow. In *Black Reconstruction*, for instance, Du Bois makes some cutting observations regarding the deliberate sanitizing and rewriting of the historical record by late nineteenth and early twentieth century historians:

> We have spoiled and misconceived the position of the historian. If we are going in the future, not simply with regard to this one question [i.e. slavery], but with regard

---

[21] The following quote from Aptheker (1971: 287) describes how the process works:

As fate would have it, at the very period of the appearance of Du Bois' *Black Reconstruction*, the *American Historical Review* (XL [April 1935], 438-449) published Theodore Clark Smith's "The Writing of American History, 1884-1934," which was an attack upon any departure from orthodoxy (Smith had in mind some recent heresies announced by Charles Beard). Smith offered as prize exhibits of "rigidly accurate, impeccably documented" history writing that was "absolutely without prejudice"—"the general onslaught on the Reconstruction period which took place at Columbia under the guidance of our former honored associate, Professor Dunning." Another of Smith's prize exhibits of unprejudiced history writing was that by U.B. Phillips, whose "works.....substituted direct observation and analysis for propaganda or emotional treatment."

Phillips was also a major influence on Abigail Curlee's 1932 UT Austin dissertation on Texas plantations. When discussing the "easier" life of Texas slaves prior to the civil war, Willoughby (1993) cites this theoretically outdated study as evidence.

> to all social problems, to be able to use human experience for the guidance of mankind, we have got clearly to distinguish between fact and desire (Du Bois 1935: 1039).

Du Bois later writes (p. 1043): "armed and warned by all this, and fortified by long study of the facts, I stand at the end of this writing, literally aghast at what American historians have done to this field."[22]

Du Bois disciple and historian Herbert Aptheker skillfully carried forward the tradition established by the old man. Much like Du Bois's work, Aptheker's "radical" histories of the United States and of slavery were iconoclastic anti-establishment narratives that stressed overt activism and openly embraced Marxist analysis:

> Marxism makes is possible to get at the heart of Southern Negro history, at the deepest reality of the institutions of slavery, of peonage, of jim crow. It is possible only in this way to see the organic connection between the appearance of capitalism and the enslavement of Africans; between the development of capitalism and

---

[22] Chomsky does not cite Du Bois often although both, of course, share similar intellectual roots. Chomsky's work on the Vietnam War, particularly as the war was raging during the 1960's, bears a striking resemblance to much of Du Bois.

> Afro-American slavery; between the birth of imperialism and the intensification of jim-crow oppression of Black people....Marxism does not ignore the great force of racism in Southern life; it does not deny or minimize the power of the irrational, of the emotional, of inherited and socially induced prejudices. Rather, this view explains racism in terms of its material origins and ruling-class functions. In doing this, it points the way to principled struggle against racism and to a practical means for its complete elimination (Aptheker 1971: 23).

Manning Marable is perhaps the most vocal and well known contemporary torch-bearer of the Du Boisian scholar-activist tradition. Marable's *How Capitalism Underdeveloped Black America* [23] is relevant for my purposes not only because it focuses on the role of slavery and slave trading in the historical underdevelopment of the American Black community, but is also helpful in its discussion of the relationship between racism, sexism and capitalism, and how these structures of modern dominance are a continuation of nineteenth century policies and socioeconomics, not a radical

---

[23] The book is dedicated to Walter Rodney, whose *How Europe Underdeveloped Africa* served as the inspiration for Marable's study.

break from them. Particularly noteworthy is Marable's feminism, which Joy James sees as more genuine than the feminism of Du Bois or Paul Gilroy:

> Contrary to Gilroy, other black male writers draw attention to the masculinist (historical) erasure of black women. Manning Marable's commentary offers on example. Given the pervasiveness of male elites, it is unusual for African-American male intellectuals to discuss black paternalism or sexual opportunism vis-a-vis black females. Counter to the norm, Marable's essay "Grounding with my Sisters" denounces the erasure of African-American women from political texts and memory. Although increasingly we find similar writings by black male profeminists, Marable's 1983 text was one of the earliest statements of such politics (James 1997: 57-58).

I produce a cursory examination of female master/slave relations in chapter seven by using the recollections of former slaves recorded by the Federal Writers Project in the 1930's. Marable also does a good job of historicizing the distinctions between the Black working class and of the Black bourgeoisie, and is particularly Du Bois-like in his ability to simultaneously maintain a pan-Africanist/African Diaspora perspective alongside a socialist analytical approach and vision for the future.

Ronald Bailey is another Black activist scholar whose influence can be felt in what follows. In his article "Out of Sight, Out of Mind: The struggle of African American intellectuals against the invisibility of the slave[ry] trade in world economic history," he advances Du Bois's 1896 study (mentioned earlier) by demonstrating more clearly how the transatlantic slave trade contributed to the development of modern capitalism; the trade influenced everything from shipbuilding and mercantilism to the development of modern finance and entrepreneurialism. Bailey also demonstrates the effects of the trade on New England's economic development and demonstrates, among other things, that the fortunes of the Brown family of Rhode Island (of Brown University fame) were extensively based on the slave trade. Bailey's analysis applies to the Texas case as well. Many prominent emigrés to Texas were New York and New England "Yankees" who established businesses and similar operations in nineteenth century Texas. The slave trade played a significant role in these capitalist "success stories" as well.

Paul Gilroy's *Black Atlantic*

The single most important insight of Gilroy's that I have found useful is his rethinking of the cultural geography of race. Particularly attractive is Gilroy's argument that "cultural historians take the Atlantic as one single, complex unit of analysis in their discussions of the modern world and use it to produce an explicitly transnational and intercultural perspective" (Gilroy 1993: 15). By extension, the same applies to the Gulf of Mexico and the Caribbean. Like Gilroy, I have found that the fixed borders of the nation-state are incapable of fully capturing the diversity and dynamics of the black experience of this region, especially the dynamics of slave trading.[24] While my narrative is of necessity fixed on "the Texas slave trade" I too try to make an earnest effort to expand

---

[24] "Getting beyond this national and nationalistic perspective is essential for two principal reasons: one is to do with the postmodern eclipse of the modern nation-state as a political, economic, and cultural unit. Neither political nor economic structures of domination are still co-extensive with borders of nation-states.....the second concerns the integrity of cultures and in particular the relationship between nationality and ethnicity" (Gilroy 1992: 188). There is considerable value in what Gilroy says here. But I'm not quite ready to totally ditch the nation-state yet.

my narrative to go beyond the geographically assigned borders of Texas. I do so not only because I believe it to be a wise theoretical move, but because the geographic position of Texas (especially in relation to Latin America) as well as the demographic and economic development of its gulf coast involved significant maritime contact and commerce with (ultimately) ships from all over the world. The time period under investigation actually makes the effort at transnationalization relatively uncomplicated: the borders defining Texas were constantly being shifted and renegotiated for most of the early to mid nineteenth century.

Additionally, like Gilroy I intend to lend a decisively <u>maritime</u> tenor to my narrative. The intent is to focus on the "roots and routes" of the constantly shifting Black Gulf/Caribbean world and to build on Gilroy's penetrating insight that "the image of the ship—a living, micro-cultural, micro-political system in motion—is especially important for historical and theoretical reasons" (Gilroy 1993: 4). The "image" Gilroy abstracts is more than just a theoretical construct: the port of Houston today ranks first in the nation in total tanker cargo and annually handles over $20 billion in export trade. The port ranks first in the United States in both categories (Houston Chronicle 1999: 22A). Ships and shipping are not just the economic motor of modern world commerce; they played a major role in the development of Texas and are also the locus of considerable angst and ambivalence in African-American history.

Michel-Rolph Trouillot's *Silencing the Past*

Trouillot's anthropological inquiry into the politics of historical production makes essentially the same points that the other writers discussed here make, but differs from them somewhat in style and presentation. Trouillot's book skillfully incorporates recent developments in anthropological theory (particularly the ideas of Michel Foucault) into its exploration of power in historical production and is, along with the Obeyesekere book mentioned earlier, more of a "how to"—or rather, "how not to"—of how to produce historical narratives that are more sensitive and aware of power imbalances.[25]

In the introduction Trouillot (1995: xix) is clear about what his book attempts to accomplish:

> This book is about history and power. It deals with the many ways in which the production of historical narratives involves the uneven contribution of competing

---

[25] Chomsky gives many lively concrete examples, makes correlations, and performs historical interpretations, but his focus is not usually on the processes of historical production, processes which he usually takes for granted (everyone knows that it's a function of power). Trouillot's narrative is useful in that it specifically focuses on the acts of historical production and the "silences" produced by unequal power relations.

> groups and individuals who have unequal access to the means for such production. The forces I will expose are less visible than gunfire, class property, or political crusades. I want to argue that they are no less powerful.

Trouillot's book is also useful for my purposes because it contains (indeed, the book begins with) a brief analysis of the most sacred of Texas myths, the Alamo myth. Texas is perhaps a good whipping-person for postcolonial scholarship, but not undeservedly so. Trouillot seems to recognize that the silencing processes he describes have had a particularly dumbing and numbing effect in the Lone Star State. His skillful dissection of the varying discourses surrounding Texas' largest tourist attraction points out that each side of the debate needs "to impose a test of credibility on certain events and narratives because it matters *to them* whether these events are true or false" (p. 11). The search for historical "truth" is thus in many ways as much about "what happened" as it is about "what is said to have happened." Given the fact that "pastness is a position," (p. 15) Trouillot argues that a "concrete focus on the process of historical production" (p. 24) can reveal "how history works" instead of a rather narrow and traditional focus on what history "is."

Given further that "a fetishism of the facts, premised on an antiquated model of the natural sciences, still dominates history and the other social sciences" (p. 151), and the uncomfortable conflicts that often arise between the two historicities he describes, Trouillot argues for the need to maximize historical "authenticity." By this, Trouillot envisions historical production that engages observers as both "actors and narrators" (p. 150) and one where "professional historians will have to position themselves more clearly within the present, lest politicians, magnates or ethnic leaders alone write history for them" (p. 152).

By explicitly focusing on positionality, Trouillot's book goes beyond many traditional historical arguments professing "awareness" or "recognition" of presentism within historical narratives. Trouillot is quite specific: historians do not just produce "partial" accounts of the past. "The past—or, more accurately, pastness—is a position" (p. 15). As the other theorists I discuss in this chapter note, the implications of this type of scholarship are clear: the search for "the facts" and historical "truth" are inextricably intertwined with power. That's how history _works_. Chomsky's leadership in this regard is direct and simple. Individuals (especially producers of history) should strive to be "moral agents, not servants of power" (Said 1993).

Michael Tadman's *Speculators and Slaves*

This book is the most extensive economic and social history of the internal slave trade as it was conducted in the eighteenth and nineteenth century United States. The research is based on extensive and innovate study of primary source material, particularly census documents, probate records, business transactions (manifests), and planter correspondence, and I rely on it extensively in this dissertation. Tadman's central argument is that the size and reach of the domestic slave trade provides convincing evidence that slaves were not engaged in "a smooth process of accommodation" as suggested by many scholars, but were in fact engaged in a process of strategic accommodation that involved "limited adjustment to the sheer power of masters" (Tadman 1996[1989]: xv, xxiv). Tadman argues that accommodationist studies have "tended to romanticize slavery and have been too generous toward the slaveholders of antebellum America. They have taken too much on trust the rationalizations by which slaveholders made themselves comfortable with slavery" (p. xix). Because much of the early historiography of slavery (particularly that of southern historian U.B. Phillips) is racist and accomodationist in nature, a central tenet of critically investigating the actual nature of slavery and slave trading in the antebellum south is finding out "what slaveowners did to slaves, rather than what they said they did" (p. xxi) in newspapers, books, or other propaganda.

Tadman's critique of (still) influential accommodationist studies is one of the most persuasive yet written. It is a direct challenge to the close accommodation theories of writers such as Eugene Genovese, Robert Fogel, and Stanley Engerman, and is in line with more resistive arguments put forth by scholars such as Angela Davis,[26] Lawrence Levine and Herbert Gutman

---

[26] As always, Davis's critique of Genovese in *Women, Race & Class* (1981: 26) is particularly hard-hitting and poignant. Regarding Genovese's paternalistic suggestion that enslaved women felt strong bonds of attachment and fondness for their masters, Davis observes "he fails to understand that there could hardly be a basis for 'delight, affection and love' as long as white men, by virtue of their economic position, had unlimited access to Black women's bodies. It was as oppressors—or, in the case of non-slaveowners, as agents of domination—that white men approached Black women's bodies."

whose approach also "emphasizes the resilience of slaves, and their fundamental resistance to the values and culture of masters" (p. xx).

Gutman's critique of Genovese and of Fogel and Engerman (and by extension of Moynihan and Glazer's "Black family pathology" thesis) is spelled out with clarity on pages 318-319 of *The Black Family in Slavery and Freedom* (1976):

> Genovese's insistence that "many slaveowners went to impressive lengths to keep slave families together," that "the more paternalistic masters betrayed evidence of considerable emotional strain" when faced with sale, and that an "impressive number of slaveowners took losses they could ill afford to keep families together" is not disputed. Such owners existed. But neither their presence nor the assertions that "planters did everything possible to encourage the slaves to live together in stable units" and that "the impressive econometric work by Robert Fogel and Stanley Engerman suggests that separations occurred less frequently than has generally been believed" are substitutes for sustained analysis of how local and interregional sale, involuntary migration with an owner, gift transfer, and estate division affected the immediate slave family and enlarged slave kin group. Such an analysis is not found in *Roll, Jordan Roll*, and is its most severe empirical shortcoming. It is not a marginal deficiency. It is as if the impact of the British industrial revolution on the working-class family were

studied without reference to child labor in the mines and factories. *Analysis of the frequency and character of involuntary slave family dissolution (especially in the years between 1830 and the Civil War) is the essential underpinning for studying how slaves perceived their owners ......no evidence in Roll, Jordan, Roll—or anywhere else for that matter—discloses that slave parents accepted the sale of their children, whatever their age, as a "fact of life"* (emphasis added).

Tadman's Gutmanesque thesis of master/slave relations is more dynamic and agentive than conventional histories of slavery and slave trading,[27] and his analysis of planter correspondence and diaries indicates clearly that "slaveholders and traders respected market prices far more than slave families" (p. xxx).

Tadman's study focuses mostly on the American Atlantic coast, particularly South Carolina.[28] However his investigation, particularly the appendixes, also contains detailed information

---

[27] This is not to say that it couldn't be more agentive still; Tadman does not incorporate evidence from historical (particularly plantation) archaeology into his argument. He also does not cite extensively from the oral history narratives collected by the Federal Writers Project, although he does use them.

[28] This is logical since South Carolina and Virginia were the center of the 18th century slave trade.

about other southern states, including Texas. Especially informative are Tadman's discussion of the New Orleans slave trade (which interacted heavily with the Texas trade), his estimates of interregional slave movements (p. 12), and his statistical analysis of the numbers of upper south slaves forcibly separated from their parent or spouse (Appendix 8).

In short, much of the statistical investigating concerning the slave trade discussed in this dissertation has already been performed by Tadman. Since Texas was not his primary focus, however, the figures he produces bear closer scrutiny and refinement, but the overall discussion of the prices, valuation, and profits of the trade and their ramifications are a fundamental bedrock of the analytical strategy I employ in my examination of slavery and slave trading in Texas.

CHAPTER 2: ASSESSMENT OF SOME OF THE LITERATURE

The main problem with most studies of slavery (and race relations generally) in Texas is that they in one way or another still subscribe to the racist "close accommodation" thesis of U.B. Phillips. This thesis, which, Tadman says, was "consciously created in order to make a white supremacist society confident about itself and at ease with its past" argued that genuine bonds of affection existed between masters and slaves and that slaves were generally treated well in return for which the slaves "gave loyalty, affection, and moderate labor" (Tadman 1996[1989]: xxiii). The publication of Randolph Campbell's *An Empire for Slavery* in 1989 marked something of a turning point. This study was the first comprehensive investigation of the peculiar institution in the Lone Star State and was also the first study to employ more modern interpretive and investigative tools. It broke new ground in that it explicitly situated slavery in the foreground of nineteenth century Texas history, and revealed how important the institution was felt to be by most white Texans. Nonetheless, in some ways this investigation still bears an uncomfortable resemblance to the racist histories produced earlier in the twentieth century. I will examine some of the flaws in Campbell's study in greater detail later in this chapter.

The underlying philosophy permeating most Texas historiography—especially any history related to racial or ethnic relations—is rampant Eurocentrism, or, more specifically, Anglo-Texas-centrism. Texas institutions and individuals have and continue to invest significant resources in the perpetuation of a romantic and frequently chauvinistic "Texas Myth" which downplays or obfuscates the realities of large scale slavery and slave trading, appropriation of land from Mexicans, and the extermination of indigenous populations. Essentially the myth is what Texas historians and the Texas history industry (which includes state agencies) like to tell each other, to Texans, and to non-Texans. The myth can be expressed with varying degrees of stridency; the range can be said to swing from "right wing redneck" to "Texas cultural pluralist," although cultural geographer D.W. Meinig appropriately described the myth in 1969 simply as "Imperial Texas:"

> Texans have long been taught to think of their homeland as an "empire" and to use that word as something more than just a grandiose name for a large area. Despite the natural tendency of other Americans to dismiss it as an irritating if harmless pretension, the Texan claim is substantial and their use of the term more than metaphorical. For, leaving aside the common political connotation, if "empire" implies not only a relative size, but a history of conquest, expansion, and dominion over a varied realm, and not only an outward movement of people, but the thrust of a self-confident aggressive people driven by a strong sense of superiority and destiny, then Texans can reasonably claim a strongly "imperial" history and character (Meinig 1969: 7).

Given the "imperial" nature of the Texas myth, the theoretical tools provided by postcolonialism and colonial discourse analysis seem particularly appropriate in analyzing slavery and slave trading in the Lone Star State, and in investigating social and economic relations in Texas generally.

In one of the better books on the subject of Eurocentrism (Shohat and Stam 1994: 3; see also Amin: 1989) the authors summarized the main features of Eurocentrism in the following manner:

> Eurocentrism sanitizes Western history while patronizing and even demonizing the non-West; it thinks of itself in terms of its noblest achievements—science, progress, humanism—but of the non-West in terms of its deficiencies, real or imagined.

One of the "achievements" still held up as a marker of Texas slaveholder benevolence is the myth of "easier" slavery in the Lone Star State for the state's enslaved population. The most well known proponent of this "close accommodation" point of view was the noted Texas historian Abigail Curlee Holbrook.

Abigail Curlee Holbrook

Abigail Curlee (later Holbrook) is perhaps the person most responsible for the perpetuation of racist misinformation on the institution of slavery in Texas. Her 1922 Master Thesis and 1932 Ph.D. dissertation on the subject, *A Study of Texas Slave Plantations, 1822-1865*, are still looked to as authoritative sources on plantation slavery in Texas. While these works are educative and useful sources of basic information on Texas plantations, they are also products of a decidedly questionable school of pro-southern historiography—one that the passage of time has unfortunately not eliminated. The tendency of regional historians to claim that slavery was less oppressive in their states is a well documented phenomenon (Aptheker 1963: 12). Curlee maintained her views of the "well treated" Texas slave well into the 1970's.[29] At a time of considerable social

---

[29] This is one place (there are others) where Campbell's more modern treatment of Texas slavery parts company with Curlee. In the conclusion of *An Empire for Slavery*, Campbell (1989: 257) observes that there is "no basis" for claiming that slavery in Texas was "milder" or "worse" than in the other Southern states and remarks that "little effort is now devoted to proving that slavery was 'better' or 'worse' in one place than another."

turmoil, the editor of the April 1973 edition of *Southwestern Historical Quarterly* (105-106) summarized Holbrook's approach as follows:

> Abigail Curlee Holbrook has devoted many years to the study of the Texas plantation system. She believes that Texas slaves were generally better treated than their brothers and sisters in other slave states but admits that even in Texas cruelty and injustice existed in the master-slave relationship. In the present article, Mrs. Holbrook describes the housing, food, clothing, health care, amusements and religion of slaves on the principal Texas plantations. She concludes that kindly feelings existed between the two races on most Texas plantations. In this respect, Mrs. Holbrook follows the lead of early twentieth-century southern historian Ulrich B. Phillips.....whose books were pioneer works on the subject.

One could spend a considerable amount of time anatomizing Holbrook's racist assumptions and assertions, but at this late twentieth century stage in time there really is no point; U.B. Phillips, outside of Eugene Barker Holbrook's most direct influence, has already been roundly criticized and dismissed by most of the current generation of historians and ethnic studies scholars.[30] Nonetheless, exactly what was the perspective of Phillips regarding slavery and master slave relations? In his assessment of the slavery literature in Appendix C of *The Black Family in Slavery and Freedom* (1976: 542) Gutman writes that Phillips was a "retrogressionist" and that this belief "affected his conception of the Afro-American historical experience."

> "A century or two ago," explained Phillips in 1904, "the negroes were savages in the wilds of Africa....Those who were brought to America, and their descendants, have acquired a certain amount of civilization....in very large measure the result of their association with civilized white people." Phillips paraphrased [Phillip A.] Bruce: "Several keen-sighted students have already detected a tendency of the negroes, where segregated in the black belt, to lapse back toward barbarism. Of course, if its prevention is possible, such retrogression must not be allowed to continue." Early in his career (and in greater detail in his later and more substantial writings) Phillips, living in the age of Jane Addams, sought to show that

---

[30] The close accommodation thesis was the dominant theory of master/slave relations for most of the twentieth century, until a more "radical" generation of scholars came into ascendance in the 1960's. It has by no means died, however, and has enjoyed a recent resurgence, brought about to some degree, in my view, by the conservative backlash of the 1980's and 90's. As some of the critique in this chapter demonstrates, "southern" historians, of course, have never really abandoned the thesis, although they have reformed it somewhat. The thesis was also challenged at the height of its influence: Du Bois was a virtual lone tree in the forest when he had the audacity to suggest in *Black Reconstruction* (1935) that slaves hated being enslaved and argued forcefully that newly emancipated African-Americans not only played an active role in their own emancipation but were active participants during reconstruction as well.

slaveowners ("the better element of the white people") "did what we call, in the modern phrase, social settlement work." The "patriarchal feature of Anglo-American enslavement was not the product of the plantation system, but served a racial function made "necessary" because "the average negro has many of the characteristics of a child, and must be guided and governed, and often guarded against himself, by a sympathetic hand." Dominance by well-bred, upper-class whites—not "whites" but "the planter and his wife and children and his neighbors—was essential "for example and precept among the negroes." Phillips wrote in 1905: "It is mistaken to apply the general philosophy of slavery to the American situation without very serious modification. A slave among the Greeks or Romans was generally a relatively civilized person, whose voluntary labor would have been far more productive than his labor under compulsion. But the negro slave was a negro first, last and always, and a slave incidentally." So began an influential strain in American historical writing that would view enslavement as beneficial to Africans and their Afro-American descendants and that would define "treatment" as the essential question for historical study. *The study of slave belief and behavior became the study of their treatment by owners* (emphasis added).

Given such a damning and demeaning past, it is worthwhile, therefore, to follow Trouillot's lead and briefly examine how Holbrook's "research" has been used and how the *weltanschauung* just described influences the present. The picture that emerges isn't pretty.

Unfortunately, the current situation is that Holbrook's assertion of an "easier" Texas slave life than in other states continues to survive.[31] In fact, not only is it surviving, but this folklore is being taught to Texas seventh graders and high school students as part of their state mandated Texas history curriculum. For instance, chapter 17 of Larry Willoughby's *Texas, Our Texas* (1993), covers the subject of slavery and secession in Texas, and not surprisingly shares the racist assumptions and omissions of fact perpetuated by scholars such as Holbrook. The entire chapter contains significant distortions of fact, strategic omissions designed to cover up the oppressive and coercive nature of the institution, as well as blatant falsehoods. I could choose many examples to illustrate

---

[31] As recently as 1986 authors such as Silverthorne (1986: xiv) could write: "Anyone who wants to learn about Texas plantations turns first to the fruits of Abigail Curlee Holbrook's lifelong exploration of the subject. In her master's thesis (1922), her doctoral dissertation (1932), and her articles in the *Southwestern Historical Quarterly* up to the 1970's, she has, with clarity and fairness, examined the operation and management of Texas plantations. The operative phrase is "operation and management"; to Curlee enslaved Africans and African-Americans matter mainly as laborers. They have no agency and do not figure prominently in her studies.

my point, but two distortions are particularly noteworthy; not only because they are so fundamental but because they also occur right away: the <u>first</u> sentence of the chapter reads "Texas had fewer slaves than most other southern states, but in 1860 one out of every four Texans was an enslaved person" (p. 350). This is not quite true. According to official 1860 census statistics the proportion of enslaved African-Americans in the Texas population was over thirty percent.[32] The proportion of slaveowners was twenty seven percent in 1860 (down from 30 percent in 1850) (Campbell 1989: 190). Ironically, Willoughby lists the actual census count figures on the same page—perhaps he expects the seventh grade history students to perform the math, since he decided to round down. Later in the chapter, on page 357 Willoughby writes "Defenders of slavery in Texas argued that slaves in the state led better lives than those in

---

[32] Many scholars of Texas slavery round up the estimate because of the unreliability of census figures, which tended to undercount slaves. An example of a fairly typical scholarly statement includes the following: "by the eve of the Civil War almost one-third of the total Texas population was made up of black slaves" (Baker and Baker 1997: xix).

other states. Records of people who witnessed slave life suggest that this may be true." Absent from Willoughby's narrative is the fact that almost all defenders of slavery believed slaves to be better off in an enslaved condition than as free men and women[33], and the fact that "the evidence" he cites is almost exclusively culled from accounts of individuals sympathetic to slavery—accounts extensively referred to by Holbrook.

Holbrook's scholarship has also made its influence felt in Texas maritime archaeology. For example in the historical background for his 1998 Texas A&M University master's thesis on the Caney Creek River Steamboat (online version), La Salle Shipwreck Project co-director Layne Hedrick cites the following passage from Holbrook's 1922 UT Austin M.A. thesis:

> the slaves worked less, made more cotton, and saved more cotton than in any other cotton region. The fiber of the cotton was superior, that on the Gulf coast approaching the Sea Island variety in length and

---

[33] Or, as was commonly the case in Texas, slavery was perceived to be "a necessity," a "necessary evil" or "bad in the abstract, but necessary" (Campbell 1989: 211).

fineness. Furthermore, sugar cane matured sweeter and several feet higher than in Louisiana; its grain was finer and clear; and it rattoonned longer (Curlee, 1922: 24, 148-149).

Hedrick's decision to reference this seventy-four year old study is not only questionable but unfortunate. What is clear beyond doubt is that for Hedrick and Curlee, enslaved Africans and African-Americans are labor and "contributors" to Texas' economic development, nothing else. They have no agency because they are not human beings. Current and ongoing racism in Texas is washed away and is given historical justification by the racist and romantic prose of Holbrook. The underlying racism is so pervasive it goes unquestioned. What is remarkable is that such antiquated thinking is still so influential and is so uncritically accepted by contemporary Texas scholars.

Similarly, Arnold's (1998) excavation of the Confederate blockade runner *Denbigh* is based on a decidedly Eurocentric and pro-southern, if not Confederate, perspective. The ship is deemed excavation-worthy because it was one of the most successful runners of the Union blockade of southern ports during the civil war. One of the excavators of the vessel is a descendant of the ship's cabin boy and has contributed money and time to the project. In a 1998 newspaper article advertising the excavation, a journalist for the *Austin American-Statesman* writes:

> Joining the archaeologists on their watery dig will be an enthusiastic amateur, John Erskine, an Aggie alumnus and a retired Army colonel from Aurora, Colo. Erskine's great-grandfather, Robert Horlock, was a 12-year-old cabin boy aboard the Denbigh (Stanley 1998: A5).

As far as I am aware, no outreach efforts were made to engage Galveston's and Texas' African-American community, who might have a different point of view as to the excavation-worthiness of this ship. To the proper sort of southern Confederate sympathizer, of course, questions such as this don't matter much anyhow; in the time period under investigation African-Americans were just slaves.

Appeals to this type of "simple romanticism" (McGhee 1997) have been part of nautical archaeology almost from the beginning, although in the case of the *Denbigh* project, the romanticism is also tinged with the ever recurring southern racist desire to relive a glorious "rebel" fantasy that minimizes the racial terror and dehumanization slavery inflicted upon African-Americans. The slave trading which was an integral component (in spirit if not in practice) of the Confederate blockade running business could not be further removed from the minds of the Denbigh project excavators and their benefactors. Indeed the major history on the subject of confederate blockade running (Wise 1989) leaves out this unmentionable history all together and is another genre book which romanticizes and glorifies neo-Confederate culture and white fantasies of antebellum agrarian prosperity and peace.

Richard Francaviglia's *From Sail to Steam*

This recent (published 1998) maritime history is a general survey of Texas seafaring between 1500-1900 and is, according to Andrew W. Hall who wrote an endorsement in the sleeve of the book, a "solid roadmap for newcomers to the field, and [will] promote a much wider appreciation for the subject." The book does contain many useful maps and photographs and I will cite it often in the material which follows. As might be expected, however, its dismissal of slavery and slave trading as a crucial factor in Texas maritime history and its non-treatment of any non-European maritime achievements reflect a serious Eurocentric bias.

Francaviglia's discussion of the indigenous inhabitants of the Texas gulf coast is particularly revealing. On page 23, he writes "although they [the Karankawa] possessed watercraft, these tribes of the Texas coast should not be thought of as seafarers," and in the opening sentence of chapter two ("The Power of the Wind") of the book he asserts that "the Native

Americans of the Texas coast had developed with no apparent concept of dominating or mastering the environment" (Francaviglia 1998: 27). That reasoning was used by the government of the United States as well as by Anglo settlers in Texas as a pretext for the extermination of what little remained of the indigenous coastal population (decimation of tribes in the interior would follow in short order), and was also used by President Tyler as an excuse for invading and conquering Mexico.[34]

The assumption of European seafaring superiority—a hallmark of much of the maritime archaeological and historical literature—finds full expression in *From Sail to Steam*. The Europeans, so the standard narrative goes, thanks to Prince Henry the Navigator, "innovated" the use of sail power (particularly the ability to sail into the wind) and were in

---

[34] In his discussion of the circumstances surrounding "the diplomacy of racism" and the politics leading to the Mexican War Brack (1974: 9-10) notes "Indeed Mexico was at that time a backward, poor, misgoverned, and chaotic country, circumstances that Americans attributed to the inferiority of the Mexican people which in turn justified depriving them of their territory for reasons similar to those used to justify the dispossession of Indians from their land: Americans would use it more productively."

possession of a superior "nautical heritage and technology" (27-28). Nowhere does Francaviglia mention that the Spanish and Portuguese innovations he lauds were themselves the product of a combination of environmental adaptation (the European continent contains an extensive coastline), repeated, costly, and bloody warfare (which necessitated the development of defensive and offensive weaponry), and borrowing/theft (the Portuguese learned how to sail into the wind from Arab traders) (Blaut 1993: 181). The actual processes underlying supposed European technological "innovations" are explained coherently by Loewen (1995: 45):

> Every textbook account of the European exploration of the Americas begins with Prince Henry the Navigator, of Portugal, between 1415 and 1460. Henry is portrayed as discovering Madeira and the Azores and sending out ships to circumnavigate Africa for the first time. The textbook authors seem unaware that ancient Phoenicians and Egyptians sailed at least as far as Ireland and England, reached Madeira and the Azores, traded with the aboriginal inhabitants of the Canary Islands, and sailed all the way around Africa before 600 B.C. Instead, the textbooks credit Bartolomeu Dias with being the first to round the Cape of Good Hope at the southern tip of

Africa in 1488. Omitting the accomplishments of the Afro-Phoenicians is ironic, because it was Prince Henry's knowledge of their feats that inspired him to replicate them.....in fact Henry's work was based mostly on ideas that were known to the ancient Egyptians and Phoenicians and had been developed further in Arabia, North Africa, and China. Even the word the Portuguese applied to their new ships, *caravel,* derived from the Egyptian *caravos.*[35]

From Sail to Steam is not all Eurocentric fodder, however. On page 263 Francaviglia does attempt to recognize that traditional seafaring accounts have been written mostly from a "white" perspective, and that the global seafaring community was far more multicultural than previously recognized: "Recent scholarship suggests that African-American crewmen may have been more common than popularly thought, their presence revealed by careful scrutiny of ships' lists—including New Orleans-bound vessels in the early to late nineteenth century." The attempt at broadening the narrative to include other voices is laudable, but insincere; the roles of African-

---

[35] That is not all. "The Portuguese 'discovery' of the sea route to India therefore was a simple feat with the aid of Swahili navigators who had traveled the Indian Ocean for centuries" (Cohn and Platzer 1978: 3).

Americans in Texas maritime history (and maritime history generally) warrant more than a passing mention and head-nod to "recent scholarship." The role of African-Americans in nineteenth century seafaring (as enslaved laborers as well as free men and women) is central, not an aside. *From Sail to Steam* is a book operating firmly within the confines of the imperial "Texas Myth."

Randolph B. Campbell's *An Empire for Slavery*

Outside of Curlee's pathbreaking work, this book is the definitive tome on slavery in Texas and thus deserves careful analysis and discussion. I shall mainly concern myself here with a brief critique of some of the theoretical propositions contained in the book, and will enter into more detailed discussion later in the dissertation.

An Empire for Slavery is for the most part a conventional narrative history of nineteenth century Anglo slavery in Texas and is presented from this perspective. Campbell is concerned with examining the extent (geographic, economic and social) of slavery in Texas, and charts its demographic development, while situating the role of the peculiar institution within contemporaneous political discussion. He discusses, for instance, the role of slavery in the Texas revolution (it was, he says, a factor in the Texan desire for independence, but not necessarily the most important one), and analyzes newspaper accounts from the 1850's as they became increasingly virulent in their advocacy of slavery and the slave trade. This is not a social history; Campbell is not much concerned with interpersonal relations, the intimate dynamics of master/slave relationships, or the ethics of slavery, although he does briefly examine basic Texas slave conditions such as living arrangements, clothing, and slave foodways (chapter eight is titled "family, religion and music"). Campbell charts the basic course of the nineteenth century evolution of the institution in Texas and situates slavery within a more broad context in Texas historiography.

Campbell supports his main thesis well: that Texas should not be exclusively thought of as being "southwestern" in orientation and that slavery played a far larger role in the development of the state than is commonly recognized. *An Empire for Slavery,* however, is not an attempt at revisionist storytelling; the people he cites and the stories he relates make it clear that Campbell is mostly interested in encapsulating the horrific history of slavery in Texas firmly within the archetypical "Texas Myth," albeit perhaps within the liberal end of the spectrum.[36]

The most unfortunate problem with Campbell's study is that it discounts the role of the internal slave trade as a factor in the nineteenth century Anglo colonization of Texas.[37] He observes that "a demographic analysis of Texas' slaves suggests that most came to the state with their owners" although "had this type of migration ended, there would have been no shortage of slaves available through the domestic trade" (Campbell 1989: 51-53). As evidence Campbell cites "demographic analysis" and his examination of 181 of the Texas WPA narratives, which he claims to have "examined in detail

---

[36] In the preface of the book Campbell writes that his study "seeks to describe and interpret the Peculiar Institution in Texas without the aid of any particular theoretical model" and that "instead of structuring a model and fitting the story to a theory, it proceeds simply by asking large questions and seeking answers in available sources" (p. 9). The anthropological critique of this stance is fairly obvious (see, for example, Trouillot's examination of "single-site historicity" in *Silencing the Past*, pp. 14-22). Despite his claims to the contrary, Campbell's study is hardly atheoretical. He still sees at least some value in Fogel and Engerman's *Time on the Cross*, for instance, particularly the book's assertions regarding the importance of the slave trade and its (non) effects on slave families.

[37] He is not alone. In their introduction to the *Slave Narratives of Texas*, Tyler and Murphy (1974: xxii) write that "hundreds, perhaps thousands, of slaves came into Texas via the domestic slave trade."

and [to have] made a quantitative summary of all important information" (52). By 1996 Campbell seems to have modified his thinking somewhat (Tadman's book had been published by this point). In his entry for "slavery" in the *New Handbook of Texas*, Campbell writes:

> the great majority of slaves in Texas came with their owners from the older slave states. Sizable numbers, however, came through the domestic slave trade. New Orleans was the center of this trade in the Deep South, but there were slave dealers in Galveston and Houston, too. A few slaves, perhaps as many as 2,000 between 1835 and 1865, came through the illegal African trade. (Handbook of Texas Online: slavery).

Notice that Campbell still asserts that the majority of slaves in Texas migrated with their owners, but he is now willing to concede that "sizable numbers" were also traded into the state. As discussed in the next chapter in greater detail, Campbell's demographic analysis and methodology is flawed.[38] Tadman's more exhaustive inquiry indicates that most slaves in Texas,

---

[38] Campbell also misinterprets the extent of African slave trading in Texas. He states that "the most careful studies estimate that no more than two thousand slaves came to Texas in this way between 1836 and 1860" (p. 53) although more careful interpretation reveals that at least five times that number was smuggled into the state during this time period.

perhaps as many as seventy percent, were speculated into the state. Furthermore, Du Bois's investigation shows that much of the early African slave trading in Texas involved slaves being smuggled through not necessarily into Texas.

The underlying issue I have with Campbell is that he suffers from the same sort of "doxological" thinking Marshall Sahlins and others have exhibited (Obeyesekere 1997: 234) in their studies of the "other." The disposition to write "about" or "for" natives and colonized populations is a deeply embedded tendency in the social sciences and humanities, and the postcolonial critique of this phenomenon is by now extensive. What is unfortunate is not only that there is plenty of oral history material available for scholars of slavery to examine[39] but that it can be used to personify and lend voice to those most directly effected by the institution. It is therefore

---

[39] Thus the challenge of representation is made considerably easier than in "typical" anthropological situations such as in Hawai'i or other contact situations. This is not to imply that the WPA slave narratives are without flaws, but they nonetheless are far better source material than the missionary accounts and ships' logs often encountered by scholars.

regrettable that Campbell decided to investigate the narratives (and only a portion thereof) mainly for quantitative information and to reveal tidbits about slave lives, such as what they wore and ate, and where and how they slept. Had he read the narratives more deeply, he would have noted, for instance, the extensive references to slave dealing and family separation they contain, and he would have revised his argument about the non-centrality of slave trading accordingly. The narratives which I cite in chapter seven of this study leave very little about the centrality of slave trading in Texas to the imagination. Campbell's decision to omit information on the extensive extent of slave dealing in Texas (information which, interestingly, is cited at length by Curlee) is unfortunate and irresponsible but all too familiar and understandable.

In an interesting comment in Appendix 1—which discusses the reliability of the slave narratives as a historical source—of his study, Campbell observes:

In spite of these problems, this study used the slave

> narratives extensively in describing the lives of slaves in Texas. The primary reason, as noted above, is simple. They are the only source available, and refusing to use them would in effect constitute a refusal to address one vitally important aspect of the Peculiar Institution in the Lone Star state (p. 262).

It is revealing that Campbell seems to view employment of the narratives as a "refusal to use them." What was perhaps intended as a defense of the narratives as a historical tool is apparently also an oblique head-nod to a Texas historical establishment which up to that point had for the most part disregarded any usage of the narratives altogether. Unlike Campbell, I have not "not refused to use" the narratives; for me they are central in the attempt to describe slavery, slave life, and what it felt like to be separated from one's parents and siblings.[40]

Another criticism I have of Campbell is that his

---

[40] Even editors and writers generally sympathetic to a less Eurocentric point of view sometimes just don't "get it." In his review of the recently reissued *Slave Narratives of Texas* (1997) edited by Tyler and Murphy, T. Lindsay Baker writes "This is not a book about slavery: this is a book about what it was like to be a slave" (Baker 1999: 121). What Baker does not seem to realize is that the experience of what it was like to be a slave is the essence of slavery.

doxological thinking and Eurocentrism prevent him from saying things that are too negative about Texas or "leaders" firmly ensconced in the pantheon of Texas myth. Campbell is, I think far too generous in his description of Stephen F. Austin's "ambiguous" (p. 16 and elsewhere) feeling about the establishment and furtherance of slavery in his colony[41], and Campbell is also reluctant to admit the simple and by now not that controversial argument that the Texas Revolution was a war by the Anglo settlers to preserve their "freedom" and "property rights," those rights being understood, among other things, as the right to own and trade slaves. Campbell simply waffles on the issue: he concludes chapter two by observing

---

[41] On pages 22 and 28 Campbell claims that if forced to "choose between the peculiar institution and Texas" Stephen F. Austin "would choose Texas." The argument seems to be that if the Mexican authorities had taken a firmer stand against slavery, Austin would have (albeit reluctantly) gone along and fulfilled his obligations as a Mexican citizen. On page 16 he observes that "Austin would later express doubts concerning slavery in Texas, yet he, more than any other individual, was responsible for gaining the approval of Mexican authorities for introducing the institution there." The truth is that Austin was not morally opposed to slavery—indeed his father had bought and sold slaves—and never really was "forced" to choose between slavery or Texas. If Austin actually had been forced to make a choice it is not obvious which course he would have followed, although his racist and proslavery sentiments certainly provide a clue. Campbell's conciliatory—even flattering—rhetoric regarding "the father of Texas" and his stance on slavery seems at best rather "peculiar."

that "in the broadest sense, the conflict resulted from a clash of cultures," and that "protecting slavery was not the primary cause of the Texas Revolution, but it certainly was a major result," although earlier he observes that "circumstantial evidence supports the abolitionists' contention that slavery was the primary cause of conflict" (pp. 48-49).

To paraphrase from Du Bois' chapter "The Propaganda of History" from *Black Reconstruction* (1935), what do we gain by ignoring or whitewashing the simple truth that the Texas Revolution was primarily fought over the issue of slavery, as most northern historians have claimed for years? More to the point, who benefits when a historian sugarcoats or narrowly conceives this history? Campbell does not have as difficult of a time distinguishing between "fact and desire" (Du Bois 1986 [1935]: 1039) as some of his racist historian predecessors, but he nonetheless still shares too many of their biases.

Campbell also neglects to mention the significant role of slavery in the push toward U.S. annexation of Texas, and the role of the institution in the ideology of "Manifest Destiny" the primary justification used by the U.S. in the Mexican-American War. Campbell's discussion of politics and slavery in the decade leading up to the Civil War is better, but is still told from an Anglo point of view and the thoughts and feelings of the slaves on the subject are rendered invisible in his narrative. Not once does Campbell cite an opinion by an African-American intellectual. It is at best intellectually irresponsible and at worst racist to ignore or whitewash the fact that Stephen Austin was a racist and expansionist who in squashing an Indian (Cherokee) uprising, for instance would stop at "nothing short of extermination or expulsion" for Richard Fields and John Hunter [the leaders of the rebellion] and their self-proclaimed "Republic of Fredonia" (Chomsky 1993: 27).[42] Another historical figure who receives the kid-gloves treatment from Campbell is Sam Houston (Campbell

---

[42] While Cantrell's (1999) description of the Fredonian Rebellion is in some ways the best yet written, it shortchanges the views of the Cherokees involved. Drinnon (1972) provides a more full account of the uprising.

1993), whose role in the extermination and displacement of the Cherokee nation while acting as Andrew Jackson's Indian sub-agent, among others, is not nearly as seriously analyzed as it should be.[43] Houston's complicated relationship with Native America does not dismiss the fact that he was a racist and expansionist (only different in degree, but not kind from blatant rednecks such as John Calhoun) who on several occasions expressed his succor for Manifest Destiny and the supposed "glory of the Anglo-Saxon race" (Takaki 1993: 174), and that the virtues of this superior race entitled it to the divine destiny to people North and Central America. It is regrettable but not surprising that Campbell's biography of Houston, while it recognizes the centrality of slavery in Houston's career, does not contain one word uttered or written by a Black person.

---

[43] Nor are Houston's shady land speculations and suspected slave trading (Nevin 1975: 53), tidbits of which he doubtlessly picked up from his mentor Andrew Jackson who was a known slave trader and paternalistic Indian hater (Zinn 1980: 125; see also Bancroft 1996[1931]:300).

Edward T. Cotham Jr.'s *Battle on the Bay*

This recent (University of Texas Press 1998) book is a study of Galveston during the Civil War. Galveston was the largest and most important "city" in Texas at this time and was a focal point for most Anglo and immigrant socioeconomic activity. Like the other books discussed in this chapter, slavery and slave trading (and matters of race generally) are not a primary focus of the historical narrative. Cotham's "big men in Texas history" tale discusses conventional subjects such as the effects of the Union blockade of the city, the battle of Kuhn's Wharf, and the actions (and eccentricities) of John Bankhead Magruder, whose "cottonclad" strategy of coastal defense spared the city from destruction and permanent occupation by Union naval forces. Slaves are mentioned in spots throughout the book, but mostly as an aside; no attempt is made to discern how the war was perceived from the slave perspective, or how developments during the war such as blockade running involved slaves or slave trading.

Cotham's understanding of slavery and of master/slave relations falls comfortably within the racist "Texas Myth" framework discussed earlier. Cotham's analysis of the 1860 census for Galveston, for instance, reveals that "Galveston's slaves were predominantly personal or household slaves, *who were for the most part well cared for and frequently treated almost as members of the family*" (emphasis added, Cotham 1998: 2). Cotham's source for these claims (especially the latter claim) is Earl W. Fornell's far superior study *The Galveston Era* (pp. 115-125). The problem is that Cotham has misinterpreted and misread what Fornell says; what Cotham has done is insert his own accommodationist master/slave ideology into his reading of the source material. What Fornell actually indicated was that there were "good reasons why the position of Galveston 'city Negroes' was envied by the slaves in the interior" (Fornell 1961: 117),[44] but he also was scrupulous in

---

[44] The desirability of urban over rural slavery among enslaved populations was a common phenomenon and is by now amply documented in the literature (for post-emancipation urbanization processes in Houston, for instance, see Beeth, Howard and Cary D. Wintz (Eds.)

maintaining that slaves were considered property and were treated as an investment. Indeed, a "1,500 Negro could pay for himself in five years" if hired out at a rate of "$250 to $300 a year plus keep" (p. 118).

Furthermore, Cotham's thesis of well contented and "family" slaves is contradicted by the actions undertaken by Confederate authorities as the city was under attack. Cotham mentions, for instance, that in 1863 the city

> was saved during this period [from further attack by Union Navy forces] by the fact that using the forced labor of thousands of slaves, as well as his own troops, Magruder and his engineers had supervised the erection of an elaborate chain of earthworks and wooden fortifications. This work was both difficult and dangerous. Internment records document that from February to April, 1863, at least sixty-two black men were buried in Galveston. Although their cause of death was listed simply as "not known," many soldiers suspected that these deaths were due to overwork, neglect and a virtual epidemic of lice" (p. 149).

Surely slaves (or their relatives) that were considered "family

---

Black Dixie) It takes a great deal of (racist) imagination to argue, however, that the slaves were "almost members of the family" as Cotham does. This thinking is wholly derived from the white romanticized "myth of the well treated slave" fantasy discussed earlier.

members" would not have been coerced into performing such dangerous and dirty work?

The same time period witnessed discussion of the feasibility of not only using slave labor for Confederate purposes, but of actually arming the slaves who had built the fortifications. Arguments concerning the arming of slaves during wartime are an American (and especially southern) tradition. Galveston attorney William Pitt Ballinger floated the idea, for example of "occupy[ing] these fortifications primarily with slaves, who would be made part of the Confederate Army and issued muskets. This part of the proposal, although controversial, Ballinger viewed as 'vital to us." (p. 158).

Thus it seems that slaves played a far greater role in "the Civil War struggle for Galveston" than Cotham lets on. Scholars who have more closely examined master/slave dynamics in Galveston before and during the war (such as Fornell) have found a rich gold mine of information. But for Cotham, like the other authors discussed in this chapter, enslaved African-

Americans are labor: earthwork builders, ditch diggers, and fortification constructors. They are contributors to the larger "Texas myth" and not worthy of special consideration and treatment. Furthermore, they were "happy" and considered "part of the family." It is remarkable that such racist historiography can be published by a major university press as recently as 1998.

Stephen R. Wise's *Lifeline of the Confederacy*

This is the standard reference work on the business of Civil War blockade running and is referenced extensively by the maritime archaeology group excavating the aforementioned *Denbigh* shipwreck. A reviewer for *The American Neptune* summed up his opinion of the book (reprinted in the book's back cover) in the following manner:

> Yeeeeeeeeee haaaaa! A Rebel Yell is an appropriate way to enthusiastically endorse Stephen R. Wise's Lifeline of the Confederacy...an excellent piece of research that will be appreciated by scholars and laymen alike...

Unlike the rhapsodic reviewer, I cannot "enthusiastically endorse" this book. Like the other books discussed in this chapter, *Lifeline of the Confederacy* does contain much information that is useful and enlightening. Its rendition of events and interpretation of actions and motives, however, are narrated from a plain and barely-concealed neo-Confederate perspective.

The most glaring deficiency of the book is its neglect of

the slave trade and of African-Americans in general. It is truly remarkable that Wise, who consulted many works on the subject of blockade running, could have literally <u>written out</u> the extensive evidence of illicit slave smuggling and military impressment of African-Americans by the Confederacy (or, more accurately, by southern citizens of the Confederacy) and the important role this played in the Civil War. One notable example is Civil War hero Robert Smalls who on March 13, 1862 sailed the steamer *Planter* which had been converted into a gunboat, out of Charleston and turned it over to blockading Union forces (Christian 1995: 192). A slave impressed into the Confederate navy in 1861, Smalls later piloted the vessel for union naval forces and eventually became captain of the ship. He later became a member of the U.S. House of Representatives during Reconstruction and served five (highly charged) terms in Congress.[45]

---

[45] Another great example is William Tillman, steward and cook of the *S.J. Waring*, homeported in New York. The ship was captured by the *Jeff Davis* a Confederate privateer, in June of 1861. Upon learning that he was to be sold as a slave when the ship pulled into

Wise seems disappointed that the business of blockade running was largely an enterprise of self-interest and was only loosely organized to assist the Confederate war effort, especially in western ports such as Galveston. His assessment of private blockade-running schemes is decidedly negative:

> Nonmilitary articles carried in by private vessels were sold on the Southern market at extremely high prices, fueling inflation. The government did not attempt to control the type of goods coming in, and valuable cargo space was given over to such luxury items as liquors, carpets, furniture, and jewelry, which brought a high return in the South (Wise 1988: 120).

Confederate secretary of the treasury George Alfred Trenholm was also distressed by the inordinate amount of speculation that was taking place throughout the south, an opportunism Wise interprets as lack of Confederate patriotism, but a phenomenon which really simply flowed naturally from the frontier-bred anti-government, "free market" and "property rights" mentality of most money-minded southerners:

Charleston, Tillman revolted, killed the captain in his sleep, wounded the mate and took control of the ship. He then sailed the vessel back to New York. The New York Tribune wrote of the event: "To this colored man was the nation indebted for the first vindication of its honor on the sea" (Brown 1969[1867]: 74-75).

> Problems arose over citizens' reluctance to sell their cotton for bonds, and with the railroads still shipping private cotton ahead of the government's. Trenholm felt the South's greatest enemy was the selfishness and apathy of the Confederate people. As he wrote to a Treasury Department agent in Augusta, Georgia: "If we break down under such circumstances, it will be our fault and we deserve nobody's compassion or sympathy" (p. 152).

There were many ironies that surrounded the blockade runner's craft, and much romanticism too. One of the ironies was that a cash-strapped and credit-poor Confederacy made extensive use of British ports (particularly Nassau, Bermuda, and Halifax) in its "trading" activities, and as the war dragged on made considerable use of Belize, Honduras, Cuba, and other Caribbean islands as well. Many blockade runners were built in British shipyards, and were purchased with cotton credit. The irony is that almost two decades before, Texas annexationists and other Democrats in Congress—led by the potentially meanest man in American political history, John C. Calhoun—argued vociferously that Great Britain was conspiring to destroy "King Cotton," slavery, and ultimately the southern way of life, and that to forestall impending disaster the United States "had" to annex Texas and later go to war with Mexico. A few years later, circumstances had changed; it turns out that the British weren't so anxious to interfere with southern internal politics after all. Indeed, British support of the Confederate cause was substantial and crucial.[46] By the time of the Civil War, a former enemy had thus become a wartime "friend." To their credit, most Confederate officials and intellectuals maintained their deluded religious adherence in the power of cotton (and its influence over British foreign policy) until pretty much the very end. Cotton bales were even creatively used in several naval engagements; the vessels, known as "cottonclads" were instrumental in the defeat of

---

[46] Many privateers flew the British flag on their way to Halifax, for instance. See the letter of Charles Platt and other leaders of insurance companies to the Secretary of the Navy in the *Official Records of the Union and Confederate Navies*, p. 60.

Union warships in Galveston and Sabine Pass, for instance.[47]

The romance associated with blockade running was unfounded. Wise observes:

> Because of the physical danger of running the blockade, a romantic atmosphere developed around the men who worked the trade. The sailors involved were seen as daredevils who sought life-and-death adventures while taking their frail vessels through a gauntlet of Union warships. In actuality, there was little danger in challenging the blockade (110).

In the end, Wise's study is essentially an examination of some of the exploits of leading blockade runners and is a retrospective assessment—by a sympathetic southerner—of why the enterprise failed and why the south ultimately lost the war. Wise's argument appears to be that a lack of Confederate unity and national loyalty was one of the main reasons why the Confederacy lost the war. Who could argue with this? The problem with this study is that it utterly ignores the slave

---

[47] This was a strategy that worked during the Texas Revolution as well. See Jackson (1985).

trade[48] and Africans and African-Americans generally; there is not a word by a Black man or woman in the book.

---

[48] Two events that could have been mentioned include the capture of the slavers *Nightingale* (a 1066 ton clipper of Boston registry captured with 961 slaves) and *Triton* (captured by *USS Constellation* at the mouth of the Congo river) off the African coast in April and May of 1861 (Official Records of the Union and Confederate Navies 1894: 11, 24).

CHAPTER 3: THE GEOGRAPHY OF THE TEXAS GULF COAST AND AN OVERVIEW OF THE TEXAS SLAVE TRADE

It remains true that geography and climate are to history what stage and props are to drama: necessary to the acting out of the play, but not the play itself.
Herbert Aptheker " Afro-American History, The Modern Era" p. 17.

Colonization and settlement is fundamentally about geography, and a basic understanding of Texas geography is essential to any attempt to grasp the dynamics of the Texas slave trade. Many of the early colonial settlements (Spanish, French, Anglo) were along the coast, and these coastal villages and towns, particularly Galveston, were the entry point for thousands of immigrants and other settlers. Texas' 624 miles of coastline and constantly shifting sandbars and estuaries also provided a haven for smugglers and pirates of every persuasion, including slave traders, during the early nineteenth century.

Physiography

It has as been long recognized that Texas is not just a cultural but also a geographic meeting place. In terms of climate, physiography, soil, and weather, Texas is the place where south meets west:

> The eastern plains of the state are a continuation of the large Atlantic and Gulf Coastal Plain which extends from the Yucatan to Cape Cod. The North Central prairies and woodlands of the state come from the vast interior lowlands of the Midwest, while the High Plains are part of the great north-south High Plains of the continent's interior. In the western part of the state is the southern extension of the Rocky Mountains. Thus, the state serves as a places of focus for some of the continent's major landforms—plains, lowlands, plateaus, and mountains (Meinig 1969: 17).

Figure 2 depicts the major physiographic regions of the U.S. and of Texas. Since the major emphasis in this dissertation is on the maritime component of the slave trade, the geographic discussion which follows will focus primarily on the Gulf Coastal Plain region of Texas and on the gulf of Mexico. Jordan et al. (1984: 31) characterize this region as:

> grassland [which is] underlain by calcareous clays derived from recently emerged limestones and shales. The region consists of two major subdivisions. Coastal marshes parallel the Texas Gulf Coast for its entire length, at no point extending very far inland. The marsh terrain is falt and poorly drained, capable of supporting only halophytic wetland grasses of little value for livestock. Toward the interior, an upland prairie emerges, with a

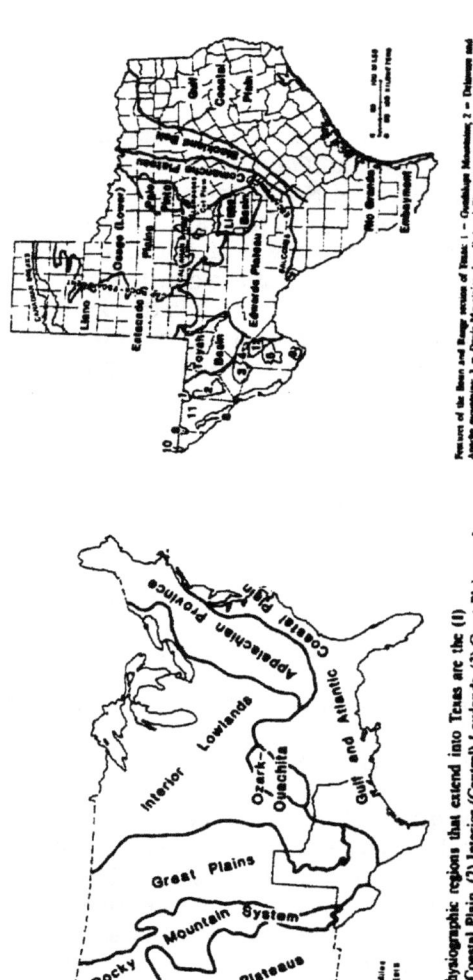

Figure 2: Major Physiographic Regions of the United States and Texas. Source: Jordan, Terry G., J.L. Bean, and William M. Holmes, 1984 *Texas: A Geography*, pp. 8-9

lush bunch-grass and bluestem cover that is excellent for livestock. Hardwoods also are found along the water courses.

Sediments in this region are generally divided into two groups, those of Pleistocene or Holocene (4,500-2,800 B.P.) deposition. "Two natural depositional systems comprise the Pleistocene system: fluvaic-deltaic and a barrier-strandplain system formed over 38,000 B.P. (Hoyt et al 1998: 20). The lengthy marsh-swamp systems which characterize the coast approach the gulf at the innermost part of the continental shelf and are composed mainly of relict Pleistocene sand and mud, and predominantly turn into muddy fine sand as one goes down the shore face floor.

Major barrier islands such as the Bolivar Peninsula, Galveston Island, and Follets Island started to be formed approximately 4,500 B.P. when sands eroded from Pleistocene deltaic headlands and the inner shelf migrated southwestward via long shore currents and wind-generated waves. These deposits are affected by changing currents and tides and facilitate the development of marine life and marsh grasses, which assist in the gradual deposition of more sediment. These phenomena are ongoing processes and are accelerated or counteracted further by weather (e.g. hurricanes) or human activity (there has been extensive dredging inside the sandbars along the Texas coast). To summarize, the physiography of the Texas gulf coast is made up of adjoining estuarine bays which are shielded from the Gulf of Mexico by a chain of barrier islands that contain narrow and shifting tidal passes. These barrier islands bear the brunt of wind and wave activity and are constantly changing.

Climate

Hot summers and mild winters are the norm along the Texas gulf coast. The area is subject to considerable levels of tropical weather activity, and between late spring and early autumn winds blow predominantly from the southeast bringing hot and muggy conditions to the area from the gulf. Sixty-five tropical storms and hurricanes struck the Texas coast between

1871 and 1982 (Hoyt et al 1998: 11), the most serious of which was the Galveston hurricane of 1900 which featured maximum sustained winds of 125 mph, a 20 foot storm surge height, and an estimated death toll in excess of 6,000 people. This hurricane is one of the worst natural disasters in American history.

Average summer humidity along the upper Texas coast averages around 70 percent at about mid-afternoon and increases to about 80 percent at night. Summer is also when most of the rain falls, averaging 40 inches at Matagorda Bay and 28 inches at Baffin Bay (Carr 1967). Starting in October the winds begin to shift to a more northeasterly direction, producing greater wave activity and resulting in a re-suspension of bottom mud and sediment along the shore. These northers which "tend to amplify ebb tides and in part, neutralize flood tides" (Hoyt et al 1998: 15) also reduce salinity levels, which has an effect on estuarine marine life.

During periods of early settlement, seasonal rains caused

flooding which turned roads into nearly impassable quagmires.

Ferdinand Roemer wrote in 1846:

> The whole prairie as far as the Brazos was under water. The creeks and bayous also had overflowed their banks and could be crossed only by swimming. These overflows occur every spring in the coastal region and disrupt communication with the interior almost entirely, or make travel very difficult (Roemer 1935).

Human Habitation And Adaption Along The Gulf Coast

The aboriginal inhabitants of the region were the Karankawa (or Spanish *Carancahua*), American Indians comprised of five major groups. Settlement in this region, according to radiocarbon dates obtained by archaeologist Robert Ricklis, dates back at least 4,000 years (Ricklis 1996: 44), although the first documented contact between gulf coast Indians and Europeans is explained by Alvar Núñez Cabeza de Vaca in his *Relación*, which documents his party's Texas coast adventures that occurred after a shipwreck in 1528.

Ricklis argues that the Karankawa followed a highly specialized prehistoric settlement and subsistence pattern which was well adapted to the coastal environment and which was gradually disturbed by increasing Spanish settlement.[49] There were less than a thousand Karankawa left when Anglo settlement began in the nineteenth century, and these were quickly displaced and eliminated by the settlers. The seasonal

---

[49] I do not entirely agree with Ricklis' interpretation of the relationship between the Karankawa and the Spanish missions. Ricklis is to be commended for suggesting that the Karankawa may have made a conscious choice to adapt to changing and difficult socioeconomic circumstances as Spanish influence grew. This is a more agentive approach that at least acknowledges some element of choice among the Karankawa. Ricklis' inattention to power relations, however, leads him to argue that "stabilizing selection" (an idea he adapts from Kirch 1980) allowed the Karankawa to essentially maintain their established sociocultural and subsistence patterns while their relationship to the Spanish moved from one based on conflict to one based on more peaceful interaction. He argues that "new sociocultural input was integrated into established patterns in a way that maintained, rather than disrupted those patterns" (Ricklis 1996: 172). Who is disturbing whose subsistence pattern here? This argument is ridiculous. European settlement in the Western Hemisphere was highly disruptive and destructive to most indigenous populations (especially diseases), and the Karankawa were no exception to this rule of thumb. A brief example: although Ricklis doesn't mention the incident, Jean Laffite's pirates and privateers routinely kidnapped and sexually exploited Karankawa women. When the Indians retaliated and killed five members of Laffite's colony, the privateers massacred the Indians with artillery (Ramsay 1996: 107). An analogue: Africans and African-Americans also engaged in a considerable amount of adaptation on plantations and also exercised agency in a multitude of ways. But following Ricklis' logic, would it be appropriate to suggest that slaves incorporated enslavement and everything associated with it into their lifeways? Such an argument would be absurd; it is obvious who held the reins on the plantation and who didn't. The element of choice was severely limited by the "sheer power of masters" discussed in Tadman's theorizations. The fact is that the Spanish erected forts, built missions, and established European agriculture in Texas with enslaved or coerced Indian labor. In the end, the "stabilizing selection" aspect of Ricklis' (otherwise well constructed) argument is a smokescreen and apologia for the unequal power relations inherent in imperialism. The same is true of Kirch's work in Hawai'i. Loewen (1999: 65) provides the most direct and honest assessment of what happened: "Anthropologists are fond of saying that the French penetrated Native American societies, the Spanish acculturated them, and the British expelled them. Or, equally accurate, the French exploited the Indians, the Spanish enslaved them, and the Anglos killed them."

Karankawa subsistence pattern extrapolated from the archaeological evidence by Ricklis basically goes as follows. The Karankawa primarily harvested fish and shellfish during fall and winter at strategic locations (fishing camps) along the coast, and dispersed into smaller coastal prairie groupings in the spring and summer to make greater use of terrestrial flora and fauna (which included bison hunting camps). The diet was supplemented by opportunistic consumption of nuts, berries, and roots throughout the year.

European Impressions Of Texas

Early (i.e. pre-nineteenth century) expeditionary observations of the Texas gulf coast were primarily impressionistic or chance descriptions that were driven by military/political concerns as opposed to economic affairs. In the early sixteenth century, Spain was still in the exploratory stages of its colonization efforts, especially in the northern reaches of its overseas empire. Cabeza de Vaca, one of the survivors of the ill fated Narvaez expedition[50] was one of the first Europeans to offer a description of Texas when he published his *Relacion* in 1539. Driven coastward in 1528 by one of the seasonal storms that periodically inundate the western gulf of Mexico, his impressions of the gulf coast, particularly its waves, were understandably not positive:

> Near dawn I thought I heard the roar of the breakers near shore, which was very loud because the coast was so low. Surprised by this, I roused the sailing master, who said he thought that we were near land.....near land a great wave took us and cast the boat out of the water as far as a horseshoe can be tossed....another strong wave caused the boat to capsize...since the surf was very rough, the sea wrapped all the men in its waves, except the three that had been pulled under by the boat, and cast them on the shore of the same island (Favata and Fernandez 1993: 22).

About 160 years later the French explorer La Salle also did not have a favorable initial impression of the gulf coast. Having overnavigated his target (the mouth of the Mississippi) by over

---

[50] Which, incidentally, included Estevanico, the first known African and slave to set foot in what is now Texas. It should be noted that the mestizaje that took place in Mexico (i.e. Texas) did not just involve Spaniards and indigenous peoples. "During the period of 1521-1821, more Africans entered Mexico than Spaniards" (Chávez Leyva, 2000: 3).

250 nautical miles, La Salle instead landed at present-day Matagorda, where one of his ships the *Aimable* promptly ran aground in a mudflat while attempting to navigate a shallow narrow barrier island inlet.

By the late eighteenth century Spain had sent several expeditions into Texas and had developed reliable maps and charts of the area.[51] It was also around this time that the Spanish crown initiated serious colonization/missionary attempts. While these attempts met with limited success, the increasing attention on Texas also fired the imaginations of pirates and privateers who were already active in other regions of the Gulf and in the Caribbean. By the mid eighteenth century, Texas was a fairly regular "hiding spot" for corsairs

---

[51] One of the more noteworthy maps of New Spain was generated early in the nineteenth century by the German traveller, scientist, and classical liberal philosopher (a major influence on Chomsky) Alexander Von Humboldt. Humboldt had at his disposal important maps that were generated between 1783 and 1786 by the Spanish pilot José de Evía who had been sent to chart the Texas coastline by Governor Bernardo de Gálvez, for whom Galveston is named (Francaviglia 1998: 74).

and other unscrupulous mariners.[52]

On the other hand, early Anglo impressions of the coast, and especially of the prairie located further inland, were positive. The Zebulon Pike expedition, which passed through Texas between 1806 and 1807, was in no small measure responsible for popularizing the agricultural potential of Texas. Pike's

> description of Texas as a good place to farm excited many Americans. Pike wrote about well watered, well-wooded fertile soil for farming, grassy meadows for grazing immense herds of wild horses, and abundant game. He claimed that Texas had one of the most delightful climates in the world. The Pike report contributed to the land hunger and profit seeking for which Americans were noted. These scientific and geographical observations made the Pike expedition second only to the Lewis and Clark expedition in contributing to the knowledge of the American frontier (Stephens and Holmes 1989: 16)

The land which Pike described as being so lush is the Texas gulf coastal prairie, which extends along the gulf from the

---

[52] The port of El Copano which was opened in 1785 at the order of Viceroy Don José de Gálvez to supply the Spanish mission at Goliad, quickly developed into a "haven for smugglers and pirates" (Francaviglia 1998: 74).

Sabine to the Lower Rio Grande Valley. "The eastern half is covered with a heavy growth of grass; the western half, which is more arid, is covered with short grass and, in some places, with small timber and brush (Ramos 1997: 63). Moses (and later Stephen) Austin were well aware of the agricultural potential of this area, and were eventually awarded a generous empresario grant along the central Texas gulf coast which embraced much of the lower Colorado and Brazos river basins.

Rivers In Texas

Texas's riverine trade networks were instrumental in the nineteenth century socioeconomic development of the state. Indeed, it is "difficult, actually impossible, in Texas to separate riverine history from other aspects of maritime history" (Francaviglia 1998: xv). Planters wasted little time in establishing facilities that would allow them to ship their plantation cotton to the coast. For example "Groce's Ferry" was a landing along the Brazos river established by Jared E. Groce shortly after he came to Texas. Groce shipped the bales downriver to Velasco on homemade flatboats (which were usually driven by slaves) to waiting schooners and steamships (which began to be used in the mid 1830's) where agents would then ship the cargo to New Orleans and beyond. Groce's plantation and the steamship *Yellowstone* also figured prominently in the Texas Revolution. Another planter who quickly established docks, sheds and storage facilities along the Brazos was Stephen Austin confidant Josiah Bell who established a plantation on the Brazos near Columbia (Silverthorne 1986: 17). Once the ax and plow had brought a significant portion of Texas land under cultivation, varying shipping magnates began to compete for the business of transporting cotton and sugar. The largest entrepreneurs (with interests in shipping, commissions, planting, and banking) in Texas were the Kentucky-born Mills brothers, David, Robert, and Andrew, who established a sugar plantation and three cotton plantations at Lowood. At the height of his power Robert Mills was the largest slaveowner in Texas with over 800 slaves and was known as the "Duke of Brazoria" (Nevin 1975: 162). What is infrequently recognized (certainly not by Francaviglia, for instance) is that cotton was not the only commodity that was traded along Texas riverways. Slaves were traded as well. The most common method of slave introduction inland mirrored the transfer of other cargo from the coast. Fast seagoing vessels would bring several hundred slaves to major ports such as Velasco or Galveston, where they were then transferred to smaller vessels (rafts, flatboats, keelboats, or steamboats) for riverine transfer to waiting plantations. In the case of Houston, Slaves were transported up Buffalo Bayou by small boat (Haygood 1992: 33-34). Significant numbers of slaves were also marched to Texas overland via Arkansas and Louisiana, however as mentioned I will be mostly restricting my focus to the maritime component of the trade.

Disease

Epidemic diseases were a major factor influencing life

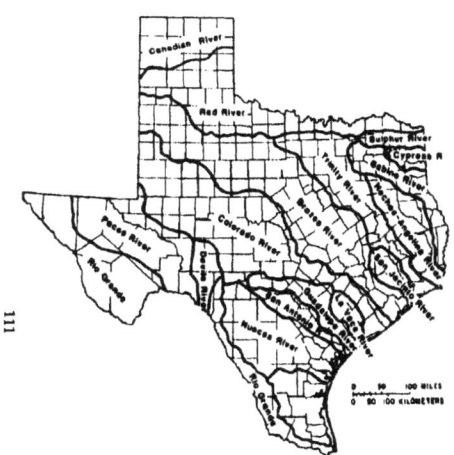
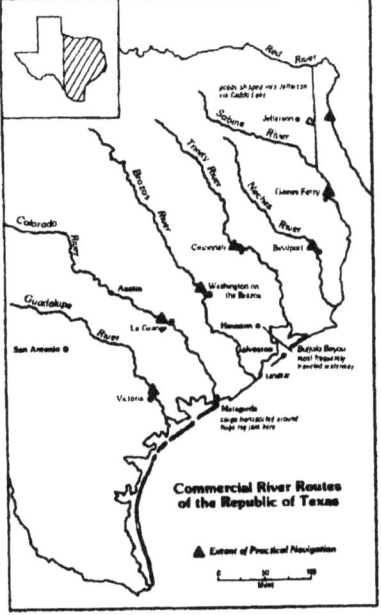

Figure 3: Rivers and Commercial River Routes in early Texas.
Sources: Jordan, Terry G., J.L. Bean, and William M. Holmes, 1984 *Texas: A Geography*, and D. Ryan Smith et.al., 1983, *Commerce*.

along the coast, and played a considerable role in trade, including the slave trade. In Galveston (but elsewhere along the coast such as Mobile as well), politicians took a laissez-faire attitude toward the enforcement of sanitation regulations that could have prevented much of the misery, but the general feeling amongst local elites was that unnecessary alarmism about yellow fever, cholera, or malaria would be bad for business. All too often the devastating effects of disease were obvious and worsening, however, and local papers published a "fever report" listing the names of those in the city who had died.

The demographic effects of disease on the coast were significant. "Almost one out of every two young Texans born on the coast during the fifties" died due to yellow fever or cholera. 400 people died of yellow fever in 1844, and 535 died in 1853 (Fornell 1961: 67). Some of the notable Galvestonians who lost children during this time period include the German editor Ferdinand Flake (5 children), William Pitt Ballinger (4 children), and E.H. Cushing (wife and son).

City ordinances were passed in 1846 and 1857 which required incoming ships to possess health certificates and which provided for cargo quarantine and other sanitation measures. The regulations, however, contained an escape clause which allowed shipowners to pay a $1 per person commutation fee. According to the British consul at Galveston, it was non-enforcement of the laws and not "excessive consumption of drink" and other often strange "causes" of disease, which were primarily responsible for periodic outbreaks of disease. The consul additionally noted that unsafe business practices (in slaughterhouses, for example) combined with the unusual climate in Galveston also contributed to the spread of diseases (Fornell 1961: 69).

The effects of yellow fever on the slave population are difficult to gauge. There is evidence that gulf coast blacks were more resistant to the scourge than Euro-Americans. Joseph J. Reynolds, assistant commissioner during Reconstruction in

Texas, wrote in 1867 during a yellow fever epidemic that the ravage held "few terrors" for blacks and that they were "almost entirely exempt from its ravages" (Crouch 1992: 31).

The effects of malaria and cholera were greatest on the plantations:

> Epidemics of the dreaded cholera caused panic in Texas cities and among plantation residents in the lower Brazos area in 1833-34 and again in 1850 and 1852. Hundreds died in Austin's colony in the first epidemic, including the eleven-year-old daughter of Emily Perry by her first marriage. Texans referred to 1833 as the year of the "Big Cholera." The towns of Brazoria and Velasco were devastated by the disease, and the plantation families suffered proportionately (Silverthorne 1986: 143).

A Smuggler's Haven

The first two decades of the nineteenth century were the golden days of smuggling in the Gulf of Mexico. The Texas coastline was used extensively by these marauders for two main reasons: 1. the aforementioned geographic advantages, which not only included concealability, but also proximity to major slaves markets such as Cuba, which was only a 4-5 day sail away, and 2. the coast was weakly guarded by Mexican authorities.

As mentioned, the shifting coast of Texas can present many problems for unvigilant or unfamiliar mariners. From afar, the coastline appears uneven, sandy, and somewhat unfettered; the topography appears cluttered and confusing in spots and one isn't sure if the coast is shielded by "islands" or by something else. Ship groundings are still a common feature along the Texas gulf coast today; a wise mariner entering Texas waters for the first time makes full use of ranges, buoys, and other aids to navigation. Above all, he/she makes sure to stay within the boundaries of the ship channel.[53]

In addition, the Brazos, Trinity, Colorado, Nueces, and Sabine rivers, among others, are navigable rivers which empty into the gulf and these provided smugglers a safe haven in case authorities successfully negotiated coastline sandbars. In the

---

[53] While serving aboard USS GLADIATOR (MCM 11) I participated in dozens of "sea and anchor" details and personally observed ship groundings, oil spills, and other incidents, attributable most of the time to a combination of tricky geography and human error.

early days sailing ships or (more frequently) small boats made the trip up the river with the contraband cargo. Beginning in the late 1830's steamships routinely traded farm equipment, cotton, and slaves up and down these waters.

In short, Texas' favorable geography made it a "fortunate" as well as logical choice for illegal activities of all sorts, including slave trading. Favorably located to the west of the United States, but still close enough to New Orleans so that illegal smuggling could be carried on profitably, these socio-geographic[54] advantages continue to play a significant role in contemporary Texas political discussions, albeit for somewhat different reasons.

---

[54] I use this term to emphasize the point that Texas was chosen as a smugglers' outpost. As Turner (1992: 7) notes in his excellent study Beyond Geography, the ideology and mythology of westward expansion are really about "the human spirit and its dark necessity to realize itself through body and place."

Characterizing and Estimating the Extent of the Slave Trade

Had the country been conceived of as existing primarily for the benefit of its actual inhabitants, it might have waited for natural increase or immigration to supply the needed hands; but both Europe and the earlier colonists themselves regarded this land as existing chiefly for the benefit of Europe, and as designed to be exploited, as rapidly and ruthlessly as possible, of the boundless wealth of its resources. This was the primary excuse for the rise of the African slave-trade to America

W.E.B. Du Bois, *Suppression of the African Slave Trade to the United States of America, 1638-1870, p. 193.*

It is notoriously difficult to produce reliable estimates of slave transfers or sales. The problem is compounded by the many interpretations of fact that are produced by how one defines and interprets the data. In Texas, the major sets of demographic data are census figures and information collected from tax rolls, although the data is of questionable reliability, especially the material from the early settlement and republic periods. Tax roll data is particularly unreliable, especially in frontier areas as infested by rogues and speculators such as Texas. Too frequently census data is also unreliable, as the manufactured northern "insanity" figures for free blacks from the 1840 census demonstrate (Merk 1972: 61-8).[55] There is also a "tendency, in the census, not to use explicit terms such as "Negro trader" [which] might reflect a stigma attached to the trade...more important, however, seems to be the tendency to use fairly general categories of occupation in the census, together with the fact that many traders had other interests, such as landowning (Tadman 1996[1989]: 35). Ultimately, from an ethical standpoint discussions of slave trading are a zero-sum numbers game; whether the figure is "sixty million and more" as declared by Toni Morrison in the introduction to *Beloved*, or something less is in the end not important.

As previously mentioned, my discussion of the numbers

---

[55] Much of the nineteenth century census data for Texas is simply implausible. It is still better than the tax roll information, however. A political study of the role of race in the decennial census would reveal many interesting tidbits. The census bureau, for instance, admits that the 1990 census was far less accurate than the 1980 census, the first time in the history of the bureau that accuracy declined instead of increased between censuses. Not only do the census bureau and the Bureau of Labor Statistics (BLS) have a reputation for flattering the American economy, they deliberately undercount the number of homeless persons, the unemployed, and members of disadvantaged minority groups generally. What is interesting is that these political debates have a long and arduous history in America (Brill 1999: 39-44), and as always have been deeply influenced by race. Another example of census data misuse occurred during World War II when the bureau conspired with the War Department to identify, relocate, and inter Japanese Americans (Holmes 2000).

leans heavily upon the research of Tadman's *Speculators and Slaves*. Although I believe that Tadman's analysis is among the best available, it is far from perfect; in a letter to me dated 16 April 99, Tadman recognizes that "in Texas in particular, I should probably have paid more attention to African importations," for instance. Estimating the precise extent of the African slave trade into Texas is a daunting task, primarily for two reasons: 1. many of the illegal Africans imported into Texas were smuggled <u>through</u> the state into nearby states such as Louisiana and Mississippi (although direct importations <u>into</u> Texas gradually increased and peaked prior to the Civil War), and 2. because the importations from Africa were illegal, the forged paperwork and counterfeit manifests or bills of sale are difficult to distinguish from regular (legal) slave sales. Thus any attempt to fix a figure is bound to be a rough estimate.[56] However the number of illegal importations is underestimated

---

[56] Fornell (1961: 242) estimated that the extent of the African trade during the 1850's "sometimes amounted to several hundred slaves each year."

significantly by establishment Texas historians such as Campbell and by Robbins (1972) whose master's thesis is the most extensive discussion of the subject.[57]

With regard to the legal African-American slave trade, in *An Empire for Slavery* (p. 51) Campbell argues that

> If Texas were importing most of its slaves from older states in the Upper South, then there should have been a high proportion of males and prime-age slave population—the assumption being that bondsmen of this sort would be more desirable as a labor force without children and old people. The fact was, however, that Texas' slave population was highly similar in age and sex characteristics to those of Upper South states such as Virginia. In other words, a demographic analysis of Texas' slaves suggests that most came to the state with

---

[57] Robbins' estimates are quite confused. In the abstract of his study he claims that "approximately three thousand slaves entered Texas illegally." In the conclusion he estimates that "five thousand or less" (p. 148) Africans were smuggled into Texas. Earlier he estimates that "the combined number of slaves imported into Texas between 1816 and 1860 may have reached five or six thousand" (p. 140). Regarding transshipment, he claims that "as many as several thousand slaves entered the United States through Texas, although the number certainly never exceeded three or four thousand" (pp. 139-140). This, then, would produce a rough estimate of 8000-9000 Africans landed along Texas shores. There are many problems with this figure. First, it is countered by Robbins' own narrative description. Ships routinely landed slave cargoes as high as 900 slaves along the Texas gulf coast, throughout this time period; Robbins cites dozens of ships which were captured or suspected of smuggling slaves into or through Texas (see Table 2). Secondly, the British consuls in Havana and Galveston, as well as the American customs collector in New Orleans, had far higher estimates of the magnitude of the trade; in 1836 the former estimated that *fifteen thousand* slaves were annually taken into Texas (Franklin 1988: 111). The truth probably lies somewhere in between, although Robbins' estimates are almost certainly too conservative.

their owners.

There is an immediate problem inherent in this line of reasoning. Campbell has mis-identified the argument; the comparison he makes is false and misleading. The question is not whether the Texas slave population was demographically similar to the enslaved population of states such as Virginia. The question is *what is the nature of the interregional movement in slaves into Texas?* Campbell illogically claims that the sex and age similarities between the slave populations of Texas and states such as Virginia indicates that slaves came to Texas primarily with their owners. Tadman (1996[1989]: 5) is more specific and reasoned in indicating where the actual controversy lies:

> We should note, first, that there has never been any real doubt that the antebellum period saw a massive interregional movement of slaves. In fact, between 1820, and 1860 that movement averaged, each decade, some 200,000 slaves (or fully 10 percent of the Upper South's slave population)....but although there has been no serious dispute about the massive expansion of slavery in this period, there has always been sharp debate over the

composition of that movement. Slave movement combined two elements—*slave trading* on the one hand and *planter migrations* on the other.

I should note that Campbell has never really been inclined to believe that large-scale slave trading existed in Texas and that his writings have been consistent on this point. For example, in a 1976 article that concerned itself, interestingly, with the question of "slave breeding," Campbell and co-author Richard Lowe observed that

> the available evidence does suggest, however, that there was little regional specialization in the buying and selling of slaves. It seems likely that most slaves who moved from the upper to the lower South migrated as plantation forces with their owners (p. 412).

Regarding Texas the authors go on to note:

> The Lone Star State, which by every indicator was the foremost importing state, did not, in general, fit the model of a buying area. The age and sex characteristics of its slave population in both 1850 and 1860, statewide, as well as among large slaveholders and cotton growers, were remarkably similar to those of the upper South. Slave migrants into Texas during the 1850's showed only a slight age imbalance (which was soon corrected by births to female immigrants) and virtually no sex imbalance. Furthermore, the fertility ratio for Texas

slaves was very close to that for the selling states in general. The fact that the foremost buying state in so many ways did not fit the model for buying states should in itself raise questions about the validity of the entire hypothesis [the "slave breeding hypothesis"] on regional specialization in the breeding and selling of slaves (p. 412).

Aside from the fact that Lowe and Campbell's statistical analysis is theoretically and methodologically flawed,[58] their essay also does not directly refute many of the studies it claims to be challenging, particularly the work of Frederic Bancroft. Additionally, by focusing much of their argument on the question of "slave breeding," Lowe and Campbell appear to be implying that studies emphasizing large-scale antebellum slave

---

[58] The authors define a "prime-age" slave as being between 15 and 49 years of age and their demographic analysis is flawed because of this assumption. The fact is that both migrants and traders brought or sold significant numbers of children into the Lower South, especially Texas (see Tadman, Appendix 2). Slaves were not just workers but were also *investments*. Settlers looking to strike it rich in the fertile lands of the Southwest had to ensure the long-term success of their ventures. It thus made both financial and pragmatic sense to bring infants along with their parents and especially children, who would be productive as workers or fetch decent prices as hires or sales in a few years. As far as the lack of a sex disparity is concerned, the only place where there was a slight tendency to favor males over females is the sugar-growing area of Louisiana; the rate of sex-based speculation overall was fairly even. For the sex ratios in Texas, see later in this chapter.

trading (of which "slave breeding" is only a part[59]) are abolitionist-tinged diatribes, full of passionate rhetoric perhaps, but not in keeping with the facts.

What is the point of studying the slave trade? The answer to the question is that 1.) the sizeable number of slaves that were traded from the upper to the lower south (roughly two million) between 1820 and 1860 constitute a major aspect of the socioeconomic development of that region of the United States and the country as a whole. 2.) The breakup of slave families, whether by migration or sale, says much about the character and development of American racism and ultimately can inform contemporary decision making, whether along personal or policy lines.[60] Tadman's study, then,

---

[59] Not that large a part, according to Tadman (121-129). There is considerable evidence that "stud farms" and other forms of breeding did exist, especially the trade in light-skinned "fancy girls" who commanded extremely high prices, but the preponderance of the trade did not involve the breeding of slaves for market.

[60] "In the context of the dynamic frontier environment of the developing South, it has sometimes been suggested that the family disruptions of slaves might not have been greatly more severe than those of whites who moved west or children sent from poor white families to become apprentices or servants. Such notions should be given little weight and do not begin to take account of the extremities of suffering inflicted upon black families. *The exodus of slaves*

"is ultimately concerned with the significance of the slave trade for the mentalities of masters and slaves" (Tadman 1996[1989]: 9).

Tadman's methodology is novel and straightforward:

> The methods used were, first an analysis of the age structure of the overall slave movement (having established that the slave trade, unlike planter migration, was highly age selective). The second method was to make a detailed count of all identifiable traders in a sample state (South Carolina) for a sample decade. (the 1850's) Traders were found to be highly active, not just in towns and cities, but throughout all of the rural South too (Bancroft 1996[1931]: xxxvi).

His findings for the internal trade into Texas reveal some fairly startling statistics:

1.) Tadman's interregional slave movement estimate (Table 2.1, p. 12) for Texas indicates that the state had one of the highest slave importation rates in the decade 1840-49, and the highest, (by far; in this decade Texas imported almost twice as

---

was forced, long-distance, and permanent. It had nothing to do with moving west so as to make one's fortune. There was, with whites, nothing remotely equivalent to the forcible breakup of marriages....and the extensive literature on white migration across the South shows, too, a very strong tendency to move, not alone, but with family and friends" (emphasis added, Tadman 1996[1989]: 161).

many slaves as the next net slave importing state, Mississippi) in the decade 1850-59. According to Tadman, Texas imported approximately 127,812 slaves in these two decades. Given that the 1860 Texas census lists the enslaved population at 182,566 persons, this then indicates that <u>approximately seventy percent of the 1860 slave population in Texas had been speculated into the state.</u> The pattern is a general one; Tadman observes that "it seems that in the 1850's, trading represented about 60 to 70 percent of some 300,000 net slave movements from the Upper to Lower South" (Tadman 1996[1989]: 31). As figure 4 indicates, the slave population grew relatively slowly until 1836 and then skyrocketed after the Texas revolution.[61]

---

[61] Slave trade studies often find it difficult differentiating between "migration" and "trading." The distinction is an important one. The former involved, so the story goes, a planter who moved into a frontier area and brought along slaves that he already owned; these slaves presumably were "part of the family" and owner concern for their welfare was present. Campbell argues that most slaves that came into Texas came as migrants with their owners. Tadman disagrees; the evidence he produces indicates that many settlers into Texas purchased their slaves at or shortly before migration. Regarding the role of the trade versus planter migration, he observes: "Phillips, the classic spokesman for the old-style paternalist concept of slavery, would, of course, have seen planter migration and not the trade as the key to expansion. He would have attributed trading, to a great extent, to "economic hardships" bearing upon masters...We could, then, from more than one ideological position dilute the slaveholder's personal responsibility for the selling

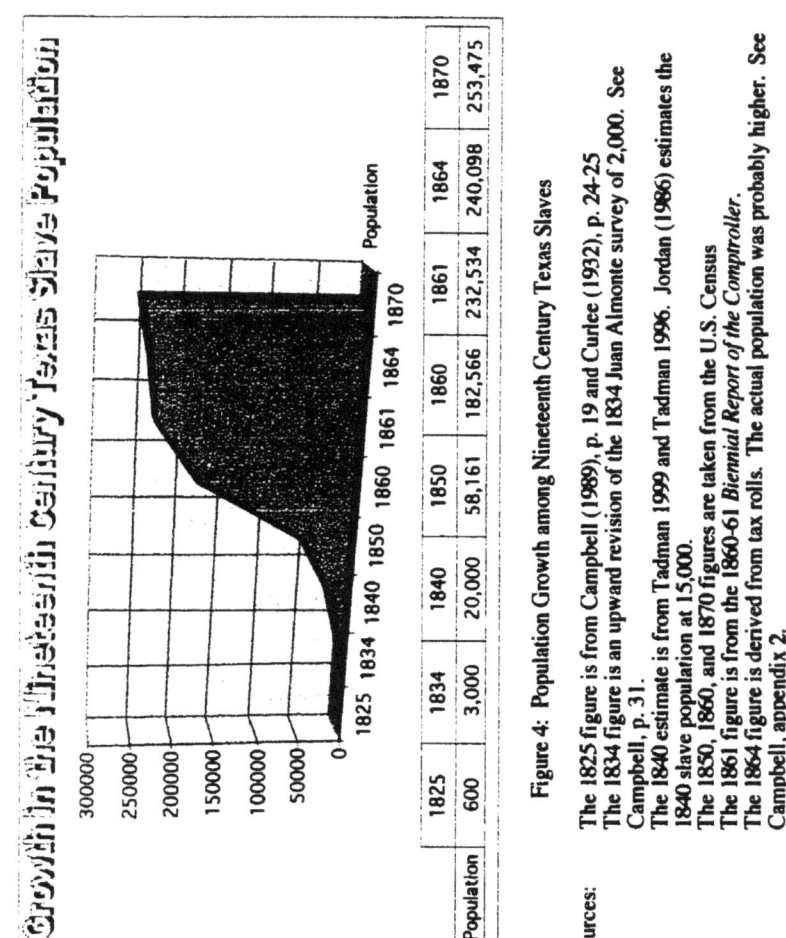

Figure 4: Population Growth among Nineteenth Century Texas Slaves

Population	1825	1834	1840	1850	1860	1861	1864	1870
	600	3,000	20,000	58,161	182,566	232,534	240,098	253,475

Sources: The 1825 figure is from Campbell (1989), p. 19 and Curlee (1932), p. 24-25
The 1834 figure is an upward revision of the 1834 Juan Almonte survey of 2,000. See Campbell, p. 31.
The 1840 estimate is from Tadman 1999 and Tadman 1996. Jordan (1986) estimates the 1840 slave population at 15,000.
The 1850, 1860, and 1870 figures are taken from the U.S. Census
The 1861 figure is from the 1860-61 *Biennial Report of the Comptroller*.
The 1864 figure is derived from tax rolls. The actual population was probably higher. See Campbell, appendix 2.

of slaves and see him as part of a wider system. Phillips's formulation goes against evidence of the trade...and his approach cannot be accepted" (Tadman 1996[1989]: 131). Obviously Campbell accepts Phillips's approach.

Another startling finding of *Speculators and Slaves* is displayed in Table A8.6 (p. 302). This chart depicts figures that indicate the net exportation and importation levels as a percentage of the state's slave population at the start of the decade. The 1850-59 figures for Texas are almost off the chart; it indicates that Texas was importing slaves of all ages (except for males older than 40 and females older than 50), especially adolescent boys and girls in roughly equal proportions. There was a slight tendency, however, to favor the importation of young boys over girls, especially in those regions of Texas engaged in significant sugar growing (primarily plantations along the Brazos river). According to the 1860 census those counties (Austin, Brazoria, Fort Bend, Grimes, Jackson, Lavaca, Matagorda, Montgomery, Walker, Washington, and Wharton) contained more per capita black male slaves than females[62] than in the state generally; these counties contained 19,079

---

[62] According to the 1860 census the Texas slave population stood at 91,189 males and 91,377 females, a nearly equal ratio.

black male slaves and 17,501 black female slaves. The mulatto slave ratio was more slanted toward females; of these there were 2,094 males and 2,559 females. The most telling statistic, however, is the age structure of Texas' enslaved African-American population. An analysis of the census figures reveals that nearly eighty percent (77.7%) of Texas slaves in 1860 were under thirty years of age. Table 1 lists the age structure of eleven of Texas' larger sugar growing counties.[63]

Table 1: Age Structure of Texas' Sugar Growing Counties in 1860.
Source: 1860 Census

County	Percentage of Prime-Age Slaves (as percentage of county slave population)
Austin	74%
Brazoria	69%
Fort Bend	71%
Grimes	79%
Jackson	78%
Lavaca	83%
Matagorda	70%
Montgomery	75%
Walker	79%

[63] It should be noted that sugar was not the only cash crop grown in these counties and was not grown in significant quantities until methods had been refined in the 1850's.

Washington	79%
Wharton	74%

Note: The prime-age percentage in Texas' largest slaveholding county (Harrison County) was 78%. "Prime-Age" is defined as slaves under thirty years of age.

How sizable was the African slave trade in Texas?[64] Although Robbins (1972) estimates that no more than about five thousand Africans were smuggled into Texas, his own narrative contradicts him. The following table is a rough estimate based on the information contained in the text of his study. The estimates in the table are conservative. I would place the total figure of African slaves smuggled into or through Texas at about 15,000-20,000 persons. Du Bois (1986[1896]: 177) estimated that "the admission of Texas added probably seventy-five thousand recently imported

---

[64] Campbell (1989: 53) observes that "the most careful studies estimate that no more than two thousand slaves came to Texas in this way between 1836 and 1860." The studies Campbell cites are wrong; they narrowly configure their scope so as to make the traffic seem as insignificant as possible. Even Barker's study, which Campbell references, quotes Sam Houston in 1837 where he observed that "it cannot be disbelieved that thousands of Africans have lately been imported to the Island of Cuba with the design to transport a large portion of them into this Republic" (Barker 1902: 155). This does not mean that the "thousands" to which Houston refers actually found their way into Texas, but there is no reason to believe that only a couple of thousand slaves were illegally traded; two thousand slaves is at best a very conservative estimate.

slaves to the Southern stock," but this figure is not borne out by the current evidence.

Table 2: Estimates of African Slaves Smuggled Into Texas

Vessel Name	Year	Number of Slaves	Reference
Belona	1817		
Calibra	1817		
Diana	1817		
Esperanza	1817		
Mosquito	1817		
Victory	1817	500	*House Doc* [HD], 15th Cong., 1st Sess., No. 12 (Serial 6), p. 14
Patronille	1817	113	
L'Enrequita	1817	174	*American State Papers* [ASP], Foreign Relations, No. 4 (Serial 4), p. 134
Unidentified	1817	650	HD, pp. 12-14
Shenandoah	1836	170	Robbins, p. 103
Unidentified	1836	200	Binkley 1936 (I): 477
Subtotal (pre-1837):		1,807	
After 1836:			
Waterwich	1837		Adams 1917: 13
Emperor	1837	100	
Neptune	1840		
Columbia	1840		
New York	1840	2000	Adams 1917: 27
Antoinette	1840's		
Ellen Frankland	1840's		

Caroline/Sarah Barnes	1840's	3000	British Consulate Papers [BCP], Kennedy to Aberdeen, July 6, 10, September 5, 1843.
Boquet	1850's	100	Howard 1963: 251-262
Jupiter	1857	70	
Merchant	1857		
William Lewis	1860	300	
Will-O-Wisp	1850's	100	Howard 1963: 50-51
Locomatara	1850's		
Thomas Watson	1850's		
Lydia Gibbs	1850's		
Nancy	1850's		
Caroline	1850's		
Lyra	1850's		
Mary Varney	1850's	5000	*Galveston Civilian*, June 6, July 14, 21, 1857
Unidentified	1860	900	*Galveston News*, August 2, 1860
Subtotal (post 1836):		11,570	
Grand Total:		13,377	

A significant portion of the enslaved population of Texas enumerated in the 1860 census was of direct African origin (usually via Cuba), although the census incorrectly only lists six such persons. The census of 1880 reveals that Texas had the highest percentage of African-born citizens of any state (Jordan

1986: 337).[65]

It seems clear, then, that Campbell's claims as to the movement of enslaved African-Americans into Texas are entirely inaccurate; Texas' slave population was highly age-selective, and was somewhat selective along sex lines as well. As elsewhere, slave trading was a fundamental, not ancillary, aspect of nineteenth century Texas slavery. Slave productivity and output were high and seemingly limitless:

> Cotton culture boomed in Texas in spite of floods, droughts, a financial panic in 1837 and a severe depression in the early 1840's. The cotton crop, estimated at 10,000 bales in 1834 jumped to 58,000 bales in 1849. In the 1850's, when the population trebled and the number of farmers doubled, Texas became one of the world's major cotton producers; its cotton production increased tenfold, reaching 431,000 bales in 1859 (Nevin 1975: 160).

---

[65] 274 Afro-Texans were listed as having been born in Africa. Louisiana listed 270. Interestingly, there were more persons listed as having been born in Asia (571) in Texas than in the other states as well. These wide ranging figures (the state with the next highest Asian population was New York which listed 81) probably have more to do with census politics than with anything else.

CHAPTER 4: PIRATES, PRIVATEERS, AND ANGLO SETTLERS; THE FIRST SLAVES COME TO TEXAS

"The wish to possess slaves is inherent in all Texas farmers who do their own work, since the profitable cultivation of cotton and sugar cane can be carried on only with slave labor. The social standing of a slave-owning planter is also quite different from that of the farmer who has to till his own soil by the sweat of his brow."
—Ferdinand Roemer, 1846

This chapter describes the time period 1816-1836 and first examines the activities of various filibusters[66] in Texas waters. The investigation then switches to discussion of the role of the slave trade in the early Anglo colonization of Texas and its role in debates leading to the Texas Revolution and secession from the Mexican Republic. My primary objectives in this chapter are to demonstrate that slavery—and by extension the slave trade—were the underlying issues in the political debates of the time period[67], and to show how the events

---

[66] Filibuster: an irregular military adventurer; *specif:* an American engaged in fomenting insurrections in Latin America in the mid-19th century (*Mirriam Webster's Collegiate Dictionary*, 10th ed.).

[67] Texas historians from Eugene Barker to Randolph Campbell (and beyond) have claimed that slavery was not the "direct" cause of the Texas revolution. They subsume the slavery question within a "larger" discussion of "cultural difference" or call the clash a "conflict of cultures." Their refusal to acknowledge the obvious role of race in this and other events—indeed throughout Texas history—is unfortunate. But it is completely understandable when looked at from the "Chomskyan" perspective outlined in chapter 1. Why should one expect these

immediately after the revolution (particularly the wording of the new Texas constitution), set the stage for massive immigration into Texas, which resulted in an enormous influx of Negro slaves.

Although the first significant slave trading activity in what is now Texas began in 1816, it is likely that the first nineteenth century slaves were imported before then. Much intrigue existed along the narrow strip of land between Louisiana and Texas known as the "neutral ground." It is well known that Thomas Jefferson, a noted Francophile and expansionist, argued that the Louisiana Purchase extended into internationally recognized Spanish territory (Jefferson argued that the border between New Spain and the United States was the Rio Grande because of La Salle's expeditions). Aaron Burr, Jefferson's Vice President, was even more expansionistic and actively plotted to invade and colonize northern New

---

establishment historians to point out the uncomfortable truth?

Spain[68] (Handbook of Texas Online: "Aaron Burr").

Hunters, trappers, Indians, outlaws and others lived in the neutral ground territory. As a result, Nacogdoches (and East Texas generally), the "city" established by the Spanish as a buffer to seventeenth century French attempts to establish a foothold in Texas, was a rough and tumble place that was "Mexican in soil but Anglo-American in culture..." many of its inhabitants were "the restless and the shiftless, the whisky peddler and the itinerant preacher," and the area was considered "volatile and conspiratorial." (Meinig 1969: 35). In 1808 fifteen slaves are listed as having run away from their master in Louisiana to Nacogdoches in a "list of fugitive slaves from Louisiana" located in the Bexar archives at the University of Texas at Austin. As a point of comparison, the 1819 San Antonio census lists seven slaves, five males and two

---

[68] Timothy Burr, a second cousin of Aaron Burr, was an early settler in the Newton County area and eventually established a plantation on the Texas side of the Sabine River.

females.[69]

The first significant slave trading activity in Texas was conducted by pirates, privateers, and Latin American revolutionaries, who intercepted merchant shipping bound for European colonies. As mentioned in chapter 3, the Texas coast offered strategic geographic advantages; Cuba and other Caribbean locales (Belize, for instance) were only about a 3-5 day sail away, and Galveston was located only approximately fifty to sixty miles from the Louisiana border, which made smuggling activities relatively effortless. The natural surroundings of the Texas coast also were well camouflaged and were treacherous sailing for unsuspecting or unfamiliar navigators.

War, especially in Europe, was the norm in the first third of the nineteenth century, and these conflicts had their counterparts in the New World, particularly in the Latin

---

[69] The Bastrop Papers at UT show the 1803 sale (not necessarily the importation) of the slave Babtiste Agai who was sold to Francois Cavet by Don Vicente Femandex Texeiro.

American colonies. The first filibusterers to establish a privateer government on Galveston Island were anti-Spanish revolutionaries such Manuel Herrera, who was the Mexican plenipotentiary in New Orleans. While working in New Orleans Herrera came into contact with Louis Michel D'Aury (ca. 1788-1821) a French-born pirate who offered his services to him after an altercation with Simón Bolívar At Aux Cayes, Haiti. Their strategy was to establish a "base camp in Texas, preferabl[y] on the coast, from which the rebels could invade Mexico (Robbins 1972: 81).

After Aury recovered from some difficulties with Black seamen which nearly scuttled the revolutionary gambit at the outset, Herrera eventually came to the island in September of 1816 and formally established a privateer government with Aury as governor. Facilities for customs collection, an admiralty court, a notary public, and disciplinary processes and procedures were established. In November, Aury's forces were augmented by troops under the leadership of Francisco Xavier

Miña (1789-1817), a well-educated Spanish nobleman and enemy of Ferdinand VII, who renounced the liberal constitution of 1812 after returning to the Spanish throne.[70] A leadership squabble ensued between Aury and Miña; the conflict was eventually resolved when Aury was named naval commander and Miña military overseer of the insurrectionist forces.

Americans also joined the insurgents. One of the revolutionaries who accompanied Miña to Galveston was Colonel Guilford Young (accompanied by other adventuring Americans) a Connecticut native who had recently been discharged from the U.S. Army. Young's detachment established a camp separate from the others, mainly because most of the Americans did not speak Spanish. The special

---

[70] "In October 1814 [Miña] arrived in England, where he became acquainted with Gen. Winfield Scott of the United States and Father José Servando Teresa de Mier Noriega y Guerra, an ardent Mexican liberal who encouraged Miña to strike at Ferdinand VII through an invasion of Mexico. Scott also is thought to have encouraged Miña and to have assured him of the support of the United States for an expedition to free Mexico from Spain" (Handbook of Texas Online: Xavier Miña). Winfield Scott, of course, would later complete the re-conquest of Mexico as commanding general of the American forces that marched inland to Mexico City during the Mexican-American War.

company under Young's charge was given the title of "The Guard of Honour of the Mexican Congress" by the privateer government (p. 87). Another American who came to Galveston with Aury was James Campbell, "a naval veteran who had seen duty on both the American warships *Constitution* and *Constellation* and had served as a sailor in the War of 1812 under Commodore Perry. Claiming an honorable discharge from the United States Navy, he became a privateer 'in the Columbian service" (Ramsay 1996: 95).

What now was needed was a source of revenue with which these "patriots" could proceed with their planned liberation of Mexico. It quickly became apparent that the best vessels to raid were Spanish commercial vessels, which in many cases contained African slaves bound for the colonies. The contraband cargo was promptly smuggled into Louisiana via intermediaries located along Sabine Pass (Hoyt and Schmidt 1997: 9) and at or near New Orleans. Profits from these ventures were used to fund the revolutionary activities of the privateer government. These activities drew the attention of the American government which made some attempts to curtail the more blatant and flamboyant trafficking by establishing extra surveillance patrols.

In the spring of 1817, however, Aury grew disillusioned with the revolutionary plot. He was more interested in piracy than in politics and decided to relocate his men and equipment further down the coast at Matagorda Bay. Into this void stepped the now legendary gentleman-pirate and "patriot" Jean Laffite, who visited Galveston shortly after Aury's departure. Laffite had recently been evicted from his previous smuggling entrepot at Barataria (near New Orleans) and had heard about the attractive business potential of Texas.

Laffite talked with some of the men Aury had temporarily left behind on the island and also conducted business, purchasing slaves from two recently arrived ships, the *Patronille* and the *L'Enrequita*. Suitably impressed with Galveston after his personal inspection, Laffite decided to relocate his base of operations from New Orleans to Galveston. Meanwhile Aury's camp at Matagorda had not worked out, primarily because of continuing Karankawa raids. Upon learning that Laffite had supplanted him on Galveston Island, Aury decided to relocate his operations off Amelia Island, near Georgia and Florida. "According to [customs] collector Chew, over 650 slaves awaited illegal entry into the United States from Galveston at the time of Aury's departure" (p. 92).

Almost immediately after establishing himself in Galveston, Laffite considerably stepped up the organizational level and volume of slave and specie smuggling from the island. Laffite possessed extensive experience as a smuggler;[71] the only thing that saved him and his brother Pierre from prosecution by American officials in Louisiana was their "loyal" and crucial service to Andrew Jackson during the War of 1812.

---

[71] Letters of marque (a legal technicality that distinguished men like Laffite from stateless "pirates") were easily obtained in Venezuela or Cartagena. In case of the latter, condemnation procedures were so liberal that prize cargoes did not have to be reported if it was inconvenient to do so, and in many cases weren't.

Furthermore, Laffite was a businessperson and entrepreneur first; he was engaged in several political intrigues (e.g. as a "spy" for the Spanish crown or as an "ally" of James Long), but these were conducted primarily to safeguard his smuggling operations or to stall for time. Although he possessed at times Cartagenian or Venezuelan letters of marque (among others),[72] Laffite was an opportunist who used the political uncertainty of the times to enrich himself and to secure a high and well respected position of influence in Latin American (particularly colonial French) high society. Tri-lingual, very attractive[73] (to both men and women), supremely manipulative, and possessed of an innate and disarming gentlemanly demeanor, Laffite

---

[72] It should be noted that privateering played a major role in the late eighteenth and early nineteenth century New World (and even before then). During the American Revolution, for example, "armed licensed merchantmen outnumbered the novice Continental Navy by ten to one. During the War of 1812, the United States issued 515 letters of marque to vessels that reported the capture of 1,345 ships" (Ramsay 1996: 158).

[73] James Campbell's wife described Laffite in 1817 as "about 40 years old, dark complexioned, handsome, over six feet tall....strongly built, black hair, side-whiskers, hazel eyes" (cited in McComb 1986: 36). Lieutenant James M. McIntosh of the American cruiser *Lynx*, which had followed one of Laffite's renegade vessels into Galveston and spent several days ashore remarked later "we passed a week with no common man; with one who, if he had his vices and also his virtues, and who possessed a courteous and gentlemanly deportment seldom equalled and not to be surpassed" (cited in Cartwright 1991: 50).

lived the good life.

It is easy to romanticize a historical figure such as Laffite, and like much of Texas history, his mysterious life has been subjected to much myth making. As might be expected, even Hollywood has gotten into the act. Yul Brynner played the part of a swashbuckling Laffite and Charlton Heston the part of Andrew Jackson in the 1958 Cecil B. DeMille production of *The Buccaneer*.[74] Needless to say, no mention was made of Laffite's slave smuggling and his extensive agglomeration of concubines throughout the Caribbean. Separating fiction from fact (or in the words of Trouillot, what happened vs. what is said to have happened) in cases such as this is at best difficult. Still, Laffite's most recent biographer has performed an admirable service by delineating some previously unknown details of Laffite's life, and more to the point, of his illegal smuggling operations.

---

[74] Friedrich March played the role of the patriotic, American flag waving Laffite in the earlier version.

The cornerstone of Laffite's operations in Louisiana was his older brother Pierre, who acted as agent and intermediary and made it known in Louisiana and Mississippi that newly imported Africans were available for purchase. Slaves were available for procurement singly or in small groups after being marched in chains overland from Galveston to Lake Sabine. Laffite always had a surplus of slaves available for purchase at Galveston; when too many slaves were filling up the slave pens (consuming resources), the Laffites arranged to sell the slaves wholesale at a fraction of their eventual retail price. Deals such as this induced planters such as J. Randall Jones to travel to Galveston and purchase Laffite's slaves personally (Ramsay 1996: 104).

Three of the better known intermediaries that worked with the Laffites were the Bowie brothers, John J., Resin P., and James, who had already accumulated significant earnings from their plantation holdings in Arkansas and Mississippi.[75] After

---

[75] One of their plantations, located near Natchez, was called Sedalia

marching a contraband slave coffle to East Texas, they would outfit several small boats and smuggle their cargo of "black ivory" along the Calcasieu and Sabine rivers. The Bowies procured the slaves from Laffite at approximately one dollar per pound, which worked out to an average of approximately $140 per slave.

> The slave runners then took advantage of the law.[76] They denounced their charges to a United States marshal or one of his deputies [informing on themselves], and then claimed a reward of one-half of the market value of the illicitly imported laborers. The captured blacks would be placed on auction where a representative of the smuggler company, knowing the site and date of the sale, would purchase the slaves. The slavers could then transport the persons who had become legal property to the plantation that would pay the highest price.....It was a lucrative business. Not only did the smuggler receive a reward for his deceptive services, but often he made a final sale of a black male for as much as $800 to $1,000. The profit was sometimes in excess of ten times the amount of the initial investment (Ramsay 1996: 104-105).

In an influential article published earlier in the twentieth

---

[76] On April 20, 1818 the U.S. Government enacted a law supposedly to curtail slave smuggling. This law "which virtually acknowledged the failure of efforts to control the trade, and sought to remedy defects by pitting cupidity against cupidity" (Du Bois 1986[1896]: 122) provided for the disbursement of half of all forfeitures and fines to the informer.

century (Barker 1902: 148), Texas historian Eugene Barker—who had the benefit of interviewing persons with direct recollections of Texas slave trading—noted that the Bowies made over $65,000 in two years while acting as intermediaries for Laffite. James Bowie would go on to later fame as a "hero" who died defending the Alamo.[77]

The United States government was aware of these activities. A report to the Secretary of the Navy related that

> the more valuable, and the slaves are smuggled in through the numerous inlets to the westward, where the people are but too much disposed to render them every possible assistance. Several hundred slaves are now at Galveston, and persons have gone from New-Orleans to purchase them (House Doc. 16 Cong. I sess. III, No. 36, p. 5).

As Du Bois (1986[1896]: 121) notes, the 1818 law was flawed

---

[77] I should note that there is a considerable divergence between Jim Bowie's "mythological" reputation as a member of the Texas pantheon of heroes and the scholarly literature on him, which is, to say the least, not at all flattering. To my mild surprise, even materials available for public consumption on Bowie at the Capitol Visitors Center acknowledge that he was a slave trader, although that is the only negative thing they say about him. A particularly incisive and devastating assessment of Bowie is J. Frank Dobie's (1957: 337-357) article "James Bowie, Big Dealer" which portrays Bowie as a philandering, arrogant, bloodthirsty, backstabbing drunk and swindler with a temper, who cheated his wife's family out of her dowry (using fabricated amounts that were accumulated via Negro and land speculation), wrote her and their children out of his will, and whose pathetic conduct at the Alamo is hardly worthy of glorification.

from the start and instead of fixing the slave smuggling problem "aggravated and complicated" it instead. Political wrangling in Congress kept serious enforcement of existing anti-African slave trading statutes from occurring and almost always allowed smugglers and their allies some type of legal loophole with which to circumvent the law.

Campeachy, Laffite's Galveston colony, was a shady and motley collection of outlaws, renegades, and other freebooters. Although it is generally recognized that greater levels of freedom were available in pirate outposts than in regular society, this multi-racial and multi-national[78] agglomeration of rogues was kept under tight administration by the force of Laffite's personality and his willingness to on occasion use shocking levels of force (as an example) to maintain discipline. Particularly unfortunate were the debased and oppressive sex

---

[78] A letter of complaint to Commodore Patterson in New Orleans observed that "vessels carrying the flags of the several new republicks pretending to have commissions from the constituted authorities there" and who were manned with "renegado crews of all nations" were roaming the Gulf and could potentially interfere with business as usual in the city (State Papers and Public Documents of the United States, Volume XI: 365).

crimes that took place, both in the beginning of the colony, and at its height of influence; nearly 1000 people and 200 buildings inhabited Campeachy at its peak, almost as many as at Laffite's previous outpost at Grand Terre. Although Laffite had outlawed sexual relations with married women, he also tolerated instances of rape, murder, and other crimes by his pirate band, especially against Indians (see footnote 50) and (enslaved and free) Blacks. It was commonplace for slave traders to take Black mistresses as domestics and concubines and Laffite himself had several. The levels of sexual violence at Laffite's previous entrepot (Grand Terre) were well known and the stuff of legend among New Orleans high society, which simultaneously deplored the more debauched forms of this depravity and yet was intrigued by Jean and Pierre's rumored lovemaking exploits (and business connections) amongst New Orleans's Creole elite.

Although the size of the slave trade emanating out of Campeachy is difficult to fix with any degree of certainty, it is certain that at the height of its power the colony was one of the largest and most efficient slave markets on the American continent (Cartwright 1991: 46). Eventually Laffite was no longer able to manipulate his way out of trouble. By 1820 he was again seen as an outlaw and renegade, and the government of the United States began operations to evict him from Galveston. The 1818 law had also been revised twice by Congress and the law now stipulated that African slave trading was punishable by death, thus the profits that had enriched the Bowies were no longer as easy and enticing. Additionally, several of Laffite's vessels were intercepted by American forces and most of the crews convicted of piracy. People began defecting from Laffite; by the end of 1820 only about twenty of his most loyal followers remained. By early 1821 Laffite had left Galveston and the few remaining structures that remained of Campeachy were left to the elements.

The Beginning of the African-American Slave Trade: Anglo Settlement

Around the time of Laffite's departure, Stephen F. Austin began Anglo settlement of an *empresario* grant his father had been able to obtain from Spanish Authorities. The story of Austin's "old three hundred" is by now a familiar one, although there are aspects of it that are usually not mentioned. Often overlooked are some of the details of what the Austin family did in Virginia and Missouri to earn a living. An ad Moses Austin placed in the Richmond Press in 1787, for instance, indicates that he was not unfamiliar with "the negro speculation:"

> One hundred Negroes, from 20 to 30 years old, for which a good price will be given. They are to be sent out of state, therefore we shall not be particular respecting the character of any of them—Hearty and well made is all that is necessary (McColley 1973: 164-65).

The majority of the Texas settlers were southerners and sympathetic to slavery, but only a handful were planters and moved to the colony with large numbers of slaves. Of these, the largest was Jared Ellison Groce who came to Texas via Virginia and Alabama with 100 slaves and settled more than 40,000 acres of land near present-day Hempstead. Thanks to the lobbying efforts of Stephen Austin, in addition to land for themselves and their family, settlers were able to receive at first fifty and eventually eighty acres of land per slave. Thus of Groce's grant, more than 7,200 acres were allotted for his bondspeople (Campbell 1989: 13-14). Groce, who had been involved in slave trading on Amelia Island prior to his migration to Texas (to avoid prosecution), engaged in both African and African-American slave trading once established on Texas soil (Robbins 1972: 105).

The colony grew quickly. The official census of 1825 lists the population at 1,800 with 443 of the residents marked as slaves. By 1831 the colony contained 5,665 inhabitants, although slaves were not enumerated. It is reasonable to assume that the proportion of slaves remained constant or increased somewhat (Curlee 1932: 5-6).

The story of the Anglo settlement of Texas has been told many times and forms a cornerstone of the Texas myth. The standard details of this enterprise are not relevant for the purposes of this discussion and can be found in innumerable conventional histories of Texas. What is relevant is the following: how many slaves "migrated" as "members of the family" to Texas with their owners, and how many were traded or speculated? Furthermore, whether migrated or traded, what were the effects of this movement on slave families? It is difficult to answer these questions definitively, but scattered evidence provides some suggestive answers.

First the numbers. Tadman argues "that trading substantially outweighed planter migrations in numerical importance"[79] (Tadman 1996[1989]: 8) and Gutman (1975: 9) correctly observes that even if planter migrations outweighed

---

[79] In fact for the New Orleans (the primary source of Texas slaves) market "*slave trading was at least three times as important as planter migration*....when a check is made of the many thousands of slaves carried by this route, at least 73 percent of the slaves carried were the property of readily identifiable traders" (emphasis added, Tadman 1996[1989]: 22-23).

the trade as Campbell suggests this does not mean that the effects on slave families were not destructive. In fact, there were many ways in which a slave family could be adversely affected other than by migration or sale. Some of these included slave hiring, gift transfer, or estate division. It is also important to note that the threat of family separation or breakup was a powerful disciplinary tool for planters and also served as "the most powerful of all labor incentives meant to encourage efficient production" (Gutman 1975: 101).

The evidence seems to indicate that many prospective Texans purchased slaves before making the journey west and/or began to purchase initial or additional slaves once they were established in Texas.[80] Tadman correctly notes that "such last-minute purchases are regarded......as being part of the trade rather than properly being a part of 'planter migrations.' (They

---

[80] Planters typically moved west with a fairly small gang of slaves, established themselves, and, if at all successful, built up their stocks with substantial help from the trade (Tadman 1996[1989]: 228). The rich soils of Texas allowed many planters in the Lone Star State to become successful.

were based on the same market transactions as the trade, and would have brought about the same sort of family separations)" (Tadman 1996[1989]: 28). One notable Texan who purchased slaves before migrating was Asa Hoxey. In a letter reproduced in the *Southwestern Historical Quarterly* in 1906, he wrote:

> I allso will have to make a trip to Virginia for the purpose of adding to my Stock of Slaves which will take up so much of my time that I cannot start sooner than the period mentioned.

Stephen Austin's nephew Guy M. Bryan was another settler who took the opportunity to purchase slaves in Baltimore and Richmond before making the journey to Texas (Tyler and Murphy 1974: xxii). In 1823 John Botts arrived in Texas with between thirty and forty slaves who were believed to have been the property of Austin's friend and partner in the first colony, Joseph Hawkins of New Orleans (Nathaniel Cox to Austin, October 20, 1836; Austin to Josiah H. Bell, January 8, 1824). Curlee (1932: 33) observed that "there is no doubt that this importation of slaves from the United States by actual settlers accounts for much of the Negro population."

> The most infamous slave trader in [early] Texas was Monroe Edwards, owner of a sugar plantation at Chenango in Brazoria County. Fishing in the troubled waters caused by the Texas Revolution, Edwards and others increased their importation of Africans during 1835 and 1836. On March 2, 1836 William S. Fisher, collector of customs at Velasco, wrote to the provisional governor, Henry Smith, that Edwards had landed a cargo of 171 Africans along the Brazos River.[81] The customs collector also reported to Governor Smith that plantation owner Sterling McNeel had landed an unknown number of slaves on the Brazos (Silverthorne 1986: 29).

The precise percentage of early settlers who made purchases prior to immigrating will probably never be known, but it is certainly a higher percentage than is usually recognized. Furthermore, as later discussion will make clear, the speculation rate increased as restrictions on slavery were removed and settlement progressed, reaching its apex in the 1850's. As a minimum, Campbell's claims of "limited" slave

---

[81] "Since no laws have emanated directly from the council [of the provisional government of Texas] in relation to this matter," he reported, "I am very much in need of instruction" (Robbins 1972: 103).

trading and benign planter migrations in Texas are inappropriate; a closer look at the numbers (and especially a reinterpretation of what precisely one means by "migration") indicate that speculation in Mexican Texas was present almost from the outset.

Anglo African Slave Trading

Another immigrant eager to enrich himself via the sale of the "black diamonds" was James W. Fannin, who arrived in Texas from Georgia in the autumn of 1834 with his wife and two daughters. Fannin and his business associate Joseph Mims jointly owned a plantation located on the west bank of the San Bernard River in southwest Brazoria county and engaged in African slave trading, with Fannin making trips to Cuba where he purchased African slaves in the recently expanding Havana slave market.[82] In a letter to Maj. Francis Belton dated August

---

[82] In their study of the Cuban slave market Bergad, García and Barcia (1995: 146) note that the African slave trade had "saturated the insular labor market" in the 1830's, which resulted in easy and profitable speculative activities on the part of Americans. As during the heyday of piracy a few years previously, a slave could be purchased in Havana for about $150 and sold for over ten times that amount in Texas or New Orleans.

27, 1835 Fannin boasted that his "last voyage from the Island of Cuba *(with 152)* succeeded admirably." Fannin attempted to sell thirty-six slaves on Caney Creek in 1835 claiming that he would use the money to purchase "war materials" for the Texas revolution (Curlee 1932: 34). Fannin's over-inflated ego and recklessness would later lead him to destruction at the hands of Santa Anna at the "Goliad massacre," although most historical treatments of Fannin's life meant for public consumption spare us the details of his incompetent and insubordinate military leadership and slave trading.[83]

Some domestic slave traders also engaged in African slave trading. Mrs. Dilue Harris who came to Texas in 1833 recollected the activities of Ben Fort Smith in an article that appeared in *The Quarterly of the Texas State Historical Association* (1900: 97-98) nearly seven decades later. She

---

[83] An exhibit titled *Rewarding Honor: Land Grants and the Texas Revolution*, held at the Capitol Visitors Center in Austin in the spring of 1999 allows visitors to recreate famous Texas land deeds, complete with Texas seal. One of these deeds ("File 70") is Fannin's 1920 acre grant in San Patricio county. The brief biography accompanying the fake grant acknowledges Fannin's failed West Point career and slave trading but does not challenge the inappropriateness (and dishonor) of heroifying such a pathetic man.

described the slaves Smith had landed on the Texas coast as being so starved, exhausted and weak from the "close confinement" of the journey that they could scarcely move. After resting a day, the group began to be marched upcountry, although the journey was made more difficult by a recent flood. The gang stopped at the home of Dr. Pleasant D. Rose, Mrs. Harris father, who butchered some beef for the visitors to eat.

> As soon as the beeves were skinned the negroes acted like dogs, they were so hungry. With the help of father and uncle, the white men kept them off till the meat was broiled, and then did not let them have as much as they could eat. Father did not have bread for them. Mother prepared dinner for the white men....[after sundown the Negroes]...went to sleep and did not wake till morning. They were so destitute of clothing, mother would not permit us children to go near them. Next day they cooked their meat before they began eating...[Smith's nephew accompanied by his personal servant Mack eventually came down with clothes for the slaves]...Mack made them go to the creek, bathe and card their heads. After they were dressed, he marched them to the house for mother and us little girls to see. He tried to teach them to make a bow. Thay laughed and chattered like monkeys. They did not understand a word of English. All the men and boys in the neighborhood came to see

the wild Africans.

William Fairfax Gray is another Virginian/Texan who made some interesting observations regarding the African slave trade. Gray first came to Texas as in 1835 as land agent for Thomas Green and Albert T. Burnley of Washington, D.C., and quickly immersed himself in Texas politics. Known as "Colonel Gray" (Gray held a commission as a lieutenant colonel in the Virginia militia, with which he served during the war of 1812), he worked in Texas primarily as an attorney. His memoirs were published in 1909 and contain the following observations about the slaves that had just been brought to Texas from Cuba by the aforementioned Monroe Edwards (Gray 1965[1909]: 158-159):

> About fifty of those poor wretches [boys and girls between the ages of ten and twenty-five] were living out of doors like cattle...boys, girls, huddled together..they are diminutive, feeble, spare, squalid, nasty, and beastly in their habits. Very few exhibit traces of intellect.....[when a beef was slaughtered] the Africans wrangled and fought for the garbage like dogs or vultures; they saved all the blood they could get, in gourds and feed on it....an old

> American Negro stood over the beef with a whip, and lashed them off like so many dogs to prevent their pulling the raw meat to pieces...this is the nearest approach to cannibalism that I have ever seen.

After landing this cargo, Edwards proceeded to erect a slave mart near present day San Leon on the west side of Galveston Bay. After swindling one of his African slave trading partners, however, Edwards was eventually forced to leave Texas permanently (Robbins 1972: 104).

American planters did not like the idea of African slaves fetching higher prices than domestic slaves. In June 1835 Alexander Calvit wrote to his son-in-law that "we have nothing New Accepts the African traid is tolerably brisk at Velasco. I think they sell for a better price than our Country raised Negroes" (Calvit to Groce, Jr. June 15, 1835).

The Role of Slavery and the Slave Trade in the Texas Revolution

Texas is a lynch state. It is in the same breath as Mississippi, no different; only they lynch you in Texas with a Texas accent and they lynch you in Mississippi with a Mississippi accent
—Malcolm X, "The Ballot or the Bullet"

Conventional explanations of the roles of slavery and the slave trade in the Texas Revolution by Texas Myth historians have changed little over the course of the twentieth century. Interesting as well are explanations of the role played in the controversy by Texas' most prominent citizen, Stephen F. Austin. Lester Bugbee (1898: 665-666) believed that Stephen F. Austin "was not an advocate of slavery" and implies that the institution was at least temporarily necessary in order to bring Texas soil under successful cultivation (Bugbee says that this essentially was Austin's attitude as well).[84] In his classic

---

[84] "Stephen F. Austin, who was the guiding spirit in the planting of the colonies in Texas, was not an advocate of slavery. He was the largest landholder in Texas and, had he wished, he could have opened plantation after plantation in the fertile bottoms of the Texas rivers; but he declined to take advantage of the opportunity and never owned more than two slaves at any time after entering Texas. From this the conclusion is not necessarily to be drawn that he refused to purchase negroes, on account to moral objections to holding them; but the fact may serve to emphasize, at least in a negative way, the sincerity of his expressed ideas on the subject" (Bugbee 1898: 664-665). Bugbee's interpretation of Austin is too generous. The reason why Austin never chose to become a planter is probably because he did not think himself suited for the rigors and demands of the planting business, and was too busy being the leader of Texas. This is not to say,

biography of Austin, Eugene Barker (1925) is direct in arguing that slavery was not the direct cause of the Texas Revolution. His thesis is that slavery was a "dull organic ache" but not the primary basis of the conflict. Liberal Texas Myth historians have deviated little from Barker since. Randolph Campbell says that "in the broadest sense, the conflict resulted from a clash of cultural traditions" and that "protecting slavery was not the primary cause of the Texas Revolution, but it certainly was a major result" (Campbell 1989: 48). The most immediate and direct cause of the conflict according to Campbell was the suspension of the Mexican constitution. Austin's most recent Texas Myth biographer (Cantrell 1999: 344) argues that while he may have on occasion used racist and expansionist language in public, Austin had a "long history of relative racial and

---

however, that he was against the lifestyle; Austin was more than willing to enjoy the fruits and comforts of plantation agriculture and plantation culture, as long as others shouldered the burdens. For example, after convincing his sister and her husband to come to his colony from Missouri, Austin generated elaborate architectural plans for the house and gardens of a plantation—called "Peach Point" because of the wild peach trees which grew on the land—the east wing of which was to be home for himself and his books and valuables (Silverthorne 1986: 17). Austin had obviously envisioned a leisurely life of "farming, "statesmanship and learning for his semi-retirement (Cantrell 1999). Peach Point went on to become one of the more successful plantations in Texas after Austin's death.

ethnic tolerance" in private.[85]

Liberal Texas myth historians are essentially indirect or silent on the question of whether the Texas Revolution was a battle for "liberty" and against "Mexican tyranny" as was claimed by propagandists then and now. This explanation (along with the Alamo myth) may have served as a good rallying tool for Texas Governor George W. Bush in a motivational speech he delivered to the 1999 U.S. Ryder Cup team, but it is for the most part no longer accepted, at least in its more virulent formulations, by Texas historians. Still, why are Texas historians so reluctant to recognize <u>directly</u> that slavery caused the Texas revolution?[86] The Texas Declaration

---

[85] Cantrell, while occasionally critical of his subject and paying lip service to "new" historical treatments of Texas history and Manifest Destiny, is still basically writing a Texas Myth biography of Austin from a white male perspective. I asked Cantrell for his opinion regarding the role of slavery in the Texas Revolution during the 1999 Texas Book Fair (Cantrell sat on a Texas biographers panel on 7 November, 1999) and he referenced Barker's "dull organic ache" thesis. This dissertation is a deliberate move away in that it foregrounds the colonial "victims'" perspective and is written "facing eastward" instead of westward (Brown 1970: xviii).

[86] It should be apparent that I believe that the Texas Revolution (and as a general rule of thumb, most power struggles) was at its core first a clash of interests, not cultures. This perspective is summarized nicely by Barrera (1979: 13): "Materialist theories in particular argue...that political movements are motivated fundamentally by interests rather than disembodied ideas. Ideas and concepts which 'catch on' enter into political debate largely as expressions or

of Independence from Mexico, although it does not mention the word "slavery" by name is certainly candid enough. Here are some phrases from the document:

> 1. "When a government has ceased to protect the lives, liberty, and property of the people from whom its legitimate powers are derived" (this is the first sentence of the document. Notice that its wording is similar to the U.S. Constitution and *not* the U.S. Declaration of Independence).
>
> 2. "It [the Mexican government] has failed and refused to secure, on a firm basis, the right of trial by jury, that palladium of civil liberty and only safe guarantee for the life, liberty, and property of the citizen"
>
> 4. "It [the Mexican government] has been, during the whole time of our connection with it, the contemptible sport and victim of successive military revolutions, and hath continually exhibited every characteristic of a weak, corrupt, and tyrannical government....we are therefore forced to the melancholy conclusion, that the Mexican people have acquiesced in the destruction of their liberty, and the substitution therefor of a military government; that they are unfit to be free, and incapable of self government.

In addition to some of the racialist overtones of especially the latter claims, the document also is critical of the "far distant

---

justifications of specific interests rather than as free-floating concepts and doctrines."

seat of government" which is carried on by a "hostile majority in an unknown tongue."[87] Clearly, in addition to the other complaints, what the Americans hated most about the Mexicans was what they saw as their inferiority and weakness. Indeed Mexicans, just like Indians and Africans, were incapable (and had proven to be so) of self government and really had no rights that a white man was bound to respect. One already sees the seeds of the "superior race of men" thesis that became a cornerstone of Manifest Destiny.

An extended analysis of these grievances would take us too far afield from the subject of slavery itself, nonetheless, since slaves were considered property it is essential to further flesh out some of the philosophical underpinnings of what "life liberty and property" meant (and means) as it is used here. It

---

[87] Of the fifty-nine delegates of Cohuila y Tejas who attended the independence convention in Washington only two, José Antonio Navarro and José Francisco Ruiz were "native" Texans. Only ten delegates had been in Texas for more than six years prior to 1836, fifteen had come in 1835. Samuel Price Carson, who was elected Secretary of State of the Texas Republic had been a citizen of Texas for about a week (Murry 1991: 10). These people did not speak Spanish and certainly had no real basis (other than their sense of inherent superiority) upon which to judge Mexican "tyranny" or "oppression."

should be apparent that in Anglo-Texan thought (and indeed in *American* thought) "human rights—often referred to as "civil liberties"—freedom of speech, of the press, of assembly, and the right to commit 'victimless' crimes are inseparable from and unthinkable outside the context of property rights" (Heider 1994: 128).[88] It is thus understandable that from their perspective the Texans thought that their freedoms were being attacked and that the Mexicans were attempting to reduce them into a condition of subjugation, even slavery. Although cautious at first (and criticized for it) Stephen Austin decided to commit himself to the Texan cause in the end, and decided to do so in vigorous and racist terms.[89] In a widely circulated

---

[88] Heider goes on to note that "the focus of the left critique of the state—the class discriminatory and antidemocratic function of the state to the advantage of the propertied class—is of little concern to the anarcho-capitalist, because for him *justice and property are identical*. (emphasis added, Heider 1994: 128). This insight, although it is meant to describe the differences between left and right wing formulations of anarchism, is an excellent description of how the concept of "property" has been historically understood in America.

[89] Cantrell (1999) argues that Austin chose to include the racist invective for political reasons, i.e. Austin felt that he needed the support of the southern slaveholders who had settled his colony. Certainly Austin, like most political leaders, tailored his remarks toward his intended audience, but there is considerable evidence that indicates that Austin actually believed what he wrote. Like Sam Houston, Austin was different in degree, but not in kind, from the more hotheaded rednecks like Groce that settled his colony. From the slave perspective, the bottom line

letter to Missouri Senator L.F. Linn (obviously intended to draw proslavery support and soldiers from the U.S.), Austin wrote:

> A war of extermination is raging in Texas......a war of barbarism and of despotic principles, waged by the mongrel Spanish-Indian and Negro race, against civilization and the Anglo-American race.....let an army of the United States march into Texas, and say to the pirate Santa Anna, "Stop:" a great and philanthropic and free people will not stand tamely by and see justice, constitutional right, and humanity, wantonly violated at her door—nor can a paternal government tolerate a state of things on its most vulnerable and important frontier, that will, and *must* bring the bloody tide of savage war and the horrors of negro insurrection within its limits (Austin to Linn, May 4, 1836, *Austin Papers* III, 344-48).90

It does not matter that Santa Anna had abolished the constitution and had established a strong centralist

---

is that Austin was a pro-slavery racist who thought that Indians and Blacks were inferior, and certainly not capable of self-government and deserving of equal treatment. Austin's occasional abstract philosophical agonizing about slavery as an institution—which was somewhat similar to Thomas Jefferson's, for similar reasons—does not dismiss this fundamental shortcoming in his temperament and character.

90   Austin's diplomatic mission to the United States to seek support for the Texas Rebellion provides some interesting lessons in moral doublethink. Of particular interest are the regular updates on the Texas situation that appeared in the New England (particularly Connecticut) press—understandable considering the Connecticut roots of the Austin family. The May 2, 1836 *Connecticut Courant* (Hartford), for example, refers to the "Fannin Massacre" and to "Slavery in Texas"—not Negro slavery, of course, but the enslavement of the Anglo Colonists, by the evil Mexican dictator Santa Anna. This and other newspaper outtakes are presented in a valuable recent publication compiled by Eric C. Caren titled *Texas Extra: A Newspaper History of the Lone Star State, 1835-1935*.

168

government. The American settlers could have—and perhaps would have—accommodated themselves to the new political reality had the new regime vigorously protected their property (i.e. slave) rights.[91]

Certainly the slaves themselves understood what was at stake, although events unfolded so rapidly that most never had the chance to escape. The first documented slave uprising in Texas occurred during the revolution. Bolstered by the freedoms Mexican victory would bring, this rebellion, which produced a sizable exodus of planter families from the Brazos river bottoms known as the "runaway scrape," caused considerable consternation among both civil and military authorities who feared (as usual) that the slaves intended to

---

[91] In the heated days prior to the outbreak of war, Lorenzo de Zavala summed up the revolutionary mood of the Texans succinctly in a September 17, 1835 letter to Austin where he wrote that "there is no unified patriotism" but "they will defend their private rights until death" (Jenkins 1973: 453-454). Zavala was also describing Austin's basic attitude on the matter; by this point Austin had decided not only that Texas needed to be independent of Mexico, but that it should be annexed to the United States. At the heart of Austin's reasoning was the question of "rights." As usual, these "rights" rested on the economic "necessity" of slavery. "Its [Texas'] inhabitants are farmers, and they need a calm and quiet life. But how can I, or any one remain indifferent, when our rights, our all appear to be in jeopardy? It is impossible?" (Austin to the people of Texas, September 8, 1835, Austin Papers III: 116-119).

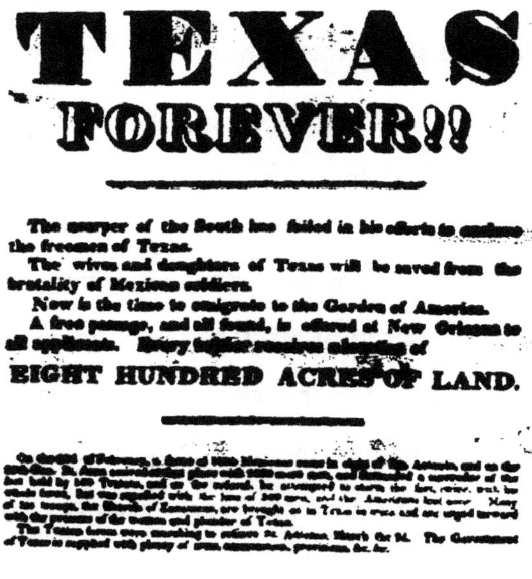

Figure 5: Recruitment Poster During the Texas Revolution. Obviously the printers of the poster had a somewhat limited understanding of what to "enslave" means.

take over the cotton farms and "intended to ship the cotton to New Orleans and make the white men serve them in turn" (B.J. White to Austin in Barker *The Austin Papers* 1926: 108). Slaves did run away to join Mexican forces,[92] and a significant number were impressed as military support personnel[93] (building fortifications) in the defense of Galveston, a pattern that was to be repeated during the Civil War.

---

[92] "Two escaped slaves died fighting with Vicente Cordova, who lead Negroes, Mexicans, and Indians in an abortive counter revolt against the Texas Republic in 1838. Texas troops executed one black prisoner and resold another into slavery. Other runaways served under Antonio Canales in his unsuccessful effort to establish the Republic of the Rio Grande in 1840" (Barr 1996: 32).

[93] Free Blacks also served on the Texas side although after the war instead of being treated as heroes most of these men became social, economic, and legal outcasts. One notable example was Greenbury Logan, who came to Texas in 1831 and settled a quarter league of land near Chocolate Bayou in Brazoria County. Logan was permanently disabled in San Antonio in 1835 when Ben Milam's forces defeated General Cos. After the war and the establishment of Texas independence, Logan bitterly wrote to congressman R.M. Forbes that "everry thing that is deare to a freeman is taken from me," that he could not even collect a debt from a white person without aid from another white person, "no vote or say in eny way, yet liable for Taxes...." Since his service wounds left him disabled, his economic situation was unbearable, for he could no longer work his land and pay his taxes. He was deeply in debt and, conquering his pride, he finally wrote to a Texas congressman appealing for tax exemption. He also asked for restoration of "what has been taken from me in the constitution," and said he "would be willing to leav the land though my blood has nearely all been shed for its rights" if his debts were erased and taxes paid. Indicative of the growing power of slaveholders in Texas and elsewhere throughout the South, his requests were never acted upon" (Katz 1996: 64-65). Logan married a German woman named Caroline. "In later years a daughter of this union married a white man after Logan had died and settled in West Texas. They had a son, who grew up in ignorance of his grandfather's color. His mother told him that her father had left some land and that the grandson journeyed to Richmond to see about getting title to the land. He learned for the first time that his grandfather was of African descent" (cited in Williams 1997: 12).

In general, I find Merk's (1972: 180) interpretation of the causes of the war to be the most fair and direct:

> The explanation of the Texan revolution, that it was an uprising against Mexican tyranny is unfounded. That explanation was propaganda, spread by the Texans in the course of the war. The Mexican administration of Texas had been weak and vacillating, the central government had been disorderly and the provincial government of Coahuila-Texas had been corrupt. But even Texan historians are now agreed that Mexican rule had not been cruel or oppressive. The revolution was basically the outcome of admitting into the rich prairies of Texas a race of aggressive and unruly American frontiersmen, a masterful race of men, who were contemptuous of Mexico and of Mexican authority. The old Latin mistake had been repeated, of admitting Gauls into the empire.

What the Texas Declaration of Independence did not mention by name, the new constitution of the republic was very careful to regulate. Here is what section 9 of the document said:

> Sec. 9. All persons of color who were slaves for life previous to their emigration to Texas, and who are now held in bondage, shall remain in the like state of servitude: *provided*, they said slave shall be the bona fide property of the person so holding said slave as aforesaid. Congress shall pass no laws to prohibit emigrants from bringing their slaves into the republic with them, and holding them by the same tenure by which such slaves were held in the United States; nor

shall congress have power to emancipate slaves; nor shall any slave holder be allowed to emancipate his or her slave or slaves without the consent of congress, unless he or she shall send his or her slave or slaves without the limits of the republic. No free person of African descent, either in whole or in part, shall be permitted to reside permanently in the republic, without the consent of congress; and the importation or admission of Africans or negroes into this republic, excepting from the United States of America, is forever prohibited, and declared to be piracy.

In his inaugural address as president of the new Texas Republic, Sam Houston urged "treaties of peace and amity" with the Indians yet later in the speech exclaimed that "the civilized world contemplated with proud emotions conduct which reflected so much glory on the Anglo-Saxon race" (Williams and Barker, *Houston Papers,* Vol. I: 449-450). Like so many "great" white men of this time, Houston wanted to have his cake and eat it too—he urged peace with the Indians, but only as long as they could be brought under the yoke of "western" culture. In other words, when Indian and American property rights came into conflict, which they increasingly did after 1836,

Houston—despite his well known support of "good faith" negotiations with the various tribes— most of the time believed that American property rights superseded the property rights of Indians. A strong sense of ego and Manifest Destiny[94] helps to explain this aspect of Houston's temperament.

Real and/or perceived conflicts of material interest—"civil rights" (defined as property rights)—were the direct cause of the Texas Revolution. To deny this or to subsume the matter under supposed "larger" conflicts is to at best tell a half truth and at worst to deliberately mislead. Disappointingly but not surprisingly, conventional wisdom among Texas Myth historians still subscribes to the Barker "dull organic ache" thesis concerning pre-revolutionary Texas slavery. Histories

---

[94] Although he would not have stated it as bluntly (having spent significant time with the Indians, Houston's attitude is perhaps best described as a form of benevolent paternalism). Houston essentially was in agreement with the governor of Georgia who wrote in the early to mid 1820's that treaties with Indians "were expedients by which ignorant, intractable, and savage people were induced without bloodshed to yield up what civilized peoples had a right to possess" (Stephanson 1995: 26). As a Cherokee with surrogate Indian parents, Houston certainly knew that Indians were not "ignorant." Nonetheless, he never let his personal feelings or affections interfere with his supreme belief that it was the karma of the Anglo-Saxon race to not only possess most of North America, but Central and South America as well, feelings he expressed in a tour of New York and New England after being elected to the U.S. Senate in 1848 (Campbell 1993: 118-119), as well as afterward.

arguing that slavery was the deciding factor in the conflict are dismissed as "conspiracy theories[95]," "naive" or criticized as being written from the perspective of a non-Texan "outsider." The debate continues, but the evidence certainly seems widespread and clear enough—it often seems that one of the initiation rites of being accepted into the club of leading Texas historians is defending the honor of the state against all attackers. Most outside observations of Texas and westward expansion have little difficulty calling the imperialist gambit of Jackson, Houston and others what it was. One leading "outside" (German) study of nineteenth century Texas, for instance, (Reichstein 1984: 186) concludes quite clearly that Jackson, Houston, and others were proslavery expansionists: "Polk,

---

[95] Charges of a Jackson and Houston conspiracy to overthrow the government of Mexico in Texas were levelled by John Quincy Adams, among others, at the time of the Texas Revolution and especially during the heated debate concerning the annexation of Texas. Within Texas historiography, one of the early and still forceful "conspiracy" arguments was laid forth by Richard Rollin Stenberg (1932) in his Ph.D. thesis, where he felt it necessary to note in the preface that his "many conclusions which are mere conjectures and have the generous tolerance but not sanction of Professor Eugene C. Barker, under whose guidance this study was done." Though he may not have agreed with its heretical conclusions, Barker signed off on Stenberg's dissertation. Regrettably Stenberg's study (and his subsequent works), which anticipated future developments in historical method and theory far better than many of Barker's works, has been mostly forgotten or dismissed.

Benton, Jackson und Sam Houston waren enge Freunde, Gegner einer Spaltung der Union über die Frage der Sklaverei und erklärte Expansionisten." Regarding the Texas Revolution Reichstein (p. 205) observes:

> Es war ein Krieg, den auf der einen Seite Santa Anna und seine Anhänger führen wollten, um oppositionelle Kräfte in Cohuila auszuschalten, für Ordnung in Texas zu sorgen, und um den unkontrollierten Landverkäufen ein Ende zu setzen, da man selbst an Landspekulation interessiert war. Auf der anderen Seite kamen die mexikanischen Truppen jenen Texanern recht, die den Krieg brauchten, um Texas von Mexiko zu lösen. *Dabei handelte es sich nicht um irgendwelche Konspirationen.* Sam Houston mußte von Andrew Jackson gar keinen Auftrag erhalten, Texas auf seine Weise den USA anzugliedern. Er wußte was sein Mentor dachte und wollte, und meinte, dies mit eigenen Unternehmungen verbinden zu können (emphasis added).

The level of defensiveness and denial about this issue is deep and widespread—especially since as Reichstag observes, one need not subscribe to any conspiracy theory whatsoever to make the argument that slavery was the primary cause of the Texas Revolution.

Over his career as a political commentator, Chomsky has

received similar responses to his institutional analyses. Author Tom Wolfe, for instance, dismisses Chomsky's theories of the manufacture of consent[96] as "some sort of cabal theory," but seems rather ignorant (or in denial) concerning what the theory actually says.[97] Contemporary race relations in

---

[96] What does this theory say? The theory basically attempts to delineate the way in which democratic institutions, as opposed to totalitarian ones, engineer assent. In a speech he delivered in December of 1984 (Chomsky 1987[1984]: 132), Chomsky described the process of "brainwashing under freedom" as follows:

> Democratic Systems are quite different. It is necessary to control not only what people do, but also what they think. Since the state lacks the capacity to ensure obedience by force, thought can lead to action and therefore the threat to order must be excised at the source. It is necessary to establish a framework for possible thought that is constrained within the principles of the state religion. These need not be asserted; it is better that they be presupposed, as the unstated framework for thinkable thought. The critics reinforce this system by tacitly accepting these doctrines, and confining their critique to tactical questions that arise within them. To achieve respectability, to be admitted to the debate, they must accept without question or inquiry the fundamental doctrine that the state is benevolent, governed by the loftiest intentions, adopting a defensive stance, not an actor in world affairs but only reacting to the crimes of others, sometimes unwisely because of personal failures, naiveté, the complexity of history or an inability to comprehend the evil nature of our enemies. If even the harshest critics tacitly adopt these premises, then, the ordinary person may ask, who am I to disagree? The more intensely the debate rages between hawks and doves, the more firmly and effectively the doctrines of the state religion are established. It is because of their notable contribution to thought control that the critics are tolerated, indeed honored—that is, those who play by the rules.

[97] On PBS Television in 1988 Wolfe told Bill Moyers that "this is—the old cabal theory that somewhere there's a room with a baize-covered desk and there's a bunch of capitalists sitting around and they're pulling strings. These rooms don't exist. I mean I hate to tell Noam Chomsky this.....I think this is the most absolute rubbish I've ever heard. This is the current fashion in universities. You know, it's patent nonsense and I think it's nothing but a fashion. It's a way that intellectuals have of feeling like clergy. I mean there has to be something wrong" (Achbar 1994: 61). In response to people who dismiss his ideas as "conspiracy theories" Chomsky observes:

Texas—with its woeful socioeconomic inequality, unfair education funding, de facto segregation, environmental destruction, and frontier justice criminal justice system—will not meaningfully improve until establishment intellectuals lay down their "Texas Pride" and recognize the foundations upon which their pride is constructed.

There's nothing more remote from what I'm discussing or what we have been discussing than a conspiracy theory. If I give an analysis of, say, the economic system, and I point out that General Motors tries to maximize profit and market share, that's not a conspiracy theory, that's an institutional analysis; it has nothing to do with conspiracies and that's precisely the sense in which we are talking about the media. The phrase conspiracy theory is one of those that's constantly brought up and I think its effect is simply to discourage institutional analysis (Achbar 1994: 131).

CHAPTER 5: THE INCREASE OF SLAVERY AND SLAVE TRADING DURING THE REPUBLIC PERIOD AND THE FLOWERING OF MANIFEST DESTINY

"The United States are in a state of progressive aggrandizement, which has no example in the history of the world. Its federal union, instead of dissolving, as had been predicted by European politicians, has strengthened with the progress of time....the mass os its population is better educated, and more elevated in its moral and intellectual character, than that of any other. If such is its political condition, is it possible that its progress can be retarded, or its aggrandizement curtailed, by the rising prosperity of Mexico?" (quoted in Stenberg 1932: 167)

With the right of slave property firmly established, the slave trade into Texas expanded rapidly. Legislators in the new Texas Senate wasted little time in enacting legislation to protect their interests—chief among these being, as argued in the last chapter, slavery and slaves:

> A threat from within that preoccupied the mostly southern and property-holding senators was that of slave revolt. Although the slave population of Texas was not yet large, the status of this group was a major determinant of the future of the Republic and received more legislative attention than the numbers might have suggested and certainly more than many people desired. A joint resolution signed by [Sam] Houston on December 14, 1837, entitled "An Act to Provide for the Punishment of Crimes and Misdemeanors by Slaves," contained a detailed list of offenses to be considered capital when committed by a slave or free person of color in an effort to impose a greater measure of control over the growing

black population (Spaw 1990: 46).

Both African and African-American slave trading continued to multiply, although the latter began to predominate, peaking in the years following the annexation of Texas to the United States. Typical examples of African-American slave trading are the following:

> Ashbel Smith, the Connecticut-born doctor and future political leader who moved to Texas in 1837, paid $2,200 for two preteenaged boys and a teenaged girl at New Orleans in April, 1838. He immediately shipped his purchases to Galveston (Campbell 1989: 50).

or

> For the next seven years [approximately 1830 to 1837] [Matthew] Cartwright was paying from four hundred and fifty dollars to eight hundred dollars "cash in hand," for young Negroes in their late teens and early twenties. Cartwright was also buying young children. He paid $185 for ten year old Jim; $320 for Milly, a year younger than Jim; and $350 for Lucy who was twelve; while he paid $1060 for the two Negroes, Mary, fifteen, and Harry, ten (Curlee 1932: 64).

As discussed in the previous chapter, such purchases, which constituted a significant proportion of slave transactions in the

Republic of Texas, should properly be considered as part of the slave trade instead of as planter migration as Campbell argues. Smith also wrote to others about land and market conditions in Texas. In a letter to Durant H. Daves (Ashbel Smith papers, Center for American History, UT Austin) Smith wrote in August of 1839 that market conditions were

> much better than it was last year...Negroes are in great demand the only difficulty in the way of sales can be the want of sound funds by purchaser...the route of the Indians and its effects on our relations with Mexico have greatly increased public confidence here so that slave sales will be readier and on better terms.

The precise number of slaves speculated into Texas during the Republic period is impossible to determine, but a rough analysis of the demographics provides a clue. As figure 4 shows, the Texas slave population began to increase significantly during the republic period, reaching somewhere in the neighborhood of 15,000-20,000 persons by 1840, and reached nearly 60,000 by 1850, according to the 1850 census. Given the fact that Texas' white population grew at a similarly high rate, it is clear that the majority of the enslaved population was transported to Texas and that natural increase was a relatively minor factor in the numbers increase. Employing Bancroft (and Tadman's) growth-rate method, one can see that highly age-selective nature of the 1850 slave population indicates that the majority of the population was traded instead of "brought" to Texas, in all likelihood in a manner similar to the slaves purchased by settlers such as Ashbel Smith.

Although the Texas constitution had outlawed the African slave trade (while simultaneously protecting slavery), Texas officials—like their American counterparts—were "criminally negligent" (Du Bois 1986[1896]: 143) in their lax enforcement of the law. Many officials, particularly customs collectors, were in fact directly benefitting from the illegal traffic, either by acceptance of payoffs or other forms of back-door dealing. As usual, the primary incentive was money; in the early days of the Texas Republic, the Texas treasury was chronically short of funds and was nearly bankrupt. As a solution to this problem, President Houston in mid-1837 began to install customs houses at all main ports of entry in Texas. "Customs accounted for half the government's revenue for the first five years of the Republic's 10-year life span; property taxes and license fees provided the rest" (Nevin 1975: 205). It was thus easy for officials to rationalize the slave trade on both personal (money in Texas was scarce and what little there was often worthless) and national grounds (the Texas treasury needed all the money it could get, especially for defense against Mexico).

Although much of the slave trade in Texas was conducted by itinerant rural traders selling their slave coffles at private sale[98], with the institution now protected, the first significant slave markets began to appear in Galveston and Houston, the primary ports of entry for new settlers. Although slaves were sold throughout the year, market conditions were most

---

[98] A pattern found throughout the south; see Tadman (1996: 12).

favorable between November and the spring months. Enslaved African Americans with sugar processing skills were deemed to be particularly valuable, especially after Texas statehood in 1845 when sugar planting began to be practiced in earnest. Slave prices in Texas were generally high, mainly for three reasons: 1.) the New Orleans slave market, the primary source of trade with Texas, had the highest slave prices in the United States 2.) there was a high demand for slaves in Texas, and 3.) there was practically no macroeconomic stability during the early years of the republic; banking facilities were almost nonexistent, and Texas money was often considered to be next to worthless (Curlee 1932: 63).

Locating slave dealers in historical records can be difficult since many of these individuals are listed as "auctioneers" or "general agents" and sold other forms of merchandise in addition to enslaved African Americans. For evidence one must look at traders' account books, correspondence, advertisements and the reports of contemporary observers (Tadman 1993: 1453). The evidence indicates that commission merchants were active as slave traders from the outset of settlement in the Republic of Texas and advertised their ties to American markets in Charleston, Richmond and New Orleans as proof of their reputability. In the December 12, 1838 Houston *Telegraph and Texas Register*, for instance, the new firm of Hedenberg and Vedder advertised a three thousand acre plantation for sale, including four male slaves. In 1839 G. Everett advertised his auctioneering services in the Bayou City and offered various goods and services, including "Negroes, horses, mules, and carriages" (*The Galvestonian*, March 27, 1839). The late thirties also saw the introduction of regular steamship services between Galveston and New Orleans (sail powered vessels, primarily schooners, still predominated however)[99]; the primary figures in the development in this traffic were entrepreneurially minded

---

[99] "The number of vessels in our [Galveston] harbor averages from twenty-five to thirty, exclusive of steam ships and steamboats" (*The Civilian and Galveston Gazette*, January 11, 1839).

New York and New England merchants such as Charles Morgan and his competitors who eagerly seized the opportunity to fill market demands for merchandise in the newly independent Texas, including slaves. As figure 2 indicates, several of Morgan's vessels were observed by contemporaries (primarily British and occasional American antislavery patrols) landing both African and African American slaves in Texas.[100]

Morgan—along with other "Lone Star Yankees" (Parmet 1997) such as William Marsh Rice—eventually grew to play a major role in the socioeconomic development of Texas and Louisiana. He was a significant booster of Manifest Destiny, hoping to benefit from adventures such as William Walker's Nicaraguan filibustering and the annexationist (particularly of Cuba) rhetoric of presidents from Polk to Buchanan. During the

---

[100] "English barrister Nicholas Maillard, who originally came to Texas searching for a healthful climate and alter strongly opposed British recognition of the Republic, filed several reports on the African slave trade into Texas with the British government. In 1840, Maillard disclosed that American steamers "of the first class" took part in the illegal slave trade into Texas. Such vessels as the *Neptune*, *Columbia*, and the *New York*, carried as many as one hundred slaves from Cuba into Texas and the United States twice a month, according to Maillard's reports" (Robbins 1972: 120).

republic period, however, Morgan was still establishing his enterprise and Texas reputation. Figure 6 is a picture of the noted steamboat *Yellowstone*, which traveled Texas waters during the republic period and played an important role during the Texas Revolution. "The steamboat had been moored at Jared Groce's landing just upstream [of the Brazos]" for instance, "taking on cotton when [General Sam] Houston had bivouacked his army at the river's edge on 31 March 1836" (Jackson 1985: 121). In the days before rail, steamboats such as *Yellowstone* were the transportation cornerstone of the growing Texas economy and began to be utilized in increasing numbers. Thus the vessel can be thought to be fairly representative of the steamboats that helped to "win" the west. In *Voyages of the Steamboat Yellowstone* Jackson (1985: 152) describes the vessel as

> a ghost ship, condemned for misdeeds aplenty: for smuggling whisky to the Indians and paying them a pittance for their season's catch. For becoming a slave ship twice a year to carry *engagés* into the wilds for hard work and wretched food. For harboring pestilence. For

being a pioneering engine of Manifest Destiny in the North and the South, toiling away in the name of a people whose urgent vision of a nation united sometimes blinded them to the dirty work that kept their dream alive and their hopes moving westward.

The architectural features of the *Yellowstone* are described in considerable detail in the appendixes of Jackson (1985) and are not particularly relevant here, although it is fairly clear that frontier vessels such as *Yellowstone* were not specifically adapted for large scale slave trading—yet. By the 1850's, however, specially built or adapted steam vessels, many of which were operated by Charles Morgan, were running regularly between New Orleans and Texas ports.

Figure 6: Historic Steamship *Yellowstone*. When fully loaded the entire ship was covered with bales of cotton and the only part of the vessel visible were the stacks. Photo Courtesy Star of the Republic Museum.

Other Evidence of African and African-American Slave Trading

Scholars have attempted to produce reasonable estimates of the African slave trade into or through Texas for years. In the sixth edition of his classic history of African-Americans, John Hope Franklin (citing Du Bois and others) remarks:

> ....New York merchants as well as those of New Orleans were benefiting from the illicit traffic. In 1836 the consul at Havana reported that whole cargoes of slaves fresh from Africa were daily being shipped to Texas in American vessels and that more than one thousand had been sent within a few months. Two months later it was estimated that fifteen thousand Africans were annually taken into Texas. Bay Island, in the Gulf of Mexico, was a depot where at times as many as sixteen thousand Africans were on hand to be shipped to Florida, Texas, Louisiana, and other markets (Franklin 1988: 111). . . . . .

There is no reason to doubt these and other reports of large-scale slave trading in Texas waters during this time period. The figure of "more than one thousand" within the space of a few months, however, requires further confirmation and, as mentioned in chapter three, is not in line with the existing evidence.

The efforts of William Kennedy, British Consular at Galveston, to check the efforts of the illegal African trade provide an important indicator of the nature of Negro speculating along the western frontier of the slave south. During the late 1830's and early 1840's, a period of sensitive negotiations between the British Crown and the Republic of Texas (mostly over the issue of slavery and slave trading), Kennedy exercised considerable energy in identifying and prosecuting African slave traders, especially if the suspected smugglers were British subjects. Charles Frankland, along with his partners Richard P. Jones and John Barnes, snuck African slaves from Barbados to Texas via New Orleans on their vessels *Antoinette, Ellen Frankland,* and *Sarah Barnes*, and were said to have landed their cargo on a small plantation a few miles up the Brazos River away from the open Gulf of Mexico. To avoid prosecution, the smugglers employed the legal ruse of registering the slaves under notarial contract until they could be sold (this was still illegal under the Texas constitution, however). When the smugglers learned of an impending investigation into their illegal activities, they switched their ships' registries from England to Texas and thus avoided legal troubles with the British (Robbins 1972: 121-122).

This episode, which is the best documented case of British slave smuggling in Texas, should be considered the exception rather than the rule. The general trend in post-revolutionary Texas was for the legal African-American slave trade to be considered the primary labor source for aspiring Texas planters. Serious African slave trading and propagandizing for its decriminalization did not reoccur until about twenty years later in the late 1850's.[101]

A major source of evidence for African-American slave

---

[101] Although abolitionists such as Featherstonhaugh and Olmstead travelled through Texas over the years and wrote influential pamphlets and books about what they saw, abolitionism as a political force never took strong root in Texas. The primary reasons why were intimidation and violence: any Texans (such as Mexicans and some Germans) who publicly expressed abolitionist sentiments were placing their lives and property in danger, slaveowning Texans were particularly vigilent in chasing down runaways (even over the border), and possessed a paranoid (even by Southern standards) fear of slave insurrection and punished suspected plotters viciously. For a description of a supposed white abolitionist plot to free Texas slaves after the John Brown raid at Harper's Ferry see Barr 1996[1973]: 33-34.

trading were advertisements placed in local papers, particularly the Houston *Telegraph*. During the republic period, Texas newspapers generally printed news of national and international interest since local news would travel faster by word of mouth. Thus most of the "news" "consisted of official government communications, political issues, and reprints of stories from American newspapers dealing with events in foreign countries" (Murry 1991: 83). As now, advertisements constituted a significant portion of a Texas newspaper: in addition to slaves, items advertised included real estate, farm implements, and animals, among others. Advertisers also offered rewards for runaways. One ad read:

> ONE HUNDRED DOLLARS REWARD WILL be given for the apprehension and delivering, negroes ARTHUR and GEORGE......They left neighborhood together, and will endeavor to get to New Orleans, where they were lately brought from (Murry 1991: 83).

Another advertisement in the May 27, 1843 *Civilian and Galveston Gazette* read:

> FOR SALE. A Negro woman, aged 27 years, a good house servant, and child 13 months old, apply to terms cash.
>
> —Lawrence Frosh[102]

Slaves did not just run away back to New Orleans. Many ran for the Mexican border. In the January 11, 1843 *Civilian and Galveston Gazette* Hamilton Stuart reported:

> It is stated by the Little Rock Gazette that 52 negroes, who robbed the store of Bigelow & Warners, at Webber's Falls and fled for Mexico across the upper and unsettled part of Texas, were pursued by a party of Creek and another of Cherokee Indians and overtaken in the Cross Timbers, about 200 miles from Fort Gibson. The negroes resisted; two of them were killed, one wounded, and twelve taken. The remainder effected their escape.[103]

---

[102] Two other Galveston speculators active in the 1840's appear to be H.A. Cobb who placed ads to both hire out and purchase Negro slaves during January and February of 1843, and the firm of Van Winkle & Bros which advertised a number of steam packets and schooners travelling between Galveston, New Orleans, and New York. Cobb's ad identifies him as an "Auction and Commission Merchant" and states that "liberal advances [will be] made on consignments." An ad he placed in the August 17, 1848 *Civilian and Galveston Gazette* reads:

> A LIKELY MULATTO WOMAN AGED about 23 or 24 years with her two children—a girl aged $4\frac{1}{2}$ and a boy aged 11 years—is offered for sale, and a female field hand will be taken in part payment—title indisputable. She is a good cook, washer, ironer, sewer and nurse
>
> —H.A. Cobb

[103] Felix Haywood, a 92 year old San Antonio slave interviewed by the Federal Writers Project in 1937 also confirmed the desire among Texas slaves to head south: "There was no reason to *run* up north. All we had to do was to *walk* south, and we'd be free as soon as we crossed the Rio Grande. In Mexico you could be free (Tyler and Murphy 1974: 69).

Texas: A Place to Make One's Fortune

By the early 1840's, newspaper editors and other new immigrants were editorializing and propagandizing the virtues and seemingly limitless economic potential of Texas. Hamilton Stuart, a recent arrival to Texas (later to become customs collector at Galveston), editorialized in his newspaper, *The Civilian and Galveston City Gazette* that

> the doctrine of Free Trade is making rapid strides, both in England and the United States, and we shall not be surprised to see it yet obtain among the most powerful and enlightened states of the world (July 15, 1843).

"Free trade," of course, meant slavery. In case Stuart's reference to laissez-faire economics was a bit too theoretical or abstract for some readers, in another editorial later in the month he addressed the issue of slavery and its relationship to "free markets" in Texas more directly:

> If the people of the Northern States find, in these circumstances, advantages in removal, there are other inducements equally great in favor of the slaveowner of Virginia. In comparison with that state, the cost of supporting slaves is seemingly, and of feeding stock

> absolutely, nothing in Texas, while besides all the agricultural products of that state, Texas presents others for the employment of slaves which yield a much better return. While there are portions of Texas which yield wheat, Indian corn and tobacco as well as Virginia, *the cotton and sugar lands of this country open a field of the employment of slave labor in which there is no danger that it will ever be supplanted by white.* Many a Virginian, who, from the poverty of his lands, finds himself poor and scarcely able to subsist with a large number of slaves, would become suddenly rich by removing to this country. The labor of a tithe of his slaves would here support the remainder, who could be employed in contributing to the support as wealth of their owner (italics added, July 29, 1843).

The early 1840's saw a drop in cotton and slave prices and editorials in the Houston *Morning Star* dismissed the alleged African trade in Texas as economically worthless; "unseasoned" Africans would not sell for more than $100 in cash in Texas, according to the editor (Campbell 1989: 70). Stuart's inducement indicates that at this stage most pro-slavery Texans were interested in enticing prospective planters from Upper South states to settle in Texas. Such settlements, of course, would have involved significant amounts of African-

American slave trading, and the demographics, as discussed, reflect this.

The Slave Trade and the Annexation of Texas

It is well known that Texas leaders desired annexation to the United States immediately after independence from Mexico but that antislavery sentiment in Congress and elsewhere prevented it from occurring right away. The battle over Texas annexation, especially whether and under what conditions the merger should occur, was a pivotal point in the history of American foreign policy and prefigured the United States' later nineteenth century imperialism and twentieth century foreign relations strategy. An investigation of the rhetoric surrounding the annexation, both pro and con, is important not only for the history of Texas slavery and the slave trade, but for American history as well. The best overall study of the role of slavery in the annexation of Texas is Merk (1972), which delves into considerable detail concerning pro and anti-annexationist propaganda and its role in the debate.[104] For the sake of focus, clarity, and brevity, I shall focus my discussion primarily on the slave trading component of the controversy.[105]

As mentioned, the Texas constitution had already outlawed the African slave trade when discussions were undertaken between officials of the Texas Republic and the

---

[104] In his *Civilian and Galveston City Gazette*, Hamilton Stuart lucidly articulated the Texas position in two increasingly strident editorials, the logic of which only hardened as the Civil War approached. The first, written September 23, 1843, articulated the well known "economic necessity" argument:

> "There are thousands of sensible men in the Northern and Eastern States opposed to slavery in the abstract, who are nevertheless unwilling to disturb the social compact which alone secures the unity, peace, and prosperity of the states, and who are as sensible of, and averse to, the evils of a free negro population as are the people of the slaveholding states."

On October 7, 1843, Stuart was more direct, almost John Calhoun-like, in outlining what was at stake:

> "The institution of slavery is engrafted upon our Constitution, *and interwoven with the very existence of the Government,* and its abolition would involve the overthrow of both, as well as bear along with it a train of evils, resulting not only in the destruction of the civil institutions of the country, but of all order and security both to persons and property" (emphasis added).

[105] I will thus be glossing over several important aspects of slavery in Texas, such as, for instance, the legislation passed February 5th of 1840 expelling all free Negroes from the state. The statute was modified in 1842 and allowed for the possibility of free African American residence in Texas—provided the claimant could pay "bond and security in the penal sum of five hundred dollars payable to the President" (*Writings of Sam Houston,* Vol. III: 241).

British Crown for the establishment of formal relations. It was well known that it was official policy on the part of the British to negotiate not only theoretical but actual agreements for the suppression of the African traffic, and the abolitionist sentiments of British officials were also matters of record. In the midst of the various intrigues that were taking place in Europe and America regarding the future role of Texas, a treaty was eventually concluded. In many ways, the wording of the treaty was a joke; the Texas Navy was practically insignificant in comparison to the Royal Navy, and the provisions for mutual search (i.e. the right of Texas vessels to search suspected British smugglers) were a pathetic formality given the fact that the Crown was by this point expending significant resources to check the illegal African traffic. Hamilton Stuart summarized the main provisions of the treaty in the April 8, 1843 *Civilian and Galveston Gazette*:

> Under the Treaty between Great Britain and this country for the suppression of the African trade it is provided that no naval ship of either nation shall have the right to

visit or examine a merchant vessel of the other, until the commander of the cruizer shall exhibit to the master of the other vessel the special orders of his Government conferring upon him the right to visit her; no officer shall exercise the right who is of a lower grade than a Lieutenant in the Navy, unless he be at the time, second in command of the visiting ship, and exhibit the special orders as above mentioned, signed by the commander; and he is required to leave with the vessel visited a certificate of his own rank, the name of his commander and that of his vessel, and the object of his visit. If it is ascertained that the papers of the vessel visited are regular and her business lawful, he is to certify these facts upon her log book, and allow her to proceed upon her course; but if sufficient grounds exist to believe that she is a slaver, she is to be detained; a list must be made out of all the papers found on board, and also a statement of the place and condition of the slaves, if any. No person is to be taken out of the vessel detained, unless necessary to preserve the health or lives of the slaves, or the safety of the persons put in charge of her.

All Texian vessels detained by the cruizers of Great Britain are to be taken to Galveston and delivered up to the authorities of Texas, but slaves found on such vessels on the coast of Brazil or of Africa, are to be sent at once, whether captured by a Texian or British cruizer, to one of the British settlements on the coast of Africa, all slaves found in such vessels to the West Indies are to be sent to Galveston; and all slaves found on *British* vessels detained by Texian cruisers shall be delivered up to the British jurisdiction at Bathurst, on the river of Gambia, if taken off the coast of Africa or at Port Royal Jamaica, if taken to the West Indies.

A merchant vessel under convoy of a cruizer of either

> nation is only liable to be searched by said cruizer.
> Any vessel attempting to carry on the slave trade shall by that act alone, lose all right to claim protection of their flag.
> The right of visit, under this treaty, is not to be exercised in the Mediterranean Sea, or those seas of Europe which lie within the straits of Gibraltar, and to the northward of the 37th parallel of north latitude, and within and to the eastward of the meridian of longitude twenty degrees west of Greenwich; nor in the Gulf of Mexico, to the northward of the 25th parallel of north latitude, nor to the westward of the 90th degree of longitude west of Greenwich.

The provisions of the treaty, which in some measures were stronger—although not much—than the existing suppression treaty between the United States and Great Britain[106] was seen by pro-annexationists as another sure sign of abolitionist conspiracy on the part of the British. The Southern propaganda machine went on overdrive and all but charged the British with making preparations to launch a full scale assault on Texas (and eventually the rest of the South) in the name of economic

---

[106] The United States flatly refused the right of search. As a consequence it was widely acknowledged that flying the American flag was a form of protection from interception by anti slave trade patrols. See Du Bois 1986[1896]: 164-165.

domination[107] and abolition. Overall, the propaganda took several interconnected directions:

> One line of argument would be directed to the Northern audience, another to the Southern. The Northern would listen appreciatively to the pocketbook argument. It would attracted by visions of Manifest Destiny. Its moralists on the slavery issue would find attractive the thesis that annexation would automatically solve both the slavery and race issues. The timid would take comfort in the thesis that annexation would avert foreign military dangers on the western frontier. The Southern audience would respond to the thesis that annexation would render the South immune to the virus of British abolitionism—also that New Orleans would be forever secure from a British invasion based on a satellite Texas. Politically minded Southerners would be attracted by the prospect that the North-South balance in the Senate would be tilted southward if Texas were annexed (Merk 1972: 46).

---

[107] In a letter to his friend and benefactor President John Tyler, Duff Green—who had been appointed an executive agent to Great Britain by Tyler but was also in London for personal business—implicated the British secretary for foreign affairs Lord Aberdeen in an elaborate abolitionist plot that would threaten the safety and security of the South. He argued that Britain had abolished slavery in the West Indies for economic not moral reasons: "If England can abolish the slave trade & it be true that by doing so she will enable her East India colonies to undersell Brazil & Cuba, it follows that England can greatly increase her manufactures" (Merk 1972: 188). He also reported "hearsay news that the British were about to make a loan of ten million dollars to Santa Anna (Merk 1972: 163).

The overall origins of Manifest Destiny[108] in Texas are by now well understood. Offers to purchase the province from Mexico were made as early as 1825[109]; Jacksonian Democrats, who wielded considerable influence in Texas, were writing in 1836 that

> Genl. Jackson says that Texas must claim the Californias on the Pacific in order to paralyze the opposition of the North and East to Annexation. That the fishing [whaling] interest of the North and East wish a harbour on the Pacific; that this claim of the Californias will give it to them, and will diminish their opposition to annexation. He is very earnest and anxious on this point of claiming the Californias and says we must not consent to less. This

---

[108] The term, of course, was coined by John O'Sullivan in a famous editorial in the *Morning Star* of December 27, 1845 where he wrote: "the right of our manifest destiny to overspread and to possess the whole continent which providence has given us for the development of the great experiment of liberty and federated self government" (Stephanson 1995: 42).

[109] In *Viage a los Estados Unidos* Lorenzo de Zavala, a Mexican liberal, federalist and active participant in the Texas Revolution ("the most interesting man in Texas" according to William Fairfax Gray), recorded many penetrating and prophetic impressions of America and Americans. "It appeared to Zavala that their lives consisted only of an endless exchange of goods and money in pursuit of profit" and that "Americans seldom discussed abstract matters or displayed much enthusiasm for any subject not calculated to advance their pecuniary interests." Based on these and other contemporary observations, Brack (1975: 60-63) observes that Mexicans "viewed slavery in the United States as the most obvious and cruel manifestation of an intense Yankee ethnocentrism that would have tragic effects on Mexico". Zavala's observations may not have always squared with his politics (he had many American friends and could hardly be considered a "progressive" on race relations within Mexico), but they nonetheless illustrate that most Mexicans (with the notable exception of the corrupt officials running the province of Coahuila and Texas), even elites, genuinely disliked and even detested slavery and understood quite well what the institution had done and was doing to the United States.

> is in strict confidence. Glory to God in the highest (Merk 1972: 47).

and by the mid 1840's claims for "reannexation" of Texas to the United States—ostensibly because Texas was considered to be part of the Louisiana Purchase—were in full swing.

Another aspect of the Texas annexation debate involved the African-American slave trade, and revolved around the adoption of the so-called "gag rules" in Congress in May of 1836. Northern radicals viewed the interstate trade in African-American slaves to be subject to congressional controls, as part of interstate commerce (Merk 1972: 7), and presented thousands of petitions on the floor of Congress for the abolition of the slave trade in the District of Columbia.[110] In response, a coalition of Southerners and Northern Democrats in the House secured passage of rules to stifle debate on the issue. In his relentless and poignant attacks on this infringement on the right to petition, John Quincy Adams, the primary standard-

---

[110] Bancroft (1996[1931]: 45) characterized the D.C. slave trade as "the most notorious" (although not the largest) and "the very seat and center" of the traffic.

bearer of the antislavery and anti-annexationist position in Congress pointed out that

> at this day the President of the United States, the President of the Senate, the Speaker of the House of Representatives, and five, out of nine, of the Judges of the supreme judicial courts of the United States, are not only citizens of the slaveholding states, but individual slaveholders themselves. So are, and constantly have been, with scarcely and exception, all the members of both Houses of Congress from the slaveholding States; and so are, in immensely disproportionate numbers, the commanding officers of the army and navy; the officers of the customs; the registers and receivers of the land offices, and post-masters throughout the slaveholding states (Merk 1972: 130).

Adams also charged that Andrew Jackson and his supporters (in Texas and elsewhere) had conspired to instigate or "aid" the Texas Revolution and that plans to annex Texas to the United States were part of a larger expansionist scheme to expand slavery and the Slave Power across North America.

There were other issues at stake, of course: the constitutional issue of whether congress had the power to annex a territory as vast as Texas to the United States, the role of Texas land speculators in funding much of the proannexationist propaganda, and the degree to which public officials had private interests in the annexation. On August 27 1845, a Texas convention finished work on a constitution to be presented to Congress. Regarding slavery and the slave trade, there was nothing of surprise in the document:

> The constitution contained a carefully drawn bill of rights. It created the traditional three departments of government. Its pattern regarding slavery and the status of free Negroes was wholly Southern. It prohibited any general legislation for emancipating slaves and any legislation restricting the right of immigrants to bring slaves with them into Texas. It gave the right of suffrage to all free white males, but not to untaxed Indians or to Africans, or to the descendants of Africans. It ordered a census to be taken every eight years in which all free inhabitants were to be enumerated, but not untaxed Indians or Africans, or the descendants of Africans. In October, a popular referendum accepted annexation and the new constitution (Merk 1972: 174)

Anson Jones, the last president of the Texas Republic presided over the ceremony of transfer of sovereignty from the Republic to the government of the United States. He made a brief speech and began to lower the flag of the Republic for the last time.

> As it [the flag] came down, the pole which had been carrying it broke in two. For a moment, before the banner of the Union was raised, the Lone Star flag shrouded the retiring President. Thirteen years later, deeply depressed over the misunderstanding of his efforts on behalf of Texas, which had reappeared in his defeat for election to the Senate of the United States, he took his own life (Merk 1972: 176).

CHAPTER 6: THE GOLDEN AGE OF THE TEXAS "SUGAR BOWL" AND KING COTTON

"The Theology was Calvin: The religion—cash"
—*Paul Robeson, Here I Stand, p. 10*

The period 1845-1865 marked the apex of classic Southern life, culture, politics, and economics in Texas. The "Black Crop" was imported into the Lone Star State in ever increasing numbers, prices for slaves were increasing, and agricultural production was beginning to hit its stride;[111] as the Civil War approached, slaveowning members of the Texas planterocracy boasted of the nearly inexhaustible agricultural potential of Texas and eagerly agitated for the re-opening of the African slave trade to the United States.

First the United States, with a newly annexed Texas, had to finish the job of crushing the "threat" posed by continued Mexican possession of the Southwest. The Mexican-American War followed and resulted in the defeat of Mexico and the finalization of U.S. hegemony over most of the usable parts of

---

[111] Texas cotton production increased 600 percent in the 1850's (Campbell, New Handbook of Texas Online: slavery).

North America. In his newspaper the *North Star* (January 21, 1848), Frederick Douglass denounced "the present disgraceful, cruel, and iniquitous war with our sister republic" and declared that

> The determination of our slaveholding President to prosecute the war, and the probability of his success in wringing from the people men and money to carry it on, is made evident, rather than doubtful, by the puny opposition arrayed against him. No politician of any considerable distinction or eminence seems willing to hazard his popularity with his party.....by an open and unqualified disapprobation of the war. None seem willing to take their stand for peace at all risks; and all seem willing that the war should be carried on, in some form or other (cited in Zinn, 1980: 155).

With Texas now officially in United States hands[112] and with the Fugitive Slave Act passed, the last remaining barriers to full-blown immigration to Texas were removed.

Historians who view the period leading up to the Civil

---

[112] The 1845 annexation of Texas by joint resolution was illegal, and was recognized as such by most observers at the time. The treaty of Guadalupe Hidalgo constitutes the official legal basis for the annexation of Texas (and the rest of the Southwest) by the United States. The terms of the treaty stipulated that Mexico would cede approximately half its territory (including present-day California, Arizona, New Mexico, Utah, Colorado, Nevada, and parts of Wyoming), in exchange for which the U.S. government would pay the government of Mexico a sum of fifteen million dollars.

War as a simple conflict over slavery or "states' rights" miss the point that slavery was primarily an *economic* institution, albeit with many social and cultural dimensions. That conflict, as in most cases, was a contest over real and perceived material interest, i.e. which version of "free market" ideology would predominate—one based on slavery or not based on slavery. Furthermore, although it is not often popularly recognized, the material interests of northern and southern elites were for the most part identical—both groups of aristocrats were dependent on slavery and slave trading. The economic fortunes of Texas, and of the South generally, were deeply intertwined with the fortunes of northern mercantile centers, particularly New York, Boston, and Philadelphia. It was well known, among historians at least, that the prosperity of New York City was "almost as dependent upon Southern slavery as Charleston itself" (cited in Foner 1968[1941]: 4) and that "the influence of the South upon New York's economic life started at the port, and proceeded uptown, touching every form of business activity on its way"

(Foner 1968[1941]: 4). The reciprocal relationship operated, roughly, as follows: plantations would produce the cotton, tobacco, or sugar (and other crops), and ship it north, while northern merchants in return would ship clothing, fruits, butter, alcohol, cheese and other finished goods back south. The cotton would be sold to New England and England textile mills where it helped to further fuel the already ongoing industrial revolution.[113] Northern merchants had no real moral objection to furnishing southern states with goods and slaves. This had been the pattern with the African slave trade all along:

> The significance of New England in the African slave trade does not, therefore, lie in the fact that she early discountenanced the system of slavery and stopped importation, but rather in the fact that her citizens being the traders of the New World, early took part in the carrying trade and furnished slaves to the other colonies" (Du Bois1986[1896]: 34).

---

113 "In 1860, 89 percent of all of Great Britain's cotton imports was produced by slaves, as was all of the cotton consumed by the US textile industry, and amount which expanded by 125 percent in each decade between 1830 and 1860....slave-produced cotton from the US South accounted for 58 percent of the dollar value of all US exports in 1860" (Bailey 1997: 254).

This was also true of the internal slave trade. As the emerging mercantile capital of British North America, the New York colony early on ensured that freedom to trade and repatriate profits were maintained: "No restriction was ever put by New York on participation in the [slave] trade outside the colony, and in spite of national laws New York merchants continued to be engaged in this traffic even down to the Civil War" (Du Bois 1986[1896]: 27).[114]

A Brief Snapshot of Antebellum Texas

There were, essentially, four socioeconomic classes in antebellum Texas. The first, and at the top of the social structure, were the planters:

> Antebellum Texas, although less than one-third of its families owned so much as a single slave, had all the characteristics of an advanced slave holding society. Slaveholders dominated the state's economy, controlled its politics, and occupied the top rung on the social ladder......In 1850, slaveholding households, which

---

[114] "The city of New York has been of late...the principal port of the world for this infamous commerce; although the cities of Portland and Boston are only second to her in that distinction" (Du Bois 1986[1896]: 178).

constituted 30 percent of the total in Texas, owned 72 percent of the state's real property. Ten years later, although slaveholding families had declined to 27 percent of the total, they still controlled 73 percent of all wealth (real and personal property combined)" (Campbell 1989: 209).[115]

The second group of "Texans" included the New Orleans, New England, or New York based "merchants" who acted as financial intermediaries and suppliers for the planters.[116] These northern capitalists were not only bound financially to the planter class; familial connections were common as well. Although not virulently pro-slavery—and in some cases against the further expansion of the institution across the rest of North America—these businessmen and women, quite simply, loved money more than they hated slavery. Thoroughgoing racists,

---

[115] The rate of ownership among slaveholding farmers remained fairly steady at about one-third between 1850 and 1860 (Campbell 1989: 209).

[116] It may seem like a contradiction in terms to label these individuals "Texans" and then to point out that they were based in New York. There is more nuance. Many northerners came to Texas, stayed permanently, and died there (e.g. Anson Jones). Some stayed for many years (William Marsh Rice lived continuously in Texas for over two decades and returned seasonally for the rest of his life) and then went back north. Others came for a relatively brief period and returned. The point is that these people (and their descendants) exercised a disproportionate degree of influence in Texas affairs and are recognized as "Texans" by Texas Myth commissars.

these individuals denounced abolitionists, routinely owned slaves (and in many cases acted as absentee landlords of plantations) themselves, and moved as comfortably through Southern high society as they did in elite circles in the north. In Texas, these "Lone Star Yankees" would end up making a fortune and playing a major role in antebellum politics.[117]

The third class of individuals included the non-slaveholding "Anglo" settlers/immigrants, Mexicans/Mexican-Americans, and Indians who constituted the majority of the non-Negro population of the state. This segment of the population was diverse and included newly arrived subsistence farmers (many of whom were aspiring planters) from across North America and abroad, small-scale businesspeople, and

---

[117] Foner's (1941: 318-319) description of the relationship between the northern merchants and their southern customers is one of the best available. He observes: "...it is true that many Northern business men were intimately tied by social and economic bonds to the Southern planters. As a consequence, they allied themselves frequently with the planters to halt the growth of movements which waged a bitter struggle against the system of slavery, and which urged the ousting of the planters from their control of the national government. These business men feared the dissolution of the Union and disruption of trade relations with the South more than they disliked slavery and more than they resented the control of the national government by the planter aristocrats."

others. Of course, only "Anglos" could vote in elections. Campbell (1989: 210) observes that although economic and political control was firmly in the hands of the planters, there was no basic conflict between slaveholding and non-slaveholding Anglo-Texans on the question of slavery. Both groups were racists, and at best considered the institution a necessary evil, and at worst considered slavery a positive good—in other words a school for civilization for ignorant and savage Africans.

> In 1850, when slaveholders headed 30 percent of Texas' households, 58 percent of all federal, state, and local officeholders owned bondsmen. Ten years later on the eve of disunion, the 27 percent of all household heads who owned slaves provided 68 percent of the officeholders. It has been argued that such control of public office does not constitute "domination" in the sense of passing laws or implementing policies that nonslaveholders opposed. This assumes, however, that somehow a serious conflict of interest existed between those who owned slaves and those who did not. No such conflict existed across Texas.

At the bottom of the social hierarchy, of course, were the enslaved Africans and African-Americans who in 1850 and

1860 constituted approximately one-third of the Texas population.

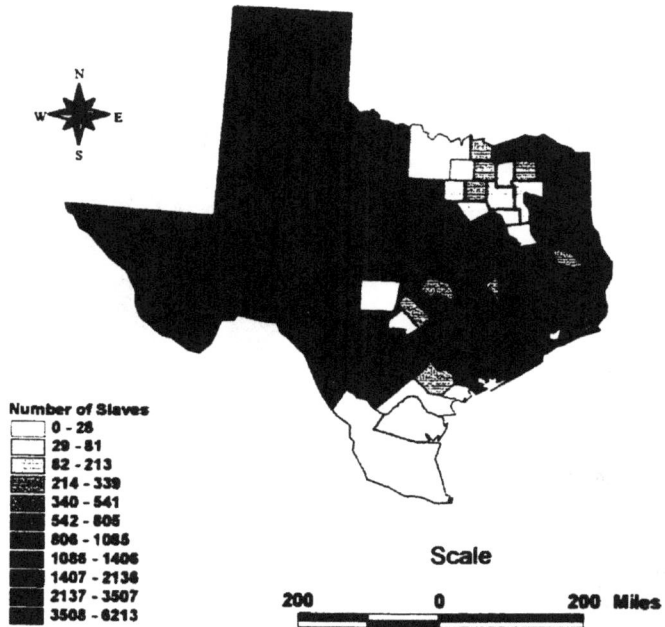

Figure 7

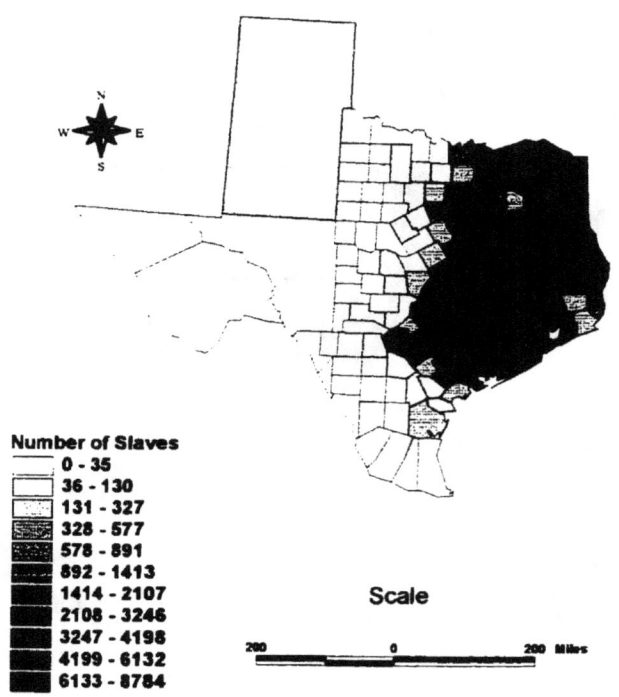

Figure 8: Distribution of the 1860 slave population by county

Foxes Minding the Henhouse: The Misadventures of Being a Free Sailor in Texas

In addition to the traditional slave trading that was the by-product of the in-migration described in previous chapters, the 1850's saw the further emergence and enlargement of an institution that had long roots in the Old South—the slave market. The primary slave markets in Texas were located in Galveston and Houston, although significant markets were located upriver in places such as Marshall, Manchester, and Hempstead as well. In fact, depending on the circumstances, (large slave coffles brought in to town, or probate proceedings, for instance) spontaneous "public outcries" for property of all kinds, including slaves, were held throughout Texas in the late 1840's and 1850's and in many cases were all day social events.[118]

According to Curlee (1932: 50) there were five

---

[118] "So lively and spirited was the bidding of a Marshall gathering in 1857 that they bid $9,085 above the appraised value of thirty slaves, and many were so interested that they neglected to vote in that day's election" (Curlee 1932: 60).

auctioneers in Texas in 1850:

> As more settlers poured in, more men opened general agencies, giving prompt and particular attention to the sale of land and Negroes. In Houston were J. Castanie, A.R. Ruthven—an Englishman and licensed auctioneer, and Wynne and Armfield—J.W. Wynne and R.B. Armfield; in Galveston, A.F. James whose agency had been established in 1842, Ira M. Freeman on Tremont Street, George H. Trabue on the Strand, and Ayres, Webb and Company of which David Ayres was a partner. Several firms kept slaves constantly on hand. In 1853, Thomas S. Gresham of Houston received direct from Virginia and Maryland a typical slave dealer's gang, consisting of 50 Negroes from ten to twenty-five years old.

Because slave prices in New Orleans were high, planters throughout the Upper South were anxious to get in on the action.[119] In turn, New Orleans auctioneers and commission merchants[120] placed many advertisements in Texas papers since Texas "was not yet saturated with Negro labor" (Curlee

---

[119] "The average price of a bondsman, regardless of age, sex, or condition, rose from approximately $400 in 1850 to nearly $800 by 1860. During the late 1850's, prime male field hands aged eighteen to thirty cost on the average $1,200, and skilled slaves such as blacksmiths often were valued at more than $2000" (Campbell, *The New Handbook of Texas Online:* slavery).

[120] F. Scranton, a Houston "Long Row" entrepreneur engaged in the auction and commission business charged two and one-half percent commission on his sales (Curlee 1932: 49).

1932: 47). In their ads, New Orleans and Shreveport dealers such as J.A. Beard & Company, Joseph Bruin, and George Pitts promised Texans continuous fresh lots of slaves, especially during the growing season. "The editor of the *Matagorda Gazette* rejoiced because every steamer leaving New Orleans for Texas brought a large cargo of Negroes" (Curlee 1932: 47).

John S. Sydnor, a former mayor of Galveston, ran the largest slave market west of New Orleans in the 1850's and also served as his own auctioneer. His voice which "was famous through the state" (cited in Fornell 1961: 115) would announce at auctions which were conducted every Tuesday and Friday morning beginning at ten A.M.

> ....in front and in the door of his store-rooms on the Strand, Sydnor held an auction sale. Because so many slaves were consigned to him, in 1860 he reduced his charges to two and a half per cent and arranged employment for the Negroes in a place directly adjoining his store. The advantages were that the Negroes could pay their board and they would "always be on hand when parties desired to see them." When directed, Sydnor hired servants about the city. His activities ceased not during the war (Curlee 1932: 51).

Sydnor doubtlessly received assistance in his business efforts from the editor and publisher of the Civilian *and Galveston City Gazette*—now Collector of Customs for the port of Galveston (and like Sydnor a former mayor of Galveston)—Hamilton Stuart. Stuart vociferously supported the reopening of the African slave trade.[121] However since he was also the principal person responsible for the enforcement of existing laws outlawing the illegal traffic, a clear conflict of interest existed between Stuart's public role as federal customs collector for Texas' largest port and his private ambitions.[122]

---

[121] Until 1859-60 when he decided to support Sam Houston for Texas governor (Houston was a "moderate" on the slavery question). By the late 1850's most editors and publishers in Texas supported the re-opening of the African slave trade; John Marshall, editor of the Austin *State Gazette* (December 18, 1858), for instance, editorialized that Texas would not reach her full economic potential unless 100,000 Africans were imported annually until the eventual goal of six million slaves was realized. One line of southern logic on the question was similar to contemporary arguments urging the decriminalization of drugs: since the trade was widespread anyway, the best solution was to legalize and then regulate the traffic (Fornell 1961: 216). The Methodist and Presbyterian Churches of Texas also strongly supported re-opening the African traffic. They argued that "slavery, as it existed in the South, is the instrument, under God, and the only instrumentality by which the savage and degraded millions of Africans can be civilized" and "the slave trade [was] not therefore a means of reducing them [Africans] to bondage, but simply of transferring them from masters as brutal and savage as themselves, to civilized masters in a country where there is law for their protection" (*Galveston News*, August 29, 1857).

[122] It should go without saying that such patterns of corruption in Texas have lasted down to the present, albeit in somewhat different form.

A good example of the contradictions involved in the corrupt administration of customs collection in Galveston are the experiences of free Black sailors who were abducted and sold into slavery. As Malloy (1990: 10) and Bolster (1997: 190) note, as early as 1822 with the passage of "Negro Seamen Acts" custom and law held that Black seamen were to be incarcerated during southern port calls. Because of the threat of contagion posed by free West Indian, northern, and Latin American sailors, among others, the port of Galveston too required captains to either deny their Black sailors shore leave while in port or to place them in jail for the duration of the ship's visit.[123]

"The kidnapping of an occasional 'coloured lad' from the West Indies Islands, with the intent to sell the boy later as a slave in Texas, was a recurring source of irritation to British

---

[123] Unscrupulous slave traders would also deliberately re-enslave free Blacks. Galveston shipmaster Captain Thomas Chubb, for instance (later famous as commander of the Confederate steamer *Royal Yacht*), "hired a colored crew at Boston, and then cooly [sold] them at Galveston." Later during the Civil War, he was captured by the Yankees and condemned to be hanged as a pirate for having engaged in the slave trade; but eventually, he was exchanged before the sentence was carried out (Fornell 1961: 230-231).

officials" (Fornell 1961: 231). Arthur Lynn, British consul in Galveston during the 1850's, exerted considerable diplomatic pressure in rescuing British nationals from enslavement and sale, and secured an apology (and a promise of prevention of such incidents in the future) from Hamilton Stuart in 1854 in the case of two British sailors of color who had been brought into Sabine by a Captain Hurd. The kidnapping of the Trinidadian mulatto Charles H. Thomas in 1857, however, sparked statewide attention and controversy and resulted in the Texas legislature enacting a fraudulent "act to permit free persons of African descent to select their own masters and become slaves."[124]

The act was promptly tested in January 1860 when the

---

[124] The act was a ruse. Abducted free Blacks brought into Galveston had no recourse in a court of law (Blacks could not testify against whites regardless of the circumstances), but Lynn's patient and persistent efforts did succeed in winning reluctant recognition of foreign citizenship from Texas officials. The response of the Texans was passage of the act, the primary presumption of which was the supposedly "voluntary" sale into slavery of previously free Black seafarers, something which everybody knew to be false. One person who voluntarily enslaved herself under the provisions of the act was Rachel Grumbles, whose son was interviewed in the 1930's by the Federal Writers Project. Ms. Grumbles enslaved herself to Aaron Burleson who had a reputation for leniency. See Winegarten (1996: 12-13).

twenty-year-old travelling artist Joseph Vincente Suarez pulled into Galveston as a member of a musical troupe of "Negro Minstrels." A native of Goa, India (and thus a Portuguese subject), Suarez was arrested after spending a few days in the city and was brought before a court:

> The deputy sheriff of Galveston County asserted that the singer "had Negro blood and was residing in the city in violation of the laws of the state." The magistrate ordered the confinement of Suarez and directed that the young man be examined by a Galveston physician. The doctor advised the magistrate that "Suarez was tinctured with over an eighth portion of Negro blood" (Fornell 1961: 237-238).

Suarez was thus scheduled to be "auctioned off on the 30th of January, 1860 at the Court House." With nobody to look after his interests (the nearest Portuguese consulate was in New Orleans) as a foreign citizen, Arthur Lynn took it upon himself to write to William Mure, the British consul in New Orleans on behalf of Suarez. Unfortunately the Portuguese authorities decided to let the matter drop and the Suarez incident disappears from history.

Another abduction and incarceration took place in August of 1860 when a free British sailor was taken from his vessel by federal officials enforcing the Texas law which made it a crime for any free Negro to enter the state.

> Lieutenant Tennison, second in command of the United States revenue cutter in Galveston harbor, upon learning that the British vessel *Alma* had a colored cook on her crew, boarded the vessel, arrested the Negro and delivered him up to the county authorities. The lieutenant explained that he boarded the British vessel because "the *Alma* had a colored cook on the crew list contrary to the municipal laws of the state" (Fornell 1961: 239).

Lynn immediately protested to Hamilton Stuart who after investigating the incident had the cook brought back to his ship. Stuart also apologized to Lynn for the "great excitement" which was pervading throughout Galveston and the state of Texas concerning "attempts recently made to incite the slaves to incendiary acts and insurrection," and acknowledged that Tennison had overstepped his bounds as a federal officer when he attempted to enforce a state law. Knowing what would happen if the vessel stayed in port, Lynn arranged for the immediate departure of the *Alma* from Galveston in order to prevent a second boarding, this time by state officials.

Perhaps the most notorious example of customs contradiction took place in the spring of 1859 when a small English schooner *Commerce* pulled into Galveston because of hull leaks; all crewmembers of the ship were free persons of color except the ship's master, J.S. Pearce, whose boss, Kingston based merchant Samuel Parsons, was a friend of Arthur Lynn's. In accordance with the law the crew was confined in the county jail. But

> since the port was at that time suffering from the fever epidemic and because confinement in the close and unhealthy quarters of the jail amounted to a virtual inoculation with the dreaded fever, Consul Lynn made a personal plea before the County Judge of Galveston to permit the crew to be confined under arrest on board the schooner *Commerce* rather than in the "unhealthy gaol of this county." The judge agreed to permit this procedure "as a special favor to Her Majesty" (Fornell 1961: 255).

Unfortunately no berths were available at the Galveston pier, so the harbormaster had the *Commerce* make fast to the *Thomas Watson*, a vessel being detained in Galveston due to suspected slave trading. But that was only the beginning of the story.

The *Thomas Watson*, along with a fleet of other ships, was owned by a pair of slave trading brothers, J.A. Machado of New York City and Bernardo José Machado of Portugal.[125] Mr. and Mrs. Thomas Watson were the seafarers who commanded the merchant firm's ships; Thomas Watson was in command of the *Lydia Gibbs* (114 tons) and his wife Mary Jane Watson captained the 348 ton schooner *Thomas Watson* which pulled into Galveston in October of 1858, ostensibly to offload a cargo of 89 camels valued at $9, 561 that had been consigned to

---

[125] "The Machado Company was represented in New York by the respected law firm of Benedict, Burr, and Benedict. These advocates protected the interests of the combination in the many conflicts their slaving fleet had with the British government. The Boston shipping firm of Ellis and Cobb also maintained business arrangements with these traders" (Fornell 1961: 251). In addition to the *Thomas Watson* and *Lydia Gibbs*, the Machado firm also sponsored other Baltimore Schooners in its Gulf of Mexico trade, including vessels such as the *Nancy* and *Lyra* (which were captured with 690 and 890 slaves, respectively, in the Caribbean in the late 1850's), *Caroline*, *Locomatara*, and the *Mary Varney*. "All of these ships bore the names of lesser known New Yorkers, thereby avoiding implication of himself in any wrong doing" (Robbins 1972: 132).

Isaac Williams and Co.[126] Consul Lynn, however, suspected that the real cargo carried by Mrs. Watson included African slaves, and ensnared the vessel in red tape[127] while he secured permission to conduct an investigation of the *Thomas Watson* and the 199 ton ship *Lucerne*, whose shallow draft permitted it to navigate the treacherous sand bars common along the Texas coast, thus allowing it to trade with the "small slaving farms"

---

[126] Obviously slaving ships' owners lied on official registration papers as to the true purpose of their ships; the *Thomas Watson* was registered as a whaler. The vessel was originally built in Baltimore in 1848 and was bought by the Machado firm in the early 1850's. It was not unusual for sailors enlisting for shipboard service to be taken by surprise by the actual commerce conducted by the ships onboard which they had rendered their services. In his now classic narrative *Six Months on a Slaver* Edward Manning described his experiences onboard the *Thomas Watson*, which he foolishly thought actually was a whaler. The New London, CT based *Thomas Watson* took on a whaling crew in 1860. Manning (romantic that he was, he registered on the ship's roster as Edward Melville) among them. Upon reaching the Azores the crew was made to break out a large supply "of rice, hard-tack, salt beef, pork, etc., in quantities enough to feed a regiment for a long time." The sailors were then ordered to lay a slave deck. The ship picked up a large quantity of slaves near the Congo River and landed over 800 of them in Cuba in December, 1860. The ship—one of the last fast schooners known to trade directly with Africa— became a Confederate blockade runner during the Civil War, ran aground outside Charleston harbor and was burned to the waterline.

[127] He refused to give the vessel a clean bill of health (necessary because of a recent yellow fever epidemic that had killed ten percent of the city). This wouldn't have been a major problem should the ship be next headed for Liverpool, as Mrs. Watson claimed on her consular paperwork. But Lynn suspected that the ship's actual next destination was Havana, which would not allow the *Thomas Watson* clearance to enter port without a clean health certificate. When Mrs. Watson demanded health clearance from Lynn (she filed an official complaint with the United States Department of State) he suggested that "since the lack of the document would cause her no difficulty in Liverpool, it was an open question as to what the real purpose of the *Thomas Watson's* next voyage might be" (Fornell 1961: 253).

(Robbins 1972: 127) located there. After inspecting the vessels, Lynn determined that the ships carried slave trading equipment and smelled like slavers; he insisted that the U.S. attorney in Galveston also inspect the vessels, which he did, but because there were no slaves actually onboard he did not press charges against Mrs. Watson or the Machados (J.A. Machado had arrived in Galveston by the spring of 1859 at Mrs. Watson's urging).

On the 31st of October, 1859 a sudden storm struck Galveston, and the *Thomas Watson's* copper sheathing[128] was ostensibly damaged by the aforementioned Jamaican schooner *Commerce* moored alongside.

> Being cognizant of both maritime law and the rules concerning the admissability of testimony by free persons of color in Texas courts, Mrs. Watson, on the 4th of November, "libeled the British schooner Commerce for damages alleged to have been caused by the latter during a severe gale." The claim was filed in the United States District Court of Galveston.

---

[128] Copper plates were common on ships by this time; the plates were installed as environmental protection from worms and other fouling. See Steffy (1994: 174-175).

> Since the only testimony which could have been produced in favor of the *Commerce* was inadmissible as evidence inasmuch as the testimony would have been that given by free persons of color, the case was decided in favor of Mrs. Watson solely on the basis of ex parte evidence. In accordance with the law, the vessel (valued at $1200) was sold to her to settle a $300 claim to which, under other circumstances, she would not have been entitled (Fornell 1961: 256).

Mrs. Watson used her proceeds from the sale of the *Commerce* to purchase the *Thomas Watson* from the Machados a year later.

Texas African Slave Trading in the 1850's

The widespread reach and extent of American participation in illegal African slave trading in the late 1850's was the worst kept secret in America.

> Senator Stephen A. Douglas of Illinois, a persistent foe of the African slave trade, declared that in 1859 more Africans entered the United States than had ever been imported during any one year before, even when the trade was legal. Douglas believed that over fifteen thousand slaves entered the United States during 1859 (Robbins 1972: 136).

Du Bois says that "it would not be true to say that there was in the South in 1860 substantial unanimity on the subject of reopening the slave-trade" (Du Bois 1986[1896]: 177), but it is clear that most planters and businesspeople in the western Gulf of Mexico—unlike their fellow slaveholders in the Upper South—were firmly in support of decriminalizing the African traffic.[129] One the one hand, Galveston and New Orleans slave dealers were in ideological sync with the leading prophets/propagandists of the reopening of the slave trade: the South Carolinians. The most influential mouths on the question were Leonidas W. Spratt, editor of the Charleston *Standard*, James D. B. DeBow, editor of the famous *DeBow's Review*, and Governor James H. Adams all of whom endorsed the official decriminalization of the African traffic at the 1857 Southern Commercial Convention in Knoxville. But Texans also

---

[129] In 1858 Governor Wickliffe of Louisiana said "it is just and right that the Federal Government and the Northern States bow to the immutable decrees of natural law and not resist the South in the spread of her institution to regions so palpably pointed to by the finger of destiny for her occupation." Prominent members of congress also lended their support. Senator Alexander Stephens, later Confederate Vice-President, argued that "slave states cannot be made without Africans....[my object] is to bring clearly to your mind the great truth that without an increase of African slaves from abroad you may not expect or look for many more slave states" (Mannix 1962: 272).

had a more practical reason for supporting the reopening of the African slave trade. The high prices fetched for domestic slaves and for white contract labor were a considerable source of displeasure to planters and merchants alike. Excessive speculation drove slave prices to all time highs in the late 1850's and early 1860's, and the Texas elite didn't like it:

> Prices continued their upward trend during 1860. Common field hands brought seventeen, eighteen, and even as high as nineteen hundred dollars on the general selling and hiring day in Harrison County. Spirited and wild bidding prevailed at the public auction on the traders' day in February, 1860; for a carpenter brought $2,755 in cash and a boy of eleven, $900 cash, thus transcending even the prices of 1835. The speculative spirit continued to stalk abroad though a few were beginning to question and to make terms. At the auction in Austin on January 2, 1860, Austin May Williams hired "a fine man who has worked at Cooks mill, I got him for $210. I would have to bid 250 rather than have lost him, I tried to hire privately but could not succeed." Only ten slaves were offered at that time. *Three months later Williams wrote that Negroes were too high and must come down* (emphasis added, Curlee 1932: 70-71).

The perhaps leading source for details on how African slaves were landed on the Texas coast (where, how) during this time period (mid 1840's to 1850's) is a questionable yet highly valuable autobiography entitled *Revelations of a Slave Smuggler* which tells the life story of one Captain Philip Drake (he is misidentified as Richard Drake in the title) who was found in "deplorable condition, both of mind and body" in a "squalid room puddled with water" which "admitted the rains freely" and was located atop a "sailor's drinking place below" by Henry Byrd West of the Protestant Home Mission (Drake 1972[1860]: iii) in 1856. West, who took down Drake's narrative before the latter died penniless and broken three months later, says that he recorded events and names fully and faithfully, although subsequent scholars have treated Drake's story with varying degrees of skepticism. Blyden Jackson, who edited the 1972 edition of the narrative, recognizes the shortfalls of *Revelations* while simultaneously acknowledging that the story "cannot be summarily dismissed as gross fabrication. Quite to the contrary, they are unquestionably convincing historical documentation." Drake's testimony about the surreptitious Texas slave trade, as well as the rest of most of his account, is backed up by a considerable body of "readily analyzable hearsay evidence" (Drake 1972[1860]: introduction) and official testimony and is not significantly contradicted by anything that currently has been found in the historical record.

Revelations begins with an interesting and revealing quote from the *New York Herald* of August 5, 1860 which in considerable detail discusses the nature of the illicit African slave trade into Texas:

> Padre Island, or rather Father Island, is called so, from being the largest of a number of similar islands along the Gulf coast of Texas, and is about a hundred and twenty-five miles long, by from one to two miles in width. It is an island, because between it and the main shore of Texas there exists a regular belt or estuary of the sea, extending from the harbor of Brazos Santiago to Corpus Christi. Its adaptability has made Padre Island a resort for the initiation of those measures which were necessary in order to make popular a matter of vital importance to the South. To have boldly ventured into New Orleans, with negroes freshly imported from Africa, would not only have brought down upon the head of the importer the vengeance of our very philanthropic Uncle Sam, but also the anathema of the whole sect of philanthropists and negrophilists everywhere. To import them for years,

however, into quiet places, evading with impunity the penalty of the law, and the ranting of the thin-skinned sympathizers with Africa, was gradually to popularize the traffic by creating a demand for laborers, and thus to pave the way for the GRADUAL REVIVAL OF THE SLAVE TRADE.

To this end, a few men, bold and energetic, determined, ten or twelve years ago, to commence the business of importing negroes, slowly at first, but surely; and for this purpose they selected a few secluded places on the coast of Florida, Georgia and Texas, for the purpose of concealing their stock until it could be sold out. Without specifying other places, let me draw your attention to a deep and abrupt pocket or indentation in the coast of Texas, about thirty miles from Brazos Santiago. Into this pocket a slaver could run at any hour of the night, because there was no hindrance at the entrance, and her she could discharge her cargo of movables upon the projecting bluff, and again proceed to sea inside of three hours. The live stock thus landed could be marched a short distance across the main island, over a porous soil which refuses to retain the recent foot-prints, until they were again placed in boats, and were concealed upon some of the innumerable little islands which thicken the waters of the Laguna in the rear. These islands, being covered with a thick growth of bushes and grass, offer and inscrutable hiding place for the "black diamonds" (Drake 1972[1860]: vii-viii).[130]

---

[130] Du Bois (1986[1896]: 180) also cites this passage. Drake also relates his experiences smuggling slaves into Florida at about the time of the War of 1812 and the opportunities this provided. He writes:

I soon learned how readily and at what profits, the Florida negroes were sold into the

Apparently this sort of trading activity had been going on for some time. During the Mexican-American War, Drake says that a primary transhipment point for slaves were the so-called Bay Islands (Roatàn, Utilia, and Guanaja) off the coast of Honduras:

> Here, a slave-depot and farm were established, to which cargoes were brought, in American clippers, from slave settlements near Cape Mesurado, in Africa. The negroes were landed, under the name of colonists; and the company had permits from Central American authorities. They had a branch farm on the Rio Grande, in Texas, which was broken up, and its stock dispersed, at the breaking out of the war between the United States and Mexico.

The object of the island outpost was to "season" the slaves (the slaves were taught limited English and Spanish and any vestiges of resistance were broken via strong discipline), upon

---

neighboring American States. The *kaffle* under charge of negro drivers, was to strike up the Escambia River, and thence cross the boundary into Georgia, where some of our wild Africans were mixed with various squads of native blacks, and driven inland, till sold off, singly or by couples, on the road. At this period (1812) the United States had declared the African slave trade illegal, and passed stringent laws to prevent the importation of negroes; yet the Spanish possessions were thriving on this inland exchange of negroes and mulattoes; Florida was sort of a nursery for slave-breeders and many American citizens grew rich by trafficking in Guinea negroes, and smuggling them continually, in small parties, through the southern United States. At the time I mention, the business was a lively one, owing to the war then going on between the States and England, and the unsettled condition of affairs on the border (Drake 1972[1860]: 51).

which the slaves were made available for transport.

> Our island was visited almost weekly, by agents from Cuba, New York, Baltimore, Philadelphia, Boston, and New Orleans. During the continuance of the Mexican war, we had 1,600 negroes in good order, and were receiving and shipping constantly. The seasoned and instructed slaves were taken to Texas, or Florida, overland, and to Cuba, in sailing-boats. As no squad contained more than half a dozen, no difficulty was found in posting them to the United States, without discovery, and generally without suspicion. A single negro, sent by special agent, as far as Savannah, would pay all his cost and expenses, and fifty per cent profit in the market....the Bay Island plantation sent ventures weekly to the Florida Keys. Slaves were taken into the great American swamps, and there kept till wanted for the market. Hundreds were sold as captured runaways from the Florida wilderness. We had agents in every slave State, and our coasters were built in Maine, and came out with lumber (Drake 1972[1860]: 97-98).

The tremendous profit rates possible even for <u>one</u> successful slaving voyage resulted in considerable advances in maritime design. American slavers of the 1850's were newer, faster clipper ships[131] instead of brigs or topsail schooners as

---

[131] Many of these clipper ships were built for the China trade and are now the stuff of maritime legend. Donald MacKay, a Boston based designer and one of the greatest maritime architects of all time is responsible for such noted ships as the *Flying Cloud, Lightning, James Baines, Donald MacKay,* and *Champion of the Seas*. Other noted clippers built elsewhere include the *Challenge* and the *Witch of the Wave* (Giggal 1988:83-94). An examination of the full extent

before, and could hold tremendous numbers of slaves: cargoes in the range of 1,000-1,500 slaves became common, and one ship, the *Martha*, had intended to purchase 1,800 (Mannix 1962: 266).

Steamships engaged in the domestic slave trade also began to be purpose-built for the traffic. According to the narrative of William Wells Brown, an enslaved African-American who worked as an assistant to a trader shipping along the Mississippi, the slaves were kept in "a large room on the lower deck...men, and women promiscuously—all chained in two." A letter written by Joshua Leavitt, an antislavery clergyman, also provides a good description of ships engaged in the domestic slave trade:

> The hold was appropriated to the slaves, and is divided into two apartments. The after-hold will carry about eighty women, and the other about one hundred men. On either side were two platforms running the whole length; one raised a few inches, and the other half way up the deck. They were about five or six feet deep. on these the slaves lie, as close as they can be stowed (Jay 1835: 149).

---

of slave trading participation by these and other ships like them remains to be written.

Mortality rates for the domestic slave trade were lower than for the Middle Passage. "Distances were shorter and slaves confronted no fundamentally new disease environment, so that death while in the hands of even the most brutal of domestic slave traders seems to have been very rare (Tadman 1996[1989]: 82).[132] As discussed in chapter three, the fundamental cruelties inherent in the domestic slave trade were family separation, forced extirpation, and movement.

The Lone Star Yankee: Two Case Studies

Charles Morgan and William Marsh Rice are two "Texans" firmly ensconced in the Texas Myth pantheon, and a brief examination of their business dealings in the Lone Star State help to illustrate how "common sensical" (Gordon 1998) slavery and slave trading were—and how easily entrepreneurially

---

[132] Nonetheless, slaves traded from the northernmost portions of the Upper South would have faced a considerably different disease environment in Texas or Louisiana. Most whites thought that all Blacks—even free Blacks from the northeastern states—had higher rates of resistance to tropical diseases than whites. During the Civil War, for instance, northern generals made this racist and flawed assumption and sent many Black troops to their deaths.

minded northerners adjusted themselves to the more notorious aspects of these institutions. The former, like Stephen F. Austin a Connecticut Yankee,[133] is the person most responsible for opening Texas to regular steamship service. Francaviglia (1998: 177), whose enthusiastic boosterism of Morgan's role in the economic and maritime development of Texas seems to at times border on worship, observes

> Entrepreneurs/capitalists like Morgan helped bring technological changes to maritime Texas, and Morgan, in fact, is one of the rather unsung visionaries in Texas history, an omission that seems to accompany the general neglect of our state's maritime history. His steamships were a familiar sight on the waters of Texas for more than forty years.

Morgan's biographer (Baughman 1968: xxvii) more succinctly—and with less hero worship—summarizes his influence and role as follows:

> He made no great technical, managerial, or humanitarian breakthroughs, but he was part of several innovative streams in his environment: functionally, he pioneered in

---

[133] Morgan was born to a family of comfortable means on April 21, 1795, in Clinton, Connecticut.

> common carriage; technologically, he contributed to improving steam transportation; geographically, he was a leader in the economic life of the Gulf South.

Before engaging in meaningful trading within the Gulf of Mexico region (political instability prevented trade with Texas in the late 1820's and early 1830's), Morgan cut his teeth in the West Indies trade—Morgan and the New York based trading house of Benjamin Aymar & Co. were the first businessmen to establish a regular packet line between New York and Kingston (Baughman 1968: 10). Morgan quickly understood the significant potential inherent in transportation specialization, something which rapid advances in steam engine technology helped to accentuate.

The Texas Revolution and the establishment of the Lone Star Republic (advertised heavily in New England and New York by Secretary of State for the Lone Star Republic Stephen F. Austin) were seen almost immediately as tremendous business opportunities. Morgan realized that steamships could make the New Orleans-Galveston run far faster than the traditional schooners that could, if the weather refused to cooperate, take almost two weeks to tack their way down the coast. Morgan's vessel *Columbia* inaugurated regular steamship service to Texas in November 1837.

> *Columbia* completed twelve round-voyages to Galveston and Velasco by June 8, 1838, when she was joined in the trade by *Cuba*—an unsuccessful New Orleans-Havana steamer then owned and operated by the Crescent City firm of Bogart & Hawthorn. The vessels formed a "New Orleans and Texas Line" and thereafter offered weekly sailings between Louisiana and the Republic (Baughman 1968: 24-25).

Morgan eventually would be owner of dozens of vessels engaged in maritime commerce in the Gulf of Mexico. In addition to "opening up" Texas to large-scale barter and exchange, Morgan, like the Lone Star Yankees that preceded him, also played a significant role in American Manifest Destiny, and, by extension, in Texas and Southwestern politics.[134] Morgan was "intimately involved in those

---

[134] "...the fact that he had a personal stake in the success of "manifest destiny" in the western Gulf of Mexico is unmistakable (Baughman 1968: 44).

movements of American capital which flowed from North to South, from commerce and industry to transport, and from older to newer transport technologies" (Baughman 1968: xxviii).

One of the first questions that might be asked about Morgan's commercial activities—one that is conveniently shirked by historians such as Francaviglia—is the following: what exactly did Morgan's steamships carry into and out of Texas? The short answer to the question is: just about everything, including tools, iron, furniture, nails, mail, etc. One item omitted from the lists of Texas Myth historians, however, is the most notorious item carried onboard Morgan's vessels: slaves. It should come as no surprise that in a political economy based on plantation agriculture that commercial intermediaries and other transportation specialists such as Morgan should be actively engaged in slave trading. As figures 9, 10, and 11 indicate, although the full extent of Morgan's activities will prove difficult to pin down exactly due to a lack of complete documentation, the scale of Morgan's slave trading activities was considerable.[135] Morgan's transportation services and slave trading constituted an integral link in the development of Texas plantation agriculture.

Morgan's stake in American westward expansion is also worthy of note. Morgan Lines steamships were used extensively during the Mexican-American War,[136] and the financial boost provided by this state subsidy of his operations allowed Morgan to dramatically extend the reach of his operations in the Gulf of Mexico. Morgan wasted little time in sponsoring varying attempts to extend the burgeoning American Empire south of the border, the most famous of these

---

[135] The Texas Slavery Project at the University of Houston has also located slave ship manifests. A copy of a manifest obtained at the Texas State Library branch in Liberty is reproduced on the project website at http://www.texasslaveryproject.uh.edu/.

[136] The shallow drafts of the steamships produced considerable military advantages.

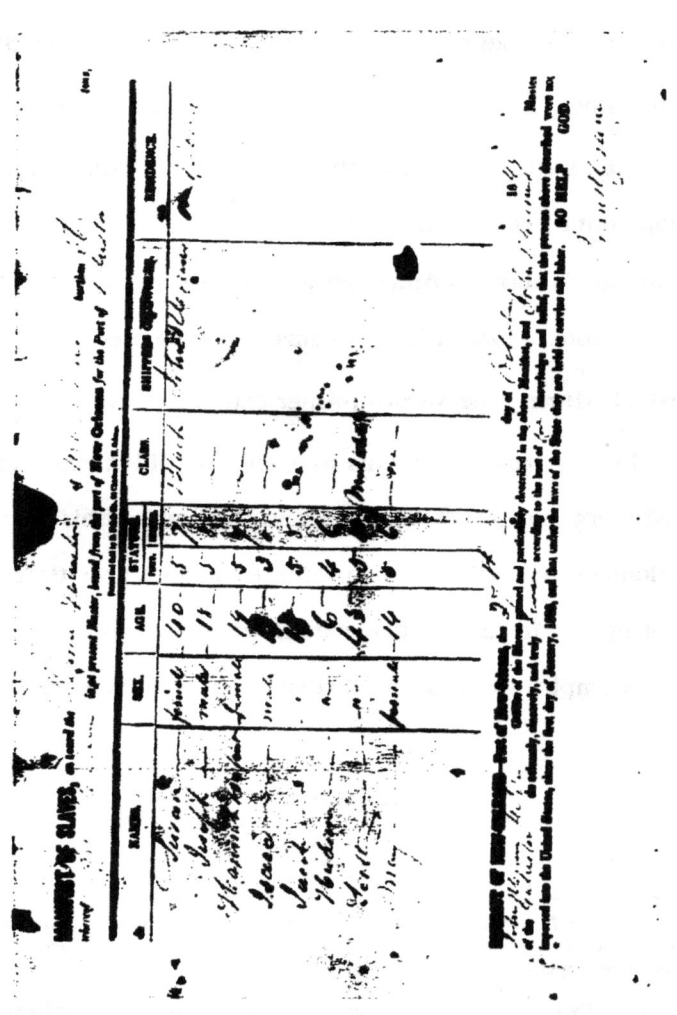

Figure 9: Manifest of Slaves for the steamer *Galveston*. Courtesy Rosenberg Library.

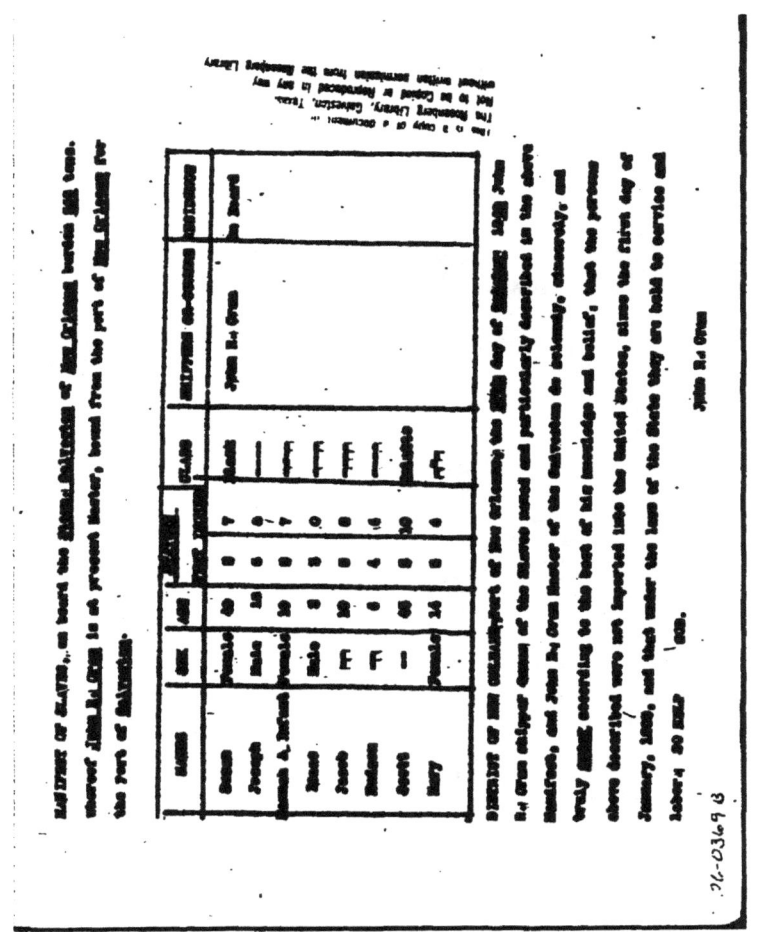

Figure 10: Transcript of Manifest for the steamer *Galveston.*, courtesy of Rosenberg Library, Galveston

Although the manifest lists the vessel as 568 tons burden, Baughman (1968: 239) lists the characteristics of the vessel as follows: 548 tons, built 1845 sunk 1851.

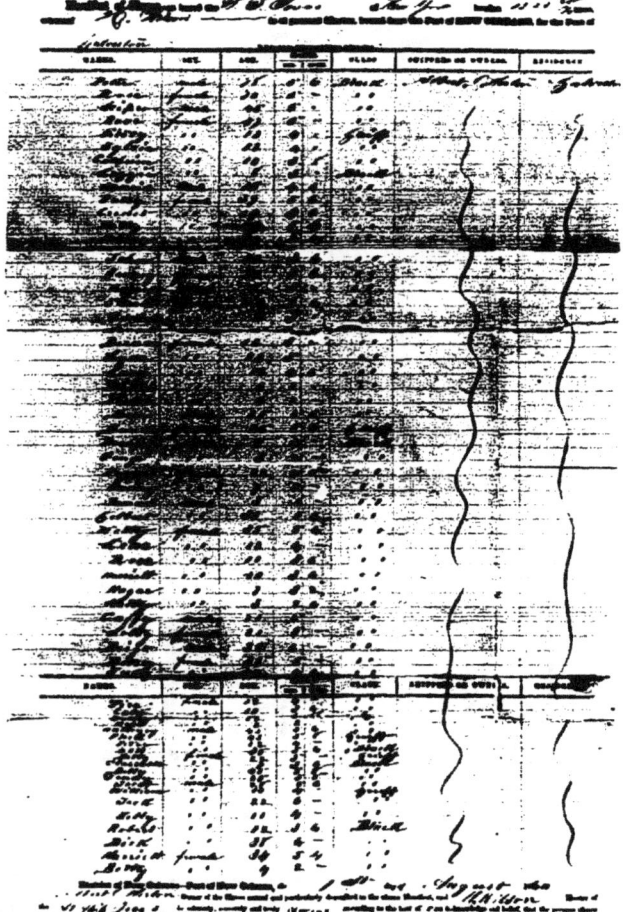

Figure 11:

Manifest of Slaves for *SS Texas*, August 1, 1860. The ship had a New York registry and was travelling from New Orleans to Galveston.

SS Texas, a 1,152 ton steamship (the manifest lists the vessel's tonnage at 1223 tons), was built in 1852 and seized in 1861.

Courtesy Rosenberg Library, Galveston.

being the wild and demented "filibustering" schemes led by William Walker, who dreamt of establishing an unregulated and economically "free" slave empire in Central America.

> During this decade [the 1850's], Cornelius Vanderbilt, having secured from the Nicaraguan government a monopolistic concession to exploit the transportation potentialities then awaiting development across the isthmus to California, established the Accessory Transit Company, a combine of shipping, railroad and stage coach transportation, providing a practical route from New York to California. The New York and San Francisco agents of this system, Charles Morgan and Cornelius K. Garrison, wishing to wrest control of the concession from Vanderbilt, entered into a conspiratorial agreement with General Walker which provided that, in return for the general's transfer of the transit concession from Vanderbilt to a new firm organized by Morgan and Garrison, these shipping magnates were to furnish Walker the shipping he needed to move potential filibuster armies from the Gulf Coast states to Nicaragua (Fornell 1961: 198).

Walker managed to get himself elected President of Nicaragua in 1856, something which enhanced his prestige and attractiveness to American expansionists and businessmen—all of whom were strong supporters of decriminalizing the African slave trade. The newly organized Garrison and Morgan line offered shipping for those interested in taking advantage of the economic "opportunities beckoning in Nicaragua" (Fornell 1961: 199); prices for passage to Nicaragua from Galveston—ships were scheduled to call into port every eighteen days—were as low as $35. Emigration and aid for the "patriots" in Nicaragua were strongly encouraged by a committee of leading Galvestonians, which included, among others, Judge David Burnet (ex-president of the Republic), General Sidney Sherman, General Hugh McLeod, John Henry Brown, Doctor William Carper, Oscar Parish, and Professor Caleb G. Forshey, the director of the Rutersville Military Institute. The committee approved the chartering of a vessel for the transportation of potential emigrants from Galveston to Nicaragua so that the country could eventually be taken from the "imbecile race" (Galveston *Civilian* May 26 and 28, 1856) that currently controlled it. Other noted citizens that enthusiastically supported "General" Walker's crusade included Henry A.

Maltby, the mayor of Corpus Christi,[137] who resigned his post in order to lead a small band of men into Galveston, and Francis Lubbock, who "made the principal address" at a meeting on February 24, 1857 where he "declared that the men assembled in Galveston were about to aid the cause of strengthening the institution of slavery and to assist in securing a needed base for the African slave trade" (Fornell 1961: 204).

Rank and file Texans were not lining up in droves to participate in these ventures. "...most Galvestonians were quite indifferent and some were revolted by the bravado and

---

[137] Some Texas Myth historians claim that the institution of slavery would or could not have spread into South and West Texas due to geographic limitations. In the case of Corpus Christi, Anglo settlers to the area certainly did not think that slavery was impossible in South Texas. A writer in the Oct. 17, 1857 *Nueces Valley* observed that "the extensive valley of the Nueces and Rio Grande are capable of subsisting a vast population, when the improvements of agriculture are once brought to bear upon them, as will be done when political skill in that science and a complete knowledge of the climate shall demonstrate the productions compatible with the country. A deep and settled prejudice, however, exists among Planters, which is very injurious to the population of the county and to themselves, besides being without foundation. *It is that slave labor cannot be safely and successfully employed*" on account of proximity to Mexico (emphasis added). Campbell (1989: 65) observes that the institution of slavery "was not threatened with an immediate or even short-term demise due to natural boundaries in Texas." My opinion is that slavery in Texas would have lasted well into the twentieth century had disunion and the Civil War not occurred. One frequently overlooked irony about Corpus Christi is that the noted abolitionist Benjamin Lundy, who published the influential anti-slavery polemic *The War in Texas* in 1836, had received permission from Mexican authorities to establish a colony of free Negroes there prior to the Texas Revolution.

boasting of these adventurers" (Fornell 1961: 201), despite the fact that Morgan and Garrison, in order to spur interest, had begun to offer free passage to Nicaragua for anybody wishing to emigrate—this in addition to a promise of $50 per month and large sums of land.[138] Walker was able to muster several hundred men in support of his Nicaraguan adventures at various points, but repeated failures[139] and the impending Civil War eventually shifted interest away from the "Nicaraguan Fever." Walker was executed in 1860. Fornell (1961: 214-15) sums up Morgan's role in the debacle as follows:

> For the most part.....the Texans were serving what they believed to be their own personal interests. In the same way, General Walker was pursuing what he must have ascertained to be his own destiny. Vanderbilt, Morgan, and Garrison, the three financiers who actually manipulated the controlling factors in these adventures, exploited not only the "destiny" of the "grey-eyed

---

[138] One of the vessels used by Morgan to ship supplies and personnel in support of the filibustering effort was the *Texas*, the slave steamship also used by Morgan in his slave trading activities (see figure 11).

[139] Sam Houston, who supported the filibustering expeditions in the early 1850's had changed his mind by 1859 and declared flatly "I am no friend of filibustering as the term is understood" (Williams and Barker 1938: 262).

general, but also the predilection for adventure of the expansion-minded Texans.[140]

Of the New York merchants distressed by the impending breakdown posed by the coming Civil War, it would be accurate to say that Charles Morgan was located decidedly in the pro-southern camp. Baughman (1968: 113) observes that Morgan's "participation in the Mexican War and of his isthmian 'fancies' clearly linked him with the course of Manifest Destiny—unlike most of his New York mercantile brethren."[141] Another factor that set Morgan apart from his fellow New Yorkers was his more than casual ownership of slaves.

> Between 1846 (or earlier) and 1861, he owned at least thirty-one slaves and condoned ownership of a like

---

[140] "Behind the legitimate facade of Morgan's reputation, however, he and Garrison participated intimately in one of the most ruthless episodes of American financial history. Morgan's role and responsibility are shadowy because of a lack of personal records. Garrison seems to have been the instigator of most of the schemes, but Morgan was always there with money and assistance" (Baughman 1968: 85).

[141] While I share Baughman's view that Morgan was decidedly more pro-southern and racist than most of his New York business contemporaries, I part company with Baughman in that I believe that most New York businesspeople in some manner believed in Manifest Destiny. Morgan was different in degree, not kind, from most of the New York merchants, who even went so far as seriously considering establishing a separate "Republic of New York" rather than disturb their financial ties to the South. For details on the plot to separate New York City from the rest of the state see Foner (1968[1941]: 295).

> number by his New Orleans agents Harris, Morgan, and Payne. Most of these Negroes were used as stevedores, deckhands, or chambermaids on Morgan's steamers, but the moral and political implications of these chattels would again seem to tie their owner closer to the southern rather than the northern democracy (Baughman 1968: 113).[142]

Once the war began, Morgan opportunistically offered his services to both sides of the conflict. His son-in-law, a committed Confederate loyalist, enthusiastically threw himself behind the southern war effort and worked to raise Confederate militias, but Morgan's primary interest was not really in participating in the southern ideological crusade: he was a businessman and above all was concerned with protecting his investments. Thus when the Confederacy started seizing some of his vessels for use in the war, Morgan protested vehemently; he expected to be properly compensated. Morgan also held extensive northern contracts and federal charters for

---

[142] According to the list of slaves in appendix 3 of Baughman (1968: 246-247), Morgan bought or sold 66 slaves between 1846 and 1862. The highest price Morgan paid for a slave during this time period was $3,750 for a twenty-two year old male named Walker. The transaction is recorded as having taken place on 4 December, 1858.

steam engine work,[143] but when the money was right he assisted the southern war effort as well. One of the vessels Morgan provided machinery for, the *Frances*, was quite successful in running the Union blockade of Galveston:

> One vessel that came to Galveston in 1864 was the steamer *Zephine*. Originally built by Harlan and Hollingsworth of Wilmington, Delaware, as the *Frances*, she was a powerful walking-beam sidewheeler. At Havana she was sold to blockade-running interests for $100,000 in gold, and given a British registry. Even with a payroll of over $36,000 in gold, the ship made money. On her first run in September 1864 she carried out over 1,000 bales of cotton, and turned a profit in excess of $300,000 in gold, more than enough to pay for the ship, the crew's wages, and the inward cargo (Wise 1988: 214).

By playing both sides, Morgan survived—even advanced—[144]his business position in Texas and the rest of the gulf. His postwar exploits are also interesting and important (Morgan played a key role in the introduction of railroad transport to Texas),

---

[143] The Morgan Iron Works had "become one of America's foremost manufacturers of marine steam engines. Its specialty was medium-sized machinery for coastal and river craft, and its engines were widely used in the United States and by American steamship companies in China" (Baughman 1968: 121).

[144] Morgan diversified his shipping interests to include cattle exports. His fleet was the first large-scale argosy to trade extensively in Aransas Bay.

but were very much in keeping with his already established business practices and sentiments. As a northerner with extensive southern investments, Morgan was one of the first, but by no means the last, of his kind.

William Marsh Rice is known today as the benefactor and founder of the Houston university that bears his name. The original charter of the university, which was specific in ensuring that only "whites" could attend,[145] was modified in the 1960's when Rice University desegregated. The career of the university's founder is another emblematic Texas story, one that reveals a great deal once the Texas-sized layers of hagiographic rubbish are washed away.

---

[145] The original incorporation charter for the "William M. Rice Institute for the Advancement of Literature, Science, and Art" dated May 13, 1891 reads as follows: "....that the interest, incomes, issues and profits thereof shall forever be devoted to the instruction and improvement of the white inhabitants of the City of Houston, and the State of Texas..." (Muir 1972: 153). Although students of Asian descent had been attending Rice for at least twenty years prior to 1962, on September 16, 1962 the Rice University board voted to remove the restrictive language from the charter, since Blacks were still denied admission to the university (equal opportunity clauses in federal contracts played a role in the decision). Two alumni (John B. Coffee and Val T. Billups) strongly opposed desegregating Rice and sued. Judge William Holland in February 1964 decided in favor of the university. The alumni appealed, but the Texas Court of Civil Appeals upheld the lower court's decision in October 1966. As a result, Rice was desegregated and could begin to charge tuition, another restriction William M. Rice had placed in the original charter (Meiners 1982: 201).

Rice was born the third in a family of ten children in Springfield Massachusetts on March 14, 1816 to a respectable family, and left school at the age of fifteen to begin work as a general store clerk; by age twenty-one he had established his own business. After the panic of 1837 (a period of financial instability due to excessive land speculation and Andrew Jackson's "hard money" policies), Rice left Springfield and headed west, perhaps as much due to financial hard times as in response to the extensive ads the Allen brothers, Augustus C. and John K, had placed in the northeastern press about their newly established town of Houston.

Houston during these years was described as "the greatest sink of dissipation and vice that modern times have ever known" (Murry 1991: 121) because of the widespread gambling and drinking that were taking place. Rice quickly adjusted to the local economic climate and on April 22, 1839 entered into an agreement to furnish the Milam Hotel with liquor in exchange for which he received three dollars per day and room and board, in addition to profits on the liquor. Rice received his official mercantile license from the city the following year, and thereafter embarked on a story-book career of import/export exchange with the local planters and in extensive land speculation (Rice also accepted land as payment for his services, another source of his large land holdings). Rice entered into business partnerships with many people, and in the early 1840's was a senior partner of the firm Rice & Nichols which "supplied plantations and settlers inland with goods from New Orleans and New York[146] and acted as banker for many of its customers" (Handbook of Texas Online: Rice, William Marsh). With Rice, Charles Morgan and others opening up Texas markets, Texas exports grew quickly. The chief export, predictably, was cotton. By 1841 Rice's lifelong friend Cornelius Ennis had succeeded in landing the first direct

---

[146] "As commission and forwarding merchants, Rice and Nichols brought in goods from New Orleans and from as far away as new York, first by boat up the Buffalo Bayou from Galveston and then by ox wagon to the settlers and plantation owners further inland" (Muir 1972: 14).

shipment of Galveston cotton in Boston.

Rice, like Charles Morgan, was keen to protect his business interests, and thus "served on a committee on resolutions in a public meeting that approved the annexation of Texas to the United States" (Muir 1972: 25). Rice, at least publicly, never adopted the fire-eating, slave-mongering language of Manifest Destiny imperialists like Sam Houston regarding the Mexican-American War—Rice was a behind-the-scenes moneymaker and boisterous public statements were not his style—but he never opposed them either. In fact, Rice did the things necessary to pass as an acceptable member of upper-crust Southern society; he dutifully served on the slave patrol for a year, was an Odd Fellow as well as a Mason, and intermittently served on the Houston City Council as an Alderman from the Second Ward.

Rice is frequently identified—like his friend Sam Houston—as being sympathetic to the Unionist side during the Civil War, but this tag is in effect meaningless. Rice had no real moral objection to slavery, especially as it intersected or conflicted with his business concerns. Like Sam Houston, he opposed the Civil War on practical grounds.[147] In other words, he opposed disunion because it was bad for business. According to the 1860 census, Rice was worth $750,000 in real and personal property, which conceivably made him the second richest man in Texas, "second only to John Hunter Herndon of

---

[147] In a famous Galveston speech recorded by Thomas North in his *Five Years in Texas*, Sam Houston expressed his sentiments regarding the political crisis:

> The drift of Houston's speech was *the inexpediency and bad policy of secession*. He told them that they could secure without secession what they proposed to secure by it, and would certainly lose through it He gave the greater force to his declarations by appealing to them to know if he had not generally been right in the past history of Texas, when any great issue was at stake. Told them he made Texas and they knew it, and it was not immodest for him to say so; that the history of old Sam Houston was the history of Texas, and they knew it; that he fought and won the battle of annexation, and they knew it; that he originally organized and established the Republic of Texas, and they knew it; that he wrested Texas from the despotic sway of Santa Anna; that he commanded at San Jacinto, where the great Mexican leader was whipped and captured, and they knew it....

> "You may," said he, "after the sacrifice of countless millions of treasure, and hundreds of thousands of precious lives, as a bare possibility, win Southern independence, if God be not against you; but I doubt it. I tell you that, while I believe with you in the doctrines of State rights, the North is determined to preserve this Union. They are not a fiery impulsive people as you are, for they live in cooler climates. But when they begin to move in a given direction, where great interests are involved, such as the present issues before the country, they move with the steady momentum and perseverance of a mighty avalanche, and what I fear is they will overwhelm the South with ignoble defeat, and I would say, amen, to the suffering and defeat I have pictured if the present difficulties could find no other solution, and that too by peaceable means. I believe they can (Gallaway 1994: 128-29).

Brazoria County, a sugar planter whose wealth lay principally in land and slaves" (Muir 1972: 26). More significantly, the 1860 census lists Rice as a slaveowner; "....he is listed as owning fifteen Negroes, some of whom he had acquired in default of payments, as he had some of his land holdings; others, the records show, he purchased outright" (Muir 1972: 30). But Rice's biggest business coup came during the Civil War, when he relocated his business operations south of the border to Matamoros and ran one of the biggest cotton smuggling operations of the war; Rice would emerge from the war as a millionaire and one of the richest men in the United States.

Most Texans were opposed to the policy adopted by the Confederate Congress that prohibited the sale of southern cotton on the world market. Texas planters and merchants felt that they should at least be allowed to conduct business with "neutral" Mexico. "The Confederate Congress consented. When it voted to prohibit cotton shipments from southern ports, it specifically exempted shipment into Mexico, ostensibly because the trade supplied several mills there" (Tyler 1970: 457). Within short order, Texas cotton practically invaded Mexico; "there was so much cotton in Texas, and so many merchants willing to go to great lengths to sell it, that some of the 'white gold' even found its way southward to the port of Tampico, situated on the Rio Pánuco, about 250 miles directly down the coast from Matamoros" (Tyler 1970: 465). The situation was utterly chaotic, and inflated prices allowed unscrupulous merchants (along with the requisite kickbacks demanded by corrupt Mexican officials) to realize nearly impossible profit margins.[148] William Marsh Rice wrote several letters to his younger brother Frederick Allyn Rice during these years. Frederick was "stationed in Houston as a captain with the

---

[148] Almost overnight the small coastal Rio Grande town of Bagdad became a cotton shipping metropolis (its 1863 population stood at about 2,000 inhabitants), where European (particularly British) and even American ships would anxiously await to onload Texas cotton that had been shipped downriver from Matamoros. In the American case, "a firm organized for the trade usually consisted of a loyal citizen of the United States who bought and sold goods in the North, a Southerner who bough cotton in Texas, and a Mexican citizen in Matamoros through whom the exchanges were made" (Cowling 1926: 93). Predictably, during these years Bagdad became one of the legendary seedy, shady, and corrupt bootlegger towns so well known in popular Texas folklore; shootings, prostitution, gambling, drinking, etc. were commonplace.

Confederate Army and served as Rice's principal business agent there while Rice was away in Mexico" (Strom 1986: 91). In one letter to his brother dated March 29, 1865, Rice, after describing business conditions in Matamoros, advises his brother to "keep the matter as close to yourself as you can" and to "keep these prices to yourself" so as to ensure that the usual mark-ups of goods (to be later sold in Texas and elsewhere) could be protected.

The illegal Mexican trade provided urgently needed supplies to the Confederate cause and grew steadily in importance as the war progressed. After the Confederate defeat in New Orleans and Union victory at Vicksburg, the Mexican lifeline was for the most part the only effective one available.[149] Men like William Marsh Rice helped to make the mercantile arrangement function (relatively) smoothly; and simultaneously made tremendous profits.

---

[149] "To the very end of the war it furnished Texas, Arkansas, Louisiana, and Mississippi with most of their manufactured goods and practically all of their munitions of war" (Cowling 1926: 123).

Perhaps one of the most lasting effects of the trade was the economic prosperity that accompanied it and remained to become the basis of financial empires on both sides of the river. Men in the cotton business accumulated "vast and immense fortunes," wrote Hunter: in Texas, Richard King, Charles Stillman, Mifflin Kenedy, and many others; on the Mexican side of the border perhaps Patricio Milmo was the most notable, but there were others. Merchants in Monterrey garnered profits that became the economic foundation of present-day Monterrey, the third largest city in Mexico and the financial capital of the north (Tyler 1970: 477).

Was William Marsh Rice a slave trader? Although I have not been able to locate direct evidence that he was, the answer, in all likelihood, is yes. Rice acted as an intermediary between Texas plantations and northern importers. He furnished the plantations with all the things necessary to run their enterprises. One would have to imagine it to be a near impossibility that someone engaged in this business in Texas in the 1840's, 50's and 60's, would not have seen to it that the planters were furnished with the number one priority of any plantation: Negro ownership and labor. Rice's biographer does not provide evidence of Rice engaging in slave trading; instead, he cites the following which neatly encapsulates the point:

> Southern Capitalism took a different turn from that developed in the North. The Texas Capitalist had two ingredients to work with, fresh lands and Negro slaves. Out of this land and forced labor he created new capital, which almost universally was reinvested in more land and more slaves....Few, if any, of these New England migrants who succeeded—as lawyers, doctors, merchants, or overseers—failed to acquire Negroes and set themselves up as Southern gentlemen. This indicates that geography more than morality permitted the American North and West to escape the incubus of Negro slavery (Fehrenbach 1968: 205-206).[150]

William Marsh Rice and Charles Morgan may be admired and even worshipped as important Texas businessmen by purveyors of the Texas Myth; but the businesses in which they were engaged mark them not just as white men of their time but as initiators of a long tradition of unscrupulous, ruthless,

---

[150] I should note, however, that Fehrenbach is also another Texas Myth historian that essentially subscribes to the "dull organic ache" thesis regarding the role of slavery in the Texas revolution and hears "conspiracy theory" whenever the role of slavery in the revolution is mentioned. This is not surprising since Fehrenbach sits on the Texas Historical Commission board. In chapter 8 I take up the issue of the more morally "pure" fight for Texas independence vs. the more clearly morally depraved role of Texas during the Civil War. The former is Disney and John Wayne—all Texans, including liberal Texas Myth adherents, are encouraged to feel pride in it. The latter is more controversial, and is for the most part only vigorously defended in public by neo-Confederates and their sympathizers, although the Confederate flag is conspicuously displayed in many public and private places in Texas, ostensibly because it has now transmogrified itself into a symbol of southern "heritage" and "pride."

and morally bankrupt Lone Star Yankees. As of this writing, one of their spiritual descendants sits in the Governor's Mansion and is the Republican candidate for President of the United States.

The Texas Planter Class

The most outstanding exemplars of the "three C's"—Commerce, Christianity,[151] and Civilization—were the Texas planter class, which, as discussed, held the reins in the state both politically and socially.[152] The intricacies of plantation agriculture involved a myriad of interwoven economic, social,

---

[151] An interesting reference to how the three C's intertwined is provided in Henson and Parmelee (1993: 38) in their description of the St. Augustine planter John Cartwright:

> John Cartwright owned about fifteen slaves, one-half the number owned by his neighbor Elisha Roberts. Like many slaveowners, John *recorded the births and deaths of his servants in his Bible.* Eight were members of one family that John may have owned since the time of his marriage. The parents, Harry and Nancy, had six children born between 1811 and 1823; the other adult slaves were acquired later and there seem to be two family units and perhaps a single man (emphasis added).

[152] "Slaveholders dominated economic, political, and social life in antebellum Texas. They produced 90 percent of the state's cotton, dominated officeholding at all levels of government, and by virtue of their wealth occupied the top rungs of the social ladder. Not surprisingly under these circumstances, most articulate Texans such as newspaper editors and ministers defended slavery with every imaginable argument, and the vast majority of the state's people either supported or quietly acquiesced in the institution" (Campbell 1989: 256).

disciplinary, and cultural practices, but the lynchpin of the system, of course, was slavery. As I pointed out in chapter 3, scholars from Bancroft to Tadman have stressed that the practice of <u>slave trading</u> was an integral component of how slavery was practiced in antebellum America. The fact that significant levels of slave trading were a <u>primary responsibility</u> of effective plantation management was not a secret among planters themselves—although Campbell (1989), like Phillips and the others criticized in this study, seems to have all but expunged this important factor from the historical record.

Brenham planter Thomas Affleck publicly printed what everyone knew (or thought they knew) in an 1855 edition of the well known Southern journal *De Bow's Review* (Affleck 1855: 339-345). The concluding paragraph of the article, which concerned itself with the proper duties of a plantation overseer, read as follows:

> A <u>fine crop</u> consists, first, in an *increase in the number, and marked improvement in the condition and value of*

the negroes;[153] second, an abundance of provisions of all sorts for man and beast, carefully saved and properly housed; third, both summer and winter clothing made at home; also, leather tanned, and shoes and harness made when practicable; fourth, an improvement in the productive qualities of the land, and in the general condition of the plantation; fifth, the teams and stock generally, with the farming implements and the buildings, in fine order at the close of the year; and young hogs more than enough for next year's killing; then, as heavy a crop of cotton, sugar, or rice, as could possibly be made under the circumstances, sent to the market in good season, and of prime quality. The time has passed when the overseer was valued solely for the number of bales of cotton, hogsheads of sugar, or tierces of rice he had made, without reference to his other qualifications (emphasis added).

The fact that Affleck defines a "fine crop" as being first and foremost conditioned upon the condition, number, and value of the slaves might lead one to believe—as the standard Texas Myth narrative does—that planters in fact were "benevolent" toward their slaves and that they exhibited genuine concern

---

[153] Affleck was reaffirming what Thomas Jefferson had noted about forty years earlier when he wrote in 1819 that "I consider the labor of a breeding woman as no object, and that a child raised every 2 years is of more profit than the crop of the best laboring man" and instructed his overseers that "it is not their labor, but their increase which is the first consideration with us." A year later Jefferson instructed his managers that "I consider a woman who brings a child every two years as more profitable than the best man on the farm" and wrote to John W. Eppes "what she produces is an addition to capital" (Jefferson to Joel Yancy, January 17, 1819 and Jefferson to John W. Eppes, June 30, 1820, in Betts 1953).

for their welfare. Even Campbell, whose general treatment of this question is for the most part on the liberal end of the Texas Myth spectrum, writes that "Slaveholders and their apologists eventually created a romantic legend concerning the trust and kindness that masters extended to their bondsmen. Like most legends, it had some basis in fact" (Campbell 1989: 197). But exactly how "factual" is the claim Campbell makes here? And why does he point out that the "legend" had at least "some basis" in fact? Tadman's analysis is far better on this question; the fact is that what "family attachments" that may have existed between white and Black families on antebellum plantations was reserved for "key slaves," that is certain overseers, drivers, and domestics. Field hands—the vast majority of a plantation's labor force—were treated as bona fide chattel, were separated and sold when it was deemed expedient by plantation management, and almost never appear in planter and/or trader correspondence (Tadman 1996[1989]:xxi). Thus the key in establishing a proper frame of reference for master/slave relations is establishing what planters and traders actually **did** to slaves rather than to point out—whether "factual" or not—what they said they did. What they in fact demonstrated is a far greater concern for slaves' market values and productivity than for the slaves' family attachments or feelings.[154] I agree with Tadman that the "basis in fact" Campbell observes is a strategic adjustment on the part of the slaves "to the sheer power of masters" and does not constitute—except in rare cases—genuine feelings of "affection" between masters and slaves. Where opportunities to exercise agency (e.g. things such as reproductive choice) and/or resistance existed, slaves exercised them.[155]

One example of planter avarice and racism ought to

---

[154] They also did not like it when their property ran away. See the ad in figure 12.

[155] The prevailing pattern in the rest of the South was that even domestic slaves abandoned their plantations (and their masters, who were shocked that "faithful servants" and "family members" would leave so callously) when opportunities to do so presented themselves. Once Union armies were rumored to be in the vicinity, thousands of slaves throughout the South affected their escape (Loewen 1999: 277). Had Texas experienced more fighting on its soil during the Civil War, the pattern would have likely been the same, as it had been during the Texas Revolutionary War where several slaves ran away to join Mexican forces (see chapter 4).

Stop the Runaway!

RANAWAY from the undersigned, on the 2d. of this month, a black boy, about twenty-one years of age, about five feet high, tolerably heavy built; square, or broad shouldered, and of rather a yellow cast. His name is SAM. He left with a horse and is supposed to be on his way to Mexico. A description of his clothes not known, as he left with more suits than one.

FIFTY DOLLARS REWARD is offered for the apprehension and delivery of said boy if taken up out of this county, and a liberal reward to any person apprehending him in the county. NANCY U. COX.
june17tf   La Grange, Fayette Co., Texas.

Figure 12: Runaway advertisment from the *Galveston Civilian* of July 21, 1857

suffice to establish the point that negro speculation in antebellum Texas was far more prevalent than is usually acknowledged. The man in question, furthermore, was not an ordinary Texas agriculturalist but sat at the uppermost rungs of the Texas planterocracy.

A.C. Horton "was unquestionably a member of the elite that directed the fortunes of antebellum Texas" (Ellenberger 1985: 363). He served as a two-term senator during the Lone Star Republic, representing Matagorda, Jackson, and Victoria counties, was elected the first lieutenant governor of the state of Texas in 1845, and was an original member of the board of trustees that established Baylor University. Horton was also a wealthy planter and operated two plantations, one at Caney Creek in what is now Wharton County (named "Sycamore Grove"), and the other in Matagorda County, near the town of Matagorda.

Horton was born in Hancock County, Georgia, on September 4, 1798, but moved to La Grange, Franklin County,

Alabama with his mother in 1823. There Horton married, acquired a modest estate (including four slaves) and served in the Alabama legislature in the early 1830's. By 1835 Horton had left for Texas and immediately involved himself in the Texan fight for independence, recruiting and organizing fighters in Alabama to assist in the expected struggle. During the war, Horton became notorious for having survived the "Goliad Massacre" where his friend and business partner James W. Fannin was executed by Santa Anna's forces; the charge of cowardice would be used against Horton by his political enemies for years to come. Horton also established himself as a merchant and operated the firm of Horton & Clements, a firm which at first engaged in retail merchandise but eventually (like William M. Rice's firm) grew to specialize in cotton trading and land speculation. By the early 1840's Horton settled the rest of his Alabama family in Texas and had established Sycamore Grove. The plantation was spectacularly profitable:

The growth of Horton's estate and the extent of his

business concerns as outlined in tax returns were staggering. An undated (through pre-1846) fragment is the first description of his estate: it was worth a little less than $17,000 with most of his property tied up in 56 town lots in Matagorda ($8,325) and slaves (10 valued at $4,000). By 1846, the core properties of his plantation were in his possession, totalling approximately 2,200 acres and valued at slightly more than $11,000; the town lots were gone, but the taxable slave total had jumped to 60, for an estate totaling $42,818. The first year Horton was listed as owning more than 100 slaves was 1855, when he possessed 113. They were valued at $56,500, slightly less than half his total wealth. Several years into the war, in 1864, Horton was recorded as owning 129 slaves and an estate valued at $160,986, a tenfold increase in perhaps a quarter of a century.

In addition to increasing his physical holdings, Horton's plantation was also very productive agriculturally:

Exact figures no longer exist, but after Horton's death the annual production of Sycamore Grove was estimated to range from 650 to 700 bales of cotton, 450 to 500 hogsheads of sugar, and about 1,600 barrels of molasses. Additionally, Horton profited from escalating land values: to take one example, donation land he had received in 1849, 640 acres in Comal County, was sold to James Calhoun for $960 in 1857. In 1850 Horton owned nearly 12,000 acres scattered about Travis, Washington, Gillespie, and Comal counties; as late as 1864 he still owned nearly 3,000 acres in the west, including 960 acres in Brown County (Ellenberger 1985: 382-383).

It appears that although Horton left Fannin to die on the Goliad battlefield, he learned at least a thing or two about Negro speculation from his fellow Georgian. Horton's rapid growth in his slaveholdings "suggests that much of this reinvested capital must have been used to buy more slaves" (Ellenberger 1985: 384). In short, Horton must have been engaged in extensive slave trading. Evidence for this can be gleaned from the 1850 and 1860 censuses, which indicate that Horton owned a disproportionate number of young slaves:[156]

> Of the 91 slaves enumerated in 1850, at least 32 were younger than twelve years old, 20 younger than four years. In 1860, 82 of the 167 slaves were younger than twelve (Ellenberger 1985: 384).

But we do not have to rely on these numbers alone to prove that Horton was a slave trader. Direct evidence of Horton's slave dealing is located in the A.C. Horton papers at the Center for American History at UT Austin, which contain a bill of sale

---

[156] Ellenberger interprets this as evidence that Horton actually cared for the welfare of his slave families. He also cites evidence, written by white Texas Myth adherents, that Horton was "remembered as a kind master to these slaves" (Ellenberger 1985: 384). We now know that such self serving romantic legend is incorrect and should be dismissed.

for 58 slaves purchased in Charleston,[157] an 1860 mortgage taken out by Horton to purchase the slaves, a will (newer than the one he executed in 1858), a property inventory of his estate, and legal correspondence. It seems that once the Civil War began, Horton defaulted on his mortgage. The mortgage holders spent the next twenty years suing Horton's family for payment. After the passage of several years—and many contrite letters on behalf of the Horton estate apologizing for the inability to pay his notes—one of the attorneys researching the matter of the defaulted mortgage produced a succinct summary of the chain of events that led to Horton's financial collapse:

> In 1860 Governor Horton came to Charleston and purchased from Josiah S. Brown a number of Negroes. In part payment of the purchase money, he executed a bond to Josiah S. Brown as agent of Mrs. S.E. Brown and others, conditioned for the payment of $16,350. He also gave three drafts for $5,000 each drawn in his own favor, on Nelson Clements & Co. of New York, dated 19th May,

---

[157] The "surety and obligator" for the slaves Horton purchased was Ziba Oakes, a well known Charleston broker and slave trader. See Tadman (1996[1989]: 36-40) who worked with the Ziba B. Oakes papers extensively.

1860, and payable as follows. Two of them on the 1st of July 1861 and the third on the 1st January 1862. He also gave a second bond, conditioned for the payment of these drafts and a further sum, which I am unable now to specify, but which was about $1,500. upon this bond Z.B. Oakes of Charleston, South Carolina was his surety. To secure these two bonds he executed a mortgage of his plantation in Wharton County, Texas.

The Negroes purchased by Governor Horton belonged to the trust estate of Mrs. Sarah E. Brown, which was created by her marriage settlement. The terms of the trust were as follows. To wit, to Mrs. S.E. Brown for life, with remainder upon her death, to the issue of her marriage with Charles Brown, living at the time of her death.

At the time of the sale of the Negroes to Gov. Horton, Mrs. Brown was a widow and had the following children then living: S. Keith Brown, S. Pinckney Brown, Josiah S. Brown, William S. Brown, Edmund L. Brown, and Sarah E. Brown. All of whom united in the bill of sale to Gov. Horton. Mrs. S.E. Brown died in 1874. E. Pinckney Brown died in 1864 unmarried. The other children are all living and reside in Charleston, South Carolina, of which state they are citizens.

The address of my firm is

       Pressley, Lord & Inglesby
       Charleston, South Carolina

I forgot to state in the proper connection that when the Drafts accepted by Nelson Clements & Co. of New York, matured, Gov. Horton wrote to Josiah S. Brown and requested that they should not be presented for payment as he had been prevented from shipping cotton to them, in consequence of the breaking out of the war and they were therefore without funds belonging to him and afterwards offered Confederate notes in payment

The bond on which Mr. Oakes was surety was not turned over to me by Mr. McLemore with the other papers. My impression is that it was kept by our Firm, for the purpose of putting it in writ against Oakes in South Carolina—on my return will forward it if it is there [the author of the letter was not the first attorney to work the case for the Browns and took a trip to Texas to research the claim in the late 1870's/early 1880's].

The Civil War may have ruined Horton financially, but at the outset of the war, he was one of the most affluent men in Texas:

The 1860 census of Texas counted a population of slightly more than 600,000 people. Of these, only 51 who owned more than 100 slaves can be identified, and only 4 owned more than Albert C. Horton. Only 25 estimated their estates at more than the $319,000 in real and personal property the census lists for Horton.

Horton was also a noted participant in the efforts of the daughter of one of the slaves he brought to Texas in the late 1830's to purchase her mother's freedom. The tale is related in the book *Louisa Picquet, the Octoroon: A Tale of Southern Slave Life*. Winegarten (1995: 39), who located a reprint of the book in a collection at the Schomburg Library in New York City, summarizes the chain of events nicely:

> Elizabeth Ramsey was sold away from her daughter, Louisa Picquet, in Georgia in 1839 and taken to Texas by her new owner. After a twenty-year separation, Picquet, who had attained her freedom and moved to Ohio, located her mother on a Matagorda, Texas, plantation. She negotiated successfully for her purchase and raised the necessary funds. After their reunion in Cincinnati, Picquet took out a notice in the Cincinnati Daily Gazette of October 15, 1860, "expressing her thanks to those ladies and gentlemen...that having accomplished through their kind aid the freedom of her mother, Elizabeth Ramsey, from slavery, by paying to her owner, Mr. A.C. Horton, of Texas, cash in hand, the sum of $900, collected by myself in small sums from different individuals, residing in this city and States of Ohio and New York...My mother also desires to say that she is most grateful to you all, and that if any of those friends who have assisted her to her freedom, feel disposed to call on her at my residence on Third Street, near Race (No. 135), she will be happy to see them and thank them personally.

Elizabeth Ramsey's letters to her daughter are also very poignant and informative. The first, dated March 8, 1859 reads as follows:

Wharton, March 8, 1859

MY DEAR DAUGHTER

I a gane take my pen in hand to drop you a few lines. I have written to you twice, but I hav not yet received an answer from you....I sent to my little grand children a ring also a button in my first letter....I said in my letter to you that Col. Horton would let you have me for $1000 dol. or a woman that could fill my place; I think you could get one cheaper where you are....than to pay him the money; I am anxios to hav you make this trade. you have no idea what my feelings are. I have not spent one happy moment since I received your kind letter. it is true I was more than rejoyest to hear from you my Dear child; but my feelings on this subject are in Expressible. no one but a mother can tell my feelings...I think that 1000 dollars is too much for me your must writ very kind to Col. Horton and try to Get me for less money...[158]

you Brother John sends his love to you and 100 kisses to your little son; Kiss my Dear little children 100 times for me particular Elizabeth say to her that she must writ to her grand mar often; I want you to hav your ambrotipe taken also your children and send them to me I would giv this world to see you and my sweet little children; may God bless you my Dear child and protect you is my prayer.

Your affectionate mother,
ELIZABETH RAMSEY

---

[158] Ramsey was right. 1000 dollars was a pretty high sum for a middle-aged to elderly slave, even in 1859.

Five days later Ms. Ramsey wrote:

> W[ha]rton, W[h]arton ..... County, March 13, '59
>
> MY DEAR DAUGHTER,
> I know of nothing on this earth that would gratify me so much as to meet with My Dear and only daughter, I fear that I should not be able to retain my senses on account of the great Joy it would create in me, But time alone will develup whether this meeting will tak plase on earth or not Hope keeps the soul alive....Direct your letter to Goven A.C. Horton, Matagorda, Texas. May God guide and protect you through Life, & Finally save You in Heaven is the prayer of your affectionate mother.
>
> ELIZABETH RAMSEY

Over a year later contact had apparently been established between Picquet and Horton. There is a stronger sense of anticipation and urgency in Ms. Ramsey's writing:

> Matagorda, April 21, 1860.
>
> DEAR DAUGHTER,
>
> [M]y master....says he is willing to take a woman in exchange for me, of my age and capasity or he will..take nine hundred dollars in *cash* for me.....he always says that money cannot buy either Arthur [her husband] or John [her son] he is training John to take charge of one of his Plantations he has unlimited confidence in him and will

not part with him untel death parts them.....Farewell My Dear Daughter.....

ELIZABETH RAMSAY

Among other things, these letters indicate that even among "key slaves" strong familial bonds and a dislike of bondage existed. Ms. Ramsey's desire for reunion with her only daughter is pretty obvious. It is likely that Ms. Ramsay was a key slave because it was very unusual for slaves to be able to read and/or write, and Ms. Ramsey's last letter indicates that Horton was unwilling to sell either her husband or son; the latter because he was being trained as an overseer. Louisa Picquet must have also been very light-skinned, as the title of the book relating her narrative indicates. Chances are that Gov. Horton and Ms. Ramsey were very well acquainted indeed.

CHAPTER 7: "SOLD FROM THEIR MAMA'S BREAST"; THE FOLKTALES AND ORAL HISTORY OF ENSLAVED TEXANS

In addition to direct "ethnographic" interaction with contemporary Afro-Texans[159] (in my opinion the best source of information on Black history in Texas) the most useful collections of indigenous information on the historical experiences of Black Texans are the slave narratives collected by the Federal Writers Project (commonly known as the "WPA Narratives") and the collection of Black Texas folktales collected and published by legendary folklorist J. Mason Brewer, who like Zora Neale Hurston, was one of the first scholars to use Black dialect in his writings.

Brewer published several collections of African-American

---

[159] I put the word in quotes because I don't consider my interactions with Black Texans to be "ethnographic" in the conventional sense. These people are my communal sisters and brothers—calling them "informants" or something like it would cheapen the perspectives I argue in this dissertation and would reduce or eliminate their respect for me, as it should. For further discussion on the politics of conducting "committed fellow traveller/resident" ethnographies as opposed to pimped and commodified studies of the "other" see Gordon (1998: viii).

folktales and his list of "firsts" is impressive.[160] Of Brewer's collections, I paid particular attention to *The Word on the Brazos* (1953) since it is generally acknowledged that this region of Texas experienced the most "classical" features of plantation slavery. Indeed in his introduction to the book, Brewer makes the same point:

> The ex-slaves who remained on Brazos River Bottom plantations after Negroes were given their freedom on June 19, 1865, were believed by Negroes residing in other sections of Texas to be the most illiterate, humble, and mistreated Negroes in the state. A common expression among Texas Negro children several decades ago, when they wanted to poke fun at their playmates for being ignorant, was, "You mus' be from de Brazos Bottoms," or "'You ack jes' lack a Brazos Bottom Nigguh" (Brewer 1953: 2-3).

Although the folktales collected by Brewer rarely if ever directly touch on the subject of slave trading, they are an essential component of any Texas revisionist historian's toolkit. These folktales help to establish a contextual framework from

---

[160] Brewer was the first Black member of the Texas Folklore Society, the Texas Institute of Letters, and was the first African-American to serve as vice president of the American Folklore Society.

which further discussion of slave life can be approached. Because so much of the historical record is distorted or told through a Eurocentric filter, folktales, oral history, and archaeology are the most direct routes by which a more well-rounded and accurate historical narrative can be constructed. As is the case with much of African-American cultural expression, folktales certainly are humorous and entertaining, but there is more beneath the surface. Many of the stories contain profound psychological, ethical, political, and sociological insights. As Lorenzo Thomas (1996: 228) notes, "it is clear that from Brewer's earliest work that he had a grasp of this fact."

One informative folktale about conditions under slavery is the story "A Sermon, a Cat, and a Churn" from *The Word on the Brazos* (Brewer 1953: 61-62). The tale, which contains humorous yet serious observances about life on the Jones plantation relates the story of a creatively lazy plantation owner:

Ah call to min' de ole Jones plannuhation down to Brazoria on de Lowuh Brazos. Ole Colonel Jones hab a bell he done meck outen de ole fam'ly silver what he hang on top of de cawn crib he done buil' in de fawm yaa'd. He put a long rope on de bell what rech from de top of de cawn crib clean on thoo de window to his baid, so's he could pull de bell evuh mawnin' 'dout ebun gittin' outen his baid. All he haf to do is to rech up whar he got de rope tied on to a nail driv in de baid pos' an' pull hit. He do dis evuh mawnin' to call de han's to work long 'fo' sunup, 'bout a hour an' a ha'f fo' daybreak. Den, he meck 'em stay in de fiel' till pitch dark. He say de moon change thirteen times a yeah an' dat he gonna git thirteen mont's work outen his Nigguhs. Sich ca'lens-on ain't in de Bottoms today. De white boss-mens what own de plannuhtations stays in town way somewhar an' 'hab a Nigguh rider to run de fawm. De Nigguh rider, he a rail obuhseer, but dey don' say so. De boss-mens fin' out de Nigguh rider mecks mo' money for 'em dan a white obuhseer; dat's de why dey change dey fashion an' hire cullud mens to look attuh dey fawms. Dey's lots of 'em in de Bottoms today. Cose dey don' come out ahaid much, but dey fares way bettuh dan befo'.

In this paragraph the storyteller relates what life was like on the Jones plantation prior to slavery, makes insightful commentary as to why plantation owners preferred Black overseers to white ones, and observes that although the situation is still bad, that times today are better than they were under slavery.

Of particular symbolic importance are the "Tales of Animals and Ranch Life" included in Brewer's collection *Dog Ghosts*. Like animal folktales in other cultures,[161] these stories of Foxes and Roosters and Snakes and Bullfrogs talk about power imbalances and temptation; you might be eaten by the fox or the snake if you are not careful. Animal tales are a more "folksy" manifestation of the diabolical dance discussed in a somewhat different way by Limón (1994).

The WPA Narratives

Although Afro-Texas folktales are an important and frequently overlooked source of information on antebellum slave life in Texas, the primary source remains the oral history narratives collected by the Federal Writers Project.[162] The

---

[161] It is interesting to compare, for instance, the famous Scottish folktale "How the Wolf Lost His Tail" (Crossley-Holland 1985: 221) with a tale included by Brewer titled "Why the Rabbit Has a Short Tail" (Brewer 1958: 50).

[162] It should be noted that the FWP was not the first attempt to collect such information. "The earliest interviews with former slaves were conducted under the auspices of Fisk University, in Nashville, Tennessee. From 1927 to 1929 Andrew P. Watson, a graduate student in anthropology at Fisk under the direction of Paul Radin, recorded autobiographical accounts and

narratives are particularly informative on the extent and significance of slave trading—many narratives mention Negro speculators by name. There are, according to a comprehensive name index edited by Howard Potts (Potts 1997: 60-73), 861 Texas narratives in the collection,[163] a significant portion of which are located at the Center for American History at the University of Texas at Austin, although the most complete collection is housed at the Library of Congress. Greenwood Press began publishing the narratives in three series in 1972 under the editorship of George P. Rawick. The collection, titled *The American Slave: A Composite Autobiography* includes all known Texas narratives, i.e. former slaves that were interviewed in Texas.

There were a significant number of interviewees who were enslaved in Texas but were not interviewed there. Thus

---

religious conversion experiences of one hundred former slaves" (Potts 1997: viii).

[163] Potts's index is organized according to where slaves lived, not where they were interviewed. "As a result, many slaves will have more than one entry if they lived in different states, counties, or the same county but with different masters within the county" (Potts 1997: xix).

a sizeable number of the Louisiana and Oklahoma narratives were in fact the life stories of enslaved Afro-Texans. "In Oklahoma about a quarter of the one hundred thirty ex-slave interviews came from men and women who had been slaves in Texas but who had later moved to Oklahoma" (Baker and Baker 1997: x). I have thus attempted to broaden the scope of the oral histories I cite beyond the "Texas" narratives. In addition to Rawick, my main sources are Tyler & Murphy (1974) which contains a sample of some of the Texas narratives, and the new collection by Baker and Baker (1997) which nicely encapsulates the Oklahoma narratives.[164]

In Appendix 1 of *An Empire for Slavery*, Campbell (1989: 262) observes that "many historians....have questioned the reliability of the slave narratives, and with good reason. First, the interviews were conducted during the late 1930's when all

---

[164] One of the nice things about the Oklahoma and Louisiana narratives is that they employed greater proportions of non-whites as interviewers. One of the concerns mentioned by scholars of the narratives is that they may not be as candid as they otherwise might have been because the majority of the interviewers were white. Baker and Baker (1997: xi) write that "Oklahoma reflected greater ethnic diversity in its staff which may have contributed to the candidness of the interviews."

the ex-slaves were at least in their seventies, and two-thirds were eighty or older. In general, they had known slavery only as children." It does not seem unreasonable for Campbell to express concern that the narratives may not be entirely accurate because the passage of time may have dulled some of the memories of the then elderly slaves.[165] But, as mentioned repeatedly in this study, Campbell's interpretation of the narratives is incomplete and too narrowly focused; his study utilizes a small portion of the narratives and, more importantly, only highlights slave behavioral patterns and material conditions without properly addressing the interviewees' extensive commentary on master/slave relations. When one looks at the veracity of the narratives with a sharp focus on the roles played by the slave trade and on the traumatic experiences of family separation, what becomes clear is that

---

[165] Baker and Baker (1997: xiv) express similar apprehensions. They observe that "because the individuals interviewed were young during slavery, they would have generally avoided some of the harsher aspects of discipline exerted on the adults, thus giving them a possibly skewed impression of life in servitude." Similarly, given the fact that the interviews took place during the great depression, some writers have noted that the former slaves may have been inclined to tell white interviewers what they wanted to hear.

even ex-slaves who had been enslaved as young children have solid and vivid recollections of the awful and bitter pains caused by being sold "away from Mama's breast." The psychological scars of being torn from one's parents and siblings last a lifetime, and the narratives, as one might expect, reflect the shock of that ordeal. The critique that the interviewees were too young to have a full understanding of life under slavery (a poor critique to begin with, in my view) is weakened considerably by the adoption of this fresher perspective.

The narratives have been subjected to a considerable amount of analysis, including by those who have focused specifically on the role of slave trading, and even slave breeding. In 1979 Paul Escott published a study (Escott 1979: 48), based on a national analysis of 499 of the narratives, that indicated that sale—not migration-was the primary cause of separation of family members. 58.5 percent of the separations were due to sale, as opposed to 9.4 percent from gifts, the next highest category.[166] For this chapter I have not examined all of the Texas narratives; instead I cite excerpts from the narratives in an attempt to let the oral history speak for itself on the issue of speculation. There are all sorts of ways in which the narratives could be employed to demonstrate the extent and intensity of the slave experience and of the role played by the slave trade. My feeling is that the life histories of the former slaves are sufficiently profound and captivating in themselves, and do not require extensive academic interpretation, embellishment, or other forms of scholasticism. The primary point I wish to make is that family separation by sale was far-reaching in Texas, and certainly more so than has been recognized by scholars. And on this point the narratives are more than clear enough.

Reeves Tucker

Reeves Tucker, 98 years old, was interviewed on August

---

[166] In her feminist analysis of antebellum slavery, Robertson (1996: 13) observes, furthermore, that "women were more likely than men to be sold (23.4 percent to 20.4 percent) and much more likely to be sold repeatedly."

2, 1937 in Marshall, TX; Harrison County (Rawick 1979: 3892).

> I'se saw lots of slaves bid off like stock, and babies sold from their mothers breast. Some of them brought $1,500, owing to how strong they was. Speculators rode all over the country buying up "Niggers." I'se seed as many as fifty in a gang being driven like convicts.

Mary Gaffney

Ms. Gaffney was born in Selville, Mississippi in 1846 and brought to Texas in 1860. She was interviewed in Madisonville, TX by B.E. Davis on January 19, 1938 (Rawick 1979: 1445).

> Yes, I'se seen slaves sold and auctioned off. The first thing they did was to make us clean up good and put clean clothes on, then they would give us some tallow from a beef and grease our face, hands and feet, then they would trot us out before the bidder so he could look us over real good; then he would offer Master a price. Maser never would take the first bid, he would always get the highest bid he could before he sold; then the fun would take place, all the hollering and bawling you never heard. Well you have sold calves from cows haves'nt you? and heard them bawl for 3 or 4 days for their calves, that was just the way with the slaves. Mostly like burying a slave, because when they sold a slave the new buyers would nearly everytime carry them clear out of the state, and the slaves that were left at home would not even know where the new Maser was carrying them or

even his name. They done that so we would not be wanting to go see our son, daughters, mother or father.

Mariah Robinson

Mariah Robinson couldn't recall how old she was, but was probably at least 90 years of age. She was born in Georgia and was interviewed in Meridian, TX. Like many Texas settlers, her master Bob Young was leaving Georgia to escape debt. Her recollections of sailing down the Atlantic to New Orleans and then to Galveston via boat can be considered to be fairly typical (Tyler and Murphy 1974: 6-7). Chapter 4 discusses the dynamics of how "settlers" and their slaves arrived in Texas, usually Galveston, via New Orleans.

> We came by rail from Monroe [Georgia] to Social Circle and then boarded the boat *Sweet Home*. There were just two boats on the line, the *Sweet Home* and the *Katie Darling*......We sailed down the Atlantic Ocean to New Orleans, myself and my Aunt Lizzie and Uncle Johns, all with Miss Josephine. When we got to New Orleans we rested and put up in the trader's office.....Coming down the Mississippi and across the Gulf we saw no land for days and we went through the Gulf of Mexico and landed at the port, Galveston, and we came to Waco on the stagecoach.

Betty Simmons

Betty Simmons said that she must have been at least 100 years of age. Ms. Simmons's master, "Massa Langford" had gone bankrupt and reluctantly gave up his slaves as payment for his debts. Her narrative was recorded in Beaumont (Tyler and Murphy 1974: 9-10).

> When we got to the crossroads, there were the massa and a nigger man. That was another slave he was going to sell, and he hated to sell us so he couldn't look us in the eye. they put us niggers inside the buggy, so if the creditors came along they couldn't see us.
> Finally those slave speculators put the nigger man and me on the train and took us to Memphis, and when we got there they took us to the nigger traders' yard. We got there at breakfast time and waited for the boat they called the *Ohio* to get there. The boat just ahead of the *Ohio*, old Captain Fabra's boat, was destroyed and that delayed our boat two hours. When it came, there were 258 niggers out of those nigger yards in Memphis who got on this boat. They put the niggers upstairs and went down the river as far as Vicksburg, that was the place, and then we got off of the boat and got on the train again, and that time we went to New Orleans.
> I was satisfied then that I had lost my people and was never going to see them any more in this world, and I never did.....At last, Col. Forescue, he bought and kept me. he was a fighter in the Mexican War, and he came to New

Orleans to buy his slaves. He took me up the Red River to Shreveport, and then by buggy to Liberty, in Texas.

William Hamilton

Interviewed in Fort Worth (Tyler and Murphy 1974: 10).

The only thing I remember about all that is that there was lots of crying when they took me away from my mammy. That's something I will never forget.

Walter Rimm

Interviewed in Fort Worth. Vivid and detailed

description of a negro speculator plying his trade (Tyler and

Murphy 1974: 25).

> Those sales are one thing that made an impression on me. I heard the folks whisper about going to have the sale, and about noon there was a crowd of folks in the front yard, and a nigger trader with his slaves. They set up a platform in the middle of the yard, and one white man got on that and another white man came up and had a white woman with him. She appeared to be about fifteen years old and had long, black hair down her back. They put her on the platform, and then I heard a scream, and a woman who looked like the gal cried out, "I'll cut my throat if my daughter is sold." The white man went and talked to her and finally allowed her to take the young gal away with her. That sure stirred up a commotion amongst the white folks, but they said that gal had just a little nigger blood and could be sold for a slave, but she

looked as white as anybody I ever saw.

Mintie Maria Miller

Ms. Miller was born in Tuscaloosa, Alabama and was brought to Texas as a young girl. She described her experiences of being on a Houston auction block when interviewed in her home in Galveston (Tyler and Murphy 1974: 25).

> They said they were going to sell me, cause Miss Nancy's father-in-law died, and they got rid of some of us. She didn't want to sell me so she told me to be sassy, and no one would buy me. They took me to Houston and to the market, and a man called George Fraser sold the slaves. The market was an open house, more like a shed. We all stood to one side till our turn came. There was nothing else you could do.
> They stood me on a block of wood, and a man bid me in. I felt mad. You see I was young then, too young to know better. I didn't know what they sold me for, but the man who bought me made me open my mouth while he looked at my teeth. They did us all that way, sold us like you sell a horse. Then my old master bade me goodby and tried to give me a dog, but I remembered what Miss Nancy had said, and I sassed him and slapped the dog out of his hand. So the man who bought me said, "When one o'clock comes you've got to sell her again, she's sassy. If she did me that way, I'd kill her." So they sold me twice in the same day.

James Brown

Mr. Brown was born in Bell County in 1853 and was taken to Waco while still an infant. He was interviewed in July, 1937 (Tyler and Murphy 1974: 25-26).

> Another thing that massa did powerful good was trade the niggers. He bought and sold them all the time. You see, there were traders that traveled from place to place them days and they took sometimes as many as 100 niggers to trade. There were sheds outside of town, where they kept the niggers when they came to town. The massa and the trader talked this way: "How you trade?" "I'll give you even trade." "No, I want $25.00 for the difference." "I'll give you $5.00." That's the way they talked on and on. Maybe they'd make the trade, and maybe they didn't.
> They had auctions sometimes, and massa always attended them. At the auction, I've seen them sell a family. Maybe one man would buy the mammy, another the pappy, and another buy all the children or maybe just one, like that. I've seen them cry like they were at a funeral when they were parted. They had to drag them away.
> When the auction began, he said: "This nigger is so and so old, he's never been abused, he's sound as a dollar. Just look at the muscle and the big shoulders. He's worth a thousand of any man's money. How much am I offered?" Then the bidding started. It went like this: $200, I hear, do I hear $250, do I hear $300." Then the nigger took his clothes—they had one extra suit—and went

with the man that bought him.

Tom Holland

Mr. Holland thought he was about 97 years old and was interviewed in Madisonville, Waller County (Tyler and Murphy 1974: 26).

> I saw slaves sold and auctioned off, because I was put up to the highest bidder myself. Massa traded me to William Green just before the war, for a hundred acres of land at $1.00 an acre. He thought I'd never be much account, cause I had the glass eye....All the hollering and bawling took place, and when he sold me it took me most a year to get over it, but there I was, belonging to another man.

Henry Lewis

102 years old and interviewed in Beaumont (Tyler and Murphy 1974: 29).

> There used to be nigger traders who came through the country with the herd of niggers, just like cattlemen with the herd of cattle. They fixed camp and the pen on the ridge outside of town and people who wanted to buy more slaves went there. They had a block and made the slaves get up on that. Maybe one said, "I'll give you $200," and when they were through, the slave was sold to the highest bidder. Old massa warned us to look out and not let the trader catch us, cause the trader'd just as soon

steal a nigger as sell him.

Wes Brady

An 88 year old Harrison County slave interviewed in Marshall who recalled seeing a slave coffle (Tyler and Murphy 1974: 50).

> I saw long lines of slaves chained together driven by a white man on a horse down the Jefferson road.

Uncle Cinto Lewis

About 101 years old, born in Fort Bend County, near Richmond. This brief excerpt indicates that Africans were mixed in with the American-born slave population and that like elsewhere they were the ones most inclined to run away or rebel.

> Some of the slaves ran away to the woods, and if they didn't catch them first, they finally got hungry and came home, and then they got a hiding. Some niggers just came from Africa, and old marse had to watch them close, cause they were the ones that mostly ran away to the woods.

Annie Hawkins

Ms. Hawkins was 90 years old when Jessie R. Ervin, a white WPA staff worker, interviewed her at Colbert, Oklahoma. In her interview, the first thing Ms. Hawkins recalls is the shock and fear of arriving in Texas from Georgia and experiencing a night when the "stars fell," perhaps a night during a meteor shower or when one of the patented Texas northers blew through Galveston (Baker and Baker 1997: 31).

> I called myself 90 but I don't know jest how old I really am but I was a good sized gal when we moved from Georgia to Texas. We come on a big boat and one night the stars fell. Talk about being scared! We all run and hid and hollered and prayed. We thought the end of the world had come.

Lewis Jenkins

Mr. Jenkins was interviewed in Oklahoma City on June 15, 1937 by Ida Belle Hunter, an African-American WPA worker. This interview, one of the best available anywhere, touches on more than just the slave trade. Mr. Jenkins, whose father was a Black coachman on the Alabama plantation where he was born, also makes insightful and frank observations about transracial identity and the contradictions involved in antebellum interracial interaction.

> I seen 'em sell people, what wasn't able to work from the block jest lak cattle. They would be chained togedder. They tuck mothers from children even just a week old and sell 'em. They stripped the slaves, women and all and let the bidders look at 'em to see iffen they was scared before they would buy 'em.

Allen V. Manning

87 years old at the time of the interview in Tulsa. Mr. Manning was born in Clarke County, Mississippi in the fall of 1850 and was brought to Texas by his master, a Baptist preacher during the second year of the Civil War. Manning's narrative is revealing in its insights into the scope and scale of migration into Texas by slaveowners who looked to escape conscription into the Confederate army or navy—many of the migrants viewed the protection of their assets (including their slaves) as being more important than fighting in a war that was primarily agitated by large planters and propagandists.

About that time [the Civil War] it look like everybody in

the world was going to Texas. When we would be going down the road we would have to walk along the side all the time to let the wagons go past, all loaded with folks going to Texas......[167]

I sells milk and makes my living, and I keeps so busy I don't think back on the old days much, but if anybody ask me why the Texas Negroes been kept down so much I can tell them. If they set like I did on the bank at that ferry across the Sabine, and see all that long line of covered wagons, miles and miles of them, crossing that river and going west with all they got left out of the War, it aint hard to understand.

Them whitefolks done had everything they had tore up, or had to run away from the places they lived, and they brung their Negroes out to Texas and then right away they lost them too. They always had them Negroes, and lots of them had mighty fine places back in the old states, and they had to go out and live in sod houses and little old boxed shotguns and turn their Negroes loose. They didn't see no justice in it then, and most of them never did until they died.

Phyllis Petite

Ms. Petite was born in Rusk County, TX and was interviewed at Fort Gibson, Oklahoma. Her narrative is

---

[167] Thousands of slaves were brought to Texas by their owners during the Civil War. Some accompanied their masters or mistresses (while the husbands fought for the Confederacy), while others were stashed there as investments/trades in slave dealers' pens or with friends. The 1860's saw a demographic decrease in the rate of slave growth in Texas although there was still a significant overall increase. According to the *Biennial Report of the Comptroller*, the 1861 slave population of Texas was 232,534. The 1870 census lists the Black population at 253,475.

additionally noteworthy in that it discusses slave trading practices among the Cherokee. Ms. Petite and her family were registered as freedmen members of the Cherokee Nation by the Dawes Commission in 1903.

> My mammy and pappy belonged to a part Cherokee named W. P. Thompson when I was born. He had kinfolks in the Cheroke Nation, and we all moved up here to a place on Fourteen-Mile Creek close to where Hulbert now is, 'way before I was big enough to remember anything. Then, so I been told, old master Thompson sell my pappy and mammy and one of my baby brothers and me back to one of his neighbors in Texas name of John Harnage.....
> Old Master Harnage bought and sold slaves most all the time, and some of the new negroes always acted up and needed a licking. The worst ones got beat up good too! They didn't have no jail to put slaves in because when the Masters got done licking them they didn't need no jail.
> My husband was George Petite. He tell me his mammy was sold away from him when he was a little boy. He looked down a long lane after her just as long as he could see her, and cried after her. He went down to the big road and set down by his mammy's barefooted tracks in the sand and set there until it got dark, and then he come on back to the quarters.

Harriet Robinson

Ms. Robinson, who was 95 years of age when interviewed

by Black WPA worker Ida Belle Hunter in June of 1937, was enslaved in Bastrop County. Her master was Samuel W. Simms, who according to the 1860 census owned 19 slaves worth $14,650. Simms was one of Bastrop's more prominent citizens, and in addition to building and operating steamboats and promoting railway construction, he helped to organize Bastrop Military Academy. Ms. Robinson suffered daily abuse at the hand of Simms's wife Julia. The portion of her narrative describing her migration experiences seems disjointed and incongruous with the rest of her narrative. Nonetheless, it pretty accurately describes the process by which slaves were transported.

> I 'member the battle being fit. The white folks buried all the jewelry and silver and all the gold in the Blue Ridge Mountains [?], in Orange [?], Texas. Master made all us niggers come together and git ready to leave 'cause sho' 'nuff slavery. Then we got on a steamship and pulled out to Galveston. Then he told the captain to feed we niggers. We was on the bay, not the ocean. We left Galveston and went on trains for Houston.
>
> Andrew Simms

Mr. Simms, age eighty, was interviewed near Sapulpa, Oklahoma during the spring or summer of 1937. He was the son of enslaved Africans that had survived the Middle Passage. His master was William Giles Driver, a Georgia-born planter who had come to Texas in the early 1850's. Apparently by the early 1860's Driver, like so many other slaveowners, had decided to relocate his Florida-based slave property to relative safety in Texas.

> My parents come over on a slave ship from Africa about twenty year before I was born on the William Driver plantation down in Florida. My folks didn't know each other in Africa but my old Mammy told me she was captured by Negro slave hunters over there and brought to some coast town where the white buyers took her and carried her to America.
>
> Then when I was four year old along come the War and Master Driver takes up his slaves and leaves the Florida country and goes way out to Texas. Mammy goes along, I goes along, all the children goes along. I don't remember nothing about the trip but I hears mammy talk about it when I gets older.
>
> In them times it was mostly the overseers and the drivers who was the mean ones. They caused all the misery. There was other whitefolks caused troubles too. Sneak around where there was lots of the black children on the plantation and steal them. Take them poor

children away off and sell them.

Liza Smith

Ms. Smith, aged 91 years, was interviewed in Muskogee, Oklahoma by Native American WPA worker Ethel Wolfe Garrison in the winter of 1937.

> Both my mammy and pappy was brought from Africa on a slave boat and sold on de Richmond (Va.) slave market. What year dey come over I don't know. My mammy was Jane Mason, belonging to Frank Mason; pappy was Frank Smith, belonging to a master wid de same name.....In Richmond, dat's where I was born, 'bout 1847, de Master said; and dat make me more dan 90-year old dis year. All de way from Richmond to a place dey call Waco, Texas, we traveled by ox-wagon and boats, and den de Master figures we all be better off over in Arkansas and goes to Pine Bluff.
> I was at Pine Bluff when de Yankees was shooting all over de place. De fighting got so hot we all had to leave; dat's the way it was all de time for us during the war—running away to some place or de next place, and we was all glad when it stopped and we could settle down in a place.

Lou Smith

83 years old, interviewed in Platter, Oklahoma.

My father was Jackson Longacre and he was born in Mississippi. My mother Caroline, was born in South

Carolina. Both of them was born slaves. My father belonged to Huriah Longacre. He had a big plantation and lots of niggers. He put up a lot of his slaves as security on a debt and he took sick and died so they put them all on de block and sold them. My father and his mother (my grandma) was sold together. My old Mistress bought my grandmother and old Mistress' sister bought my grandma's sister.

They was a white man come into our settlement and bought a plantation and some slaves. My, but he treated them bad. He owned a boy about fifteen years old. One day he sent him on a errand. On the way home he got off his mule and set down in the shade of a tree to rest. He fell asleep and the mule went home. When he woke up he was scared to go home and he stayed out in de woods for several days. Finally they caught him and took him home and his master beat him nearly to death. He then dug a hole and put him in it and piled corn shucks all around him. This nearly killed him 'cause his body was cut up so with the whip. One of the niggers slipped off and went to the jining plantation and told about the way the boy was being treated and a bunch of white men came over and made him take the child out and doctor his wounds. This man lived there about ten years and he was so mean to his slaves 'til all the white men round who owned niggers finally went to him and told him they would just give him so long to sell out and leave. They made him sell his slaves to people there in the community, and he went back north.

My mother told me that he owned a woman who was the mother of several chillun and when her babies would get about a year or two of age he'd sell them and it would break her heart. She never got to keep them. When her fourth baby was born and was about two months old she

> just studied all the time about how she would have to give it up and one day she said, "I just decided I'm not going to let old Master sell this baby; he just ain't going to do it." She got up and give it something out of a bottle and purty soon it was dead. 'Course didn't nobody tell on her or he'd of beat her nearly to death. There wasn't many folks that was mean to their slaves.

The last sentence is interesting commentary and bespeaks how different slaves could have varying impressions of enslavement. Ms. Smith's observations about the cruelty of masters was doubtlessly influenced by the fact that her father was one of the "key slaves" on the plantation. In her narrative she remarks that "Old Master was his own overseer, but my daddy was the overlooker." Regarding slave sales she recalled

> I never saw any niggers on the block but I remember once they had a sale in town and I see them pass our house in gangs, the little ones in wagons and others walking. I've seen slaves who run away from their masters and they'd have to work in the field with a big ball and chain on their leg. They'd hoe out to the end of the chain and then drag it up a piece and hoe on to the end of the row.

Mollie Watson

Ms. Watson was interviewed in Colbert Oklahoma in the

Autumn of 1937 by Jessie R. Ervin. She was enslaved in Centerville, Leon County, and was owned by Squire (Thomas) Garner. Sebastian Stroud, Garner's son, was her master. This interview was never sent to Washington (Baker & Baker 1997: 145) and the copy in the Oklahoma archives is the only known copy.

> Speciators uster buy up niggers jest lak dey was animals and dey would travel around over de country an' sell 'em. I've seen 'em come through there in droves lak cattle. De owners would ride in wagons or buggies. Dey would come into town an' camp over night an' nex' mornin' dey would parade 'em round town an' take 'em to de town square an' put 'em on de block an' sell 'em. I've seen men, wives an' little children sold away from each other...When de sales would be goin' on me an' Billy an' Sue [Sebastian Stroud's children] would ride our stick horses up purty close an' watch 'em. I wasn't scared cause I knowed Ole Miss an' Squire Garner was settin' on de gallery a watchin' it jest lak we was an' I knowed she would keep me safe.

John White

Mr. White, who was 121 years of age when he was interviewed by the Federal Writers Project during the summer of 1937, was born in Augusta, Georgia and was sold to Texas based planter's wife Sarah Davenport when he was eleven. His original master—and perhaps his father—was James White. Ms. Davenport and her husband lived in north Texas, probably Cass county. Upon being sold by his old master, Mr. White recalled the anguish of seeing his mother for the last time (Baker & Baker 1997: 120-127):

> Master White always selling and trading to folks all over the country. I hates to leave on account of Mammy and the good way Master White fared the slaves—they was good people. Mammy cry but I has to go just the same. The tears are on my face a long time after the leaving. I was hoping all the time to see Mammy again, but that's the last time.
> We travels and travels on the stage coach. Once we cross the Big River (Mississippi) on the boat and pick up with the horses on the other side. A new outfit and we rides some more. Seems like we going to wear out all the horses before we gets to the place.
> The Davenport plantation was way north of Linden, Texas, up in the Red River country. That's where I stayed for thirty-eight year. There I was drug through the hackles by the meanest master that ever lived. The mistress was the best white woman I ever knew but Master Presley used his whip all the time, reason or no reason, and I got scars to remember by!

It appears that Mr. White's master was not only cruel, but

unprincipled. It appears that Presley Davenport, unlike some planters, sold his children into slavery.

> After a while they'd be a new baby. Yellow. When the child got old enough for chore work the master would sell him (or her). No difference was it his own flesh and blood—if the price was right!

The Peculiar Experiences of Female Enslavement

Women and girls faced particular obstacles and difficulties under conditions of slavery, problems which male slaves for the most part did not face. In this regard, Du Bois's (1986[1920]: 958) landmark essay "The Damnation of Women" remains one of the most impassioned intellectual and moral ass-chewings of the twentieth century. Regarding miscegenation, Du Bois writes:

> Many a man and woman in the South have lived in wedlock as holy as Adam and Eve and brought forth their brown and golden children, but because the darker woman was helpless, her chivalrous and whiter mate could cast her off at his pleasure and publicly sneer at the body he had privately blasphemed.

Du Bois goes on to note, in one of his more famous passages:

> I shall forgive the white South much in its final judgment day: I shall forgive its slavery, for slavery is a world-old habit; I shall forgive its fighting for a well-lost cause, and for remembering that struggle with tender tears; I shall forgive its so-called "pride of race," the passion of its hot blood, and even its dear, old laughable strutting and posing; but one thing I shall never forgive, neither in this world nor the world to come: its wanton and continued and persistent insulting of the black womanhood which it sought and seeks to prostitute to its lust. I cannot forget that it is such Southern gentlemen into whose hands smug Northern hypcrites of today are seeking to place our women's eternal destiny,—men who insist upon withholding from my mother and wife and daughter those signs and appelations of courtesy and respect which elsewhere he withholds only from bawds and courtesans.

Du Bois seems pretty clear here; the most egregious insult suffered under slavery, male or female, was the devaluation and sexualization of the enslaved Negro female. But in the following paragraph, Du Bois—in a tone that seems strangely "Foucauldian" today—notes that the unearned suffering endured by enslaved women was also redemptive (as Martin Luther King famously proclaimed) and "produced" certain positive traits:

> The result of this history of insult and degradation has

> been both fearful and glorious. It has birthed the haunting prostitute, the brawler, and the beast of burden; but it has also given the world an efficient womanhood, whose strength lies in its freedom and whose chastity was won in the teeth of temptation and not in prison and swadding clothes.[168]

When Du Bois wrote *Damnation*, he was still in what might be termed a "pre-Marxist" phase. Subsequent scholars such as Angela Davis (1981: 6) have put a more recognizably Marxist spin on the lack of sexual freedom experienced by female slaves:

> Where work was concerned, strength and productivity under the threat of the whip outweighed considerations of sex. In this sense, the oppression of women was identical to the oppression of men......But women suffered in different ways as well, for they were victims of sexual abuse and other barbarous mistreatment that could only be inflicted on women. Expediency governed the slaveholders' posture toward female slaves: when it was profitable to exploit them as if they were men, they were regarded, in effect, as genderless, but when they could be exploited, punished and repressed in ways suited only for women, they were locked into their exclusively female roles.

---

[168] Earlier Du Bois (1986[1920]: 957) observes: "Yet to save from the past the shreds and vestiges of self-respect has been a terrible task. I most sincerely doubt if any other race of women could have brought its fineness up through so devilish a fire."

Davis goes on to note (1981: 25) that "virtually all the slave narratives of the nineteenth century contain accounts of slave women's sexual victimization at the hands of masters and overseers." The same could be said of the WPA narratives of the late 1930's. Many of the women enslaved in Texas, for instance, had strong recollections of sexual abuse, either as victims or as friends or relatives of women who had been molested.

Another theme that is fairly consistent throughout the narratives is the physical and verbal abuse suffered by enslaved women at the hands of their white mistresses, particularly during the Civil War. Perhaps the harsh pressures of Texas frontier life, the stresses of being separated from husbands off fighting in a losing war, the rampant sexism of nineteenth century white American society, and exploitation at the hands of their husbands led white mistresses to lash out at their house and (occasionally) their field slaves. Then again, probably not. While the aforementioned factors doubtlessly played a role in the physical abuse and other forms of exploitative treatment white mistresses meted out to their female slaves, Black feminists[169] have been pointing out the real (and primary) reason why Black women suffered oftentimes cruel and harsh treatment at the hands of their mistresses: racism. The following narratives are representative of the sorts of experiences African-American women and girls faced under enslavement and describe, among other things, forced breeding and marriage, physical abuse, and sexual exploitation.[170]

---

[169] Ida B. Wells's poignant and influential analyses of the sexual politics of lynching are particularly noteworthy here, especially since they were one of the earlier critiques of white female "virtue." Many of Wells's ideas were picked up by later twentieth century Black feminists. Joy James (1997: 46-54), while otherwise praising Du Bois, constructively criticizes and castigates him for not mentioning the key role of Wells in the anti-lynching crusade at the turn of the twentieth century, for at least passively letting Wells be excluded from the Niagara Movement and the NAACP, and for being an elitist generally.

[170] My citation of these narratives is not intended to portray a monolithic and passive picture of female life under slavery. Women found all sorts of ways, big and small, to exercise their agency even under the emotional and psychological shackles of enslavement. The point I wish to make here is that female slaves were people and mostly acted and reacted to their peculiar situation in the way that most people under similar circumstances would behave. No more, no less. Another point I wish to emphasize is that both male and female slaves were keenly aware of the exploitative and hypocritical nature of their bondage, and where possible resisted it at every turn (for the most part). Slave "passivity" and seeming "lack of agency" should be seen as being part of the system of "limited adjustment to the sheer power of masters" described by Tadman 1996[1989]: xv, xxiv) and described in preceding chapters.

Rose Williams

Ms. Williams, 90 years of age, was enslaved in Bell County and was interviewed in Fort Worth. Her narrative provides an excellent example of the degree to which masters valued fecundity in their female slaves and points out the lengths to which masters went to encourage their female slaves to reproduce (Tyler & Murphy 1974: 21).

> There's one thing Massa Hawkins did to me that I can't shut from my mind. I know he didn't do it for meanness, but I always held it against him. What he did was force me to live with that nigger Rufus, against my wants. After I had been at his place about a year, the massa came to me and said, "You're going to live with Rufus in that cabin over yonder. Go fix it for living." I was just sixteen years old and had no learning, And I was just an ignorant child. I thought that meant for me to tend the cabin for Rufus and some other niggers. Well, that was the start of pestigation for me.
> I took charge of the cabin after work was done and fixed supper. Now, I didn't like that Rufus, cause he was a bully. He was big and cause of that he thought everybody should do what he said. We had supper, then I went here and there talking till I was ready for sleep, and then I got in the bunk. After I was in, that nigger came and crawled in the bunk with me before I knew it. I said, "What do you mean, you fool nigger." He said for me to hush the mouth. "This is my bunk, too," he said.

"You're touched in the head. Get out." I told him, and I put the feet against him and gave him a shove and out he went on the floor before he knew what I was doing. That nigger jumped up, and he was mad. He looked like a wild boar. He started for the bunk, and I jumped quickly for the poker. It was about three feet long, and when he came at me I let him have it over the head. Did that nigger stop in his tracks? I'll say he did. He looked at me steady for a minute, and you could tell he was thinking hard. Then he went and sat on the bench and said, "Just wait. You think you is smart, but you are foolish in the head. They're going to learn you something."
"Hush your big mouth and stay away from this nigger. That's all I want," I said, and just sat and held that poker in the hand. He just sat, looking like the bull. There we sat and sat for about an hour, then he went out, and I barred the door.
The next day I went to see the missy and told her what Rufus wanted, and missy said that was the massa's wishes. She said, "You are the portly gal, and Rufus is the portly man. The massa wants you to bring forth portly children."
I was thinking about what the missy said, but said to myself, "I'm not going to live with that Rufus." That night when he came in the cabin I grabbed the poker and sat on the bench and said, "Get away from me nigger, before I bust your brains out and stomp on them." He said nothing and got out.
The next day the massa called me and told me, "Woman, I've paid big money for you, and I've done that for the cause I want you to raise me children. I've put you to live with Rufus for that purpose. Now, if you don't want a whipping at the stake, you do what I want."
I thought about massa buying me off of the block and

saving me from being separated from my folks and about whipping at the stake. There I was. What was I to do? So I decided to do as massa wished, and so I yielded.

Betty Powers

Eighty years of age and complaining of a failing memory, Ms. Powers was enslaved and interviewed in Harrison County (Tyler & Murphy 1974: 36).

> ....Did we have weddings?....You know better than that. Those colored folks were just put together. The massa said, "Jim and Nancy, you go live together," and when that order was given, it better be done. They thought nothing on the plantation about the feelings of the women, and there was no respect for them. The overseer and white men took advantage of the women like they wanted to. The women had better not make a fuss about such. If she did, it was the whipping for her. I sure thank the Lord surrender came before I was old enough to stand for such. Yes sir, surrender saved this nigger from such.

Lizzie Jones

Ms. Jones was born in Harrison County and was interviewed near Karnack. She was 86 years of age at the time of the interview. She also confirms that slaves had very little agency in deciding upon a marriage partner (Tyler & Murphy

1974: 41).

> Slaves weren't married by no Good Book or law neither. They'd just take up with each other and go up to the Big House and ask massa to let them marry. If they were old enough, he'd say to the boy, "Take her and go home."

Lewis Jones

Mr. Jones was born in 1851 on a Colorado River plantation and was interviewed in Forth Worth. His master was Fred Tate. In his narrative, Mr. Jones indicates that his master bred slaves and that his father had sired nearly fifty children (Tyler & Murphy 1974: 45-46).

> How many brothers and sisters? Lord, all mighty. I'll tell you because you asked, and this nigger gives facts as this. Let's see. I can't recollect the number. My pappy had 12 children by my mammy and 12 by another nigger named Mary. You keep the count. Then there was Liza, he had 10 by her; and there was Mandy, he had 8 by her; and there was Betty, he had six by her. Now let me recollect some more. I can't bring the names to mind, but there were two or three others who had had one or two children by my pappy. That was right. Close to 50 children, cause my mammy done told me. It was thisaway, my pappy was the breeding nigger.

Katie Darling

88 years of age at the time of her interview, Ms. Darling (whose name was the same as a ship mentioned by Mariah Robinson in her narrative) was raised in Marshall. Her narrative relates the reaction of her mistress to Civil War fighting.

> I remember that fight at Mansfield like it was yesterday. Massa's field was all torn up with cannon holes and every time a cannon fired, missy went off in a rage. One time when a cannon fired, she said to me, "You little black wench, you niggers aren't going to be free. You're made to work for white folks." About that time she looked up and saw a Yankee soldier standing in the door with a pistol. She said "Katie, I didn't say anything did I?" I said, "I'm not telling a lie; you said niggers aren't going to get free."

Mary Gaffney

Ms. Gaffney's observations about slave trading were cited earlier in this chapter. The following is the portion of her narrative dealing with her forced marriage (Rawick 1979: 1453).

> When I married it was just home wedding, fact is I just hated the man I married but it was what Maser said do. When he came to Texas he took up big lots of land and he

was going to-get rich. He put another negro man with my mother, then he put one with me. I would not let that negro touch me and he told Maser and Maser gave me a real good whipping, so that night I let that negro have his way. Maser was going to raise him a lot more slaves, but still I cheated Maser, I never did have any slaves to grow and Maser he wondered what was the matter. I tell you son, I kept cotton roots and chewed them all the time but I was careful not to let Maser know or catch me, so I never did have any children while I was a slave. Then when slavery was over I just kept on living with that negro, his name was Paul Gaffney.

Fannie Norman

Ms. Norman, interviewed in Fort Worth, was born in Austin in 1859 and was owned by James Jackson, a professional gambler. Her mother was purchased by Jackson in a New Orleans slave market. Although "only" 78 at the time of the interview, Ms. Norman's interview provides valuable information on the manner in which slaves were brought into Texas and further confirmation that female slaves were often forced into marriages and other domestic arrangements (Rawick 1979: 2927).

Thar am not much to de story of my slave life. Ise bo'n

in 1859 so dat makes me jus' si yeahs old w'en freedom come to weuns an' my age am now 78. Ise bo'n in Austin, Travis County, Texas. Marster James Jackson owned my mammy an' me. Weuns am de only slaves dat Marster owned. He bought my mammy at de slave market in New O'leans f'om a nigger driver. What am a nigger driver? De nigger driver am a party dat goes 'round de country buyin' an' sellin' slaves. W'en my mammy am sold dat parts her f'om all her fouah chillun. 'Bout her husband, 'twas de rule on many plantations in slave times dat de women can't have any regular husband. Dey am fo'ced to live wid de one de Marster tells dem to an' m'ybe dey live first wid one an' tudder man.

Ida Henry

Ms. Henry was born in Marshall in 1854. She and her mother were purchased in South Carolina and were brought to Texas by the white slaveowning Hall family.[171] Ms. Henry worked as a house slave and performed duties such as sewing, nursing, and cooking. Her narrative indicates the sort of snappy and racist reactions to which house slaves could be

---

[171] According to Baker & Baker (1997:135) there were four white "Hall" families enumerated in the 1860 census, although none of them appear to have held as many slaves as Ms. Henry says were on the plantation on which she worked. According to Ms. Henry "Master's plantation was about 300 acres and he had 'bout 160 slaves," although of the four Halls mentioned in the census the largest slaveholder was M.J. Hall who is listed as owning 34 bondspeople. Who was correct? The census taker or the slave?

subjected at the hands of their mistresses.

> Me Mistress was sometimes good and sometimes mean. One day de cook was waiting de table and when passing around de potatoes, old Mistress felt of one and as hit wasn't soft done, she exclaimed to de cook, "What you bring these raw potatoes out her for?" and grab a fork and stuck it in her eye and put hit out. She, de cook, lived about 10 years and died.

Harriet Robinson

A brief biographical sketch of Ms. Robinson was provided earlier. Her mistress was a particularly cruel and racist woman:

> Slaves was punished by whip and starving. Deck was sho' a mean slave-holder. He lived close to us. Master Sam didn't never whup me, but Miss Julia whipped me every day in the mawning. During the war she beat us so terrible. She say, "You master's out fighting and losing blood trying to save you from them Yankees, so you kin git your'n here." Miss Julia would take me by my ears and butt my head against the wall. She wanted to whip my mother, but old Master told her, naw sir. When his father done give my mammy to Master Sam, he told him not to beat her, and iffen he got to whar he just had to, jest bring her back and place her in his yard from whar he got her.
> White folks didn't 'low you to read or write. Them what did know come from Virginny. Mistress Julia used to drill her chillun in spelling any words. At every word

them chillun missed, she gived me a lick 'cross the heads for it. Meanest woman I ever seen in my whole life.

Lou Smith

Ms. Smith had particularly harsh recollections of mistreatment at the hands of her mistress, and his gruesome portion of her narrative indicates the cruelties white women could inflict on slave children. Ms. Smith was interviewed by Jessie R. Ervin in Platter, Oklahoma in the spring or summer of 1937.

> Miss Jo wasn't a good Mistress and mother and me wasn't happy. When young Master was there he made her treat us good but when he was gone she made our lives a misery to us. She was what we called a "low-brow." She never had been used to slaves and she treated us like dogs. She said us kids didn't need to wear any clothes and one day she told us we could jest take 'em off as it cost too much to clothe us. I was jest a little child but I knowed I oughten to go without clothes. We wore little enough as it was. In summer we just wore one garment, a sort of slip without any sleeves. Well, anyway, she made me take off my clothes and I just crept off and cried.
> She wouldn't feed us niggers. She'd make me set in a corner like a little dog. I got so hungry and howled so loud they had to feed me. When the surrender come, I was eleven years old, and they told us we was free. I ran

off and hid in the plum orchard and I said over'n over, "I'se free, I'se free; I ain't never going back to Miss Jo."

CHAPTER 8: THE USE AND ABUSE OF TEXAS HISTORY ..

The process of creating and entrenching highly selective, reshaped or completely fabricated memories of the past is what we call "indoctrination" or "propaganda" when it is conducted by official enemies, and "education," "moral instruction" or "character building," when we do it ourselves. It is a valuable mechanism of control, since it effectively blocks any understanding of what is happening in the world."
—*Noam Chomsky (Peck 1987: 124)*

In one of the less quoted portions of his most famous speech,[172] Frederick Douglass (Andrews 1996[1852]: 119-120) declaimed the two-faced and cruel practice of the internal slave trade and denounced the supposed universality of America's self-proclaimed freedoms as being the most cruel of shams:

> Go where you may, search where you will, roam through all the monarchies and despotisms of the old world, travel through South America, search out every abuse, and when you have found the last, lay your facts by the side of every day practices of this nation, and you will

---

[172] This speech, "What to the Slave is the Fourth of July?" is not only significant as one of the masterpieces of American abolitionist oratory; like Lincoln's Gettysburg Address, the speech should also be seen as an American literary classic. One of the many strengths of the speech are its numerous and powerful usages of maritime metaphor and alliteration. Early in the speech, for instance, Douglass simultaneously informs white Americans to take justified pride in their Fourth of July celebrations, but also warns that dark and gloomy clouds lie ahead:

> From the round top of your ship of state, dark and threatening clouds may be seen. Heavy billows, like mountains in the distance, disclose to the leeward huge forms of flinty rocks! That *bolt* drawn, that *chain* broken, and all is lost. *Cling to this day—cling to it,* and to its principles, with the grasp of a storm-tossed mariner to a spar at midnight.

say with me, that, for revolting barbarity and shameless hypocrisy, American reigns without a rival.

Regarding the barbarity of the internal slave trade, Douglass observed:

> I was born amid such sights and scenes. To me the American slave trade is a terrible reality. When a child, my soul was often pierced with a sense of its horrors. I lived on Philpot Street, Fell's Point, Baltimore, and have watched from the wharves, the slave ships in the Basin, anchored from the shore, with their cargoes of human flesh, waiting for favorable winds to waft them down the Chesapeake. There was, at that time, a grand slave mart kept at the head of Pratt Street, by Austin Woolfolk. His agents were sent into every town and county in Maryland, announcing their arrival, through the papers, and on flaming *"hand bills,"* headed CASH FOR NEGROES. These men were generally well dressed men, and very captivating in their manners. Ever ready to drink, to treat, and to gamble.

It is truly regrettable that the processes of the "Invention of Tradition" (Hobsbawm & Ranger 1983) in Texas have written out the extensive history of slavery and slave trading in the Lone Star State and have produced in a significant portion of the Texas population a boisterous and manufactured pride and self-congratulation that in its softer variants can be seen as simply funny, but in its harder versions can also be quite mean-spirited and callous. In a sense, the "Texas" Myth of the Alamo and of free-ranging cattle and cowboys is not just a Texas phenomenon; men such as John Wayne, the person perhaps most responsible for the epic filming of the Disney version of the Alamo story, viewed the story of Texas independence as nothing less than the story of America itself (Graham 2000).

From a more contemporary African-American perspective, the Texas Myth takes on some added dimensions, especially politically. Prominent Afro-Texans that directly and straightforwardly question or criticize the master narrative are taking a significant political risk. The "white" power structure[173] understands this, which is why it continues to invent and reinvent new or reformulated Texas traditions and invests so much energy in ensuring that Texas schoolchildren

---

[173] This power structure is not made up exclusively of white males. It includes a variety of individuals from all races, ethnicities, and genders.

are brought up "right"; i.e. as proud and proper Texans.[174] The strategy employed by the commissars seems to be—as it has always been—to compel Black leadership in Texas to remain silent (or meaninglessly vocal) on many of the most fundamental and deep-seated grievances experienced by the Black community at large. In exchange for this, political crumbs and table scraps such as contracts, prestigious positions, and other financial or political rewards are thrown in the direction of Black leaders, who then play their own political patronage games at the local level. Many of these "leaders" are

---

[174] Baker & Baker (1997: xx) repeat the conventional historical wisdom regarding the sacrosanct Texas Revolution: "When revolution broke out between Texas settlers and Mexico in 1835, slavery was not the cause, but it was a contributing influence." This is the Anglo version. The Mexican and Black versions are different. Why do almost all Anglo Texas scholars feel such a seemingly deep-seated need to perpetuate and re-perpetuate this falsehood? Slavery and race are the defining sociopolitical realities of American history, yet we are to believe that Texas was somehow spared this unfortunate curse? As I discuss in chapter 4, although the Texas Declaration of Independence and Constitutions are clearly based on their American predecessors, they are NOT the same documents either philosophically or functionally. The John Wayne/Disney version of Texas history would have us believe that the Texan battle for independence was a noble and idealistic struggle to extend [white] American freedoms across the North American continent. It would have us believe that the conflict did not involve specific and identifiable interests, and that it was a battle for universal and enduring rights and freedoms. It wasn't. That war was controversial from the outset and in many ways presaged the Civil War. But John Wayne surely was perceptive enough: a significant portion of American identity is embodied in the "story of Texas" (the theme of the Bob Bullock Texas history museum currently under construction as of this writing).

in one way or another affiliated with certain segments of the Black church.[175] One of the conditions of allowing certain Black leaders access to the portals of Texas power is the requirement that the leadership do its dutiful part to convince its constituency to accept the Texas Myth, i.e. to cast their own stake in the dominant narrative of Texas exceptionalism and ultimate munificence. In other words, the challenge becomes getting the Black masses in Texas to understand that the price for race and class progress in the near and distant future is acceptance of the basic tenets of "Imperial Texas" and so forth. The implication of this "one Texas" type of ideology is that a special belief in the unique history and destiny of Texas—not concrete political gains and a more redistributive social policy—can be the solvent for racism.

---

[175] One of the more insightful analyses of "the ambiguous politics of the Black church" is in Marable (1983:206) where he observes that "more than other Blacks, the clergy commonly shared an unstated antipathy for atheism in any form, and possessed a class-oriented commitment to the acquisition of private property and Black petty capitalism." He goes on to note that "they are not prepared to repudiate the system which rewards their own political accommodation at the expense of the continued exploitation of Black working class and poor people" (Marable 1983: 211).

With relatively few exceptions, this sort of patronage masquerade explains much of the structure of post-Civil War Black politics in Texas, especially in the twentieth century. As might be expected, one of the largest organizations invested in this sort of civil rights strategy is the Texas NAACP. As of this writing, Gary Bledsoe, the chair of the organization, has written current Governor and Republican presidential nominee George W. Bush about the offensiveness of the Confederate battle flag (Stanley 2000: B5) which still flies in various official places of business in Texas, most notably on a plaque at the Texas Supreme Court. But regarding the Lone Star Flag, Bledsoe is not as adamant in voicing his displeasure—in fact he instead encourages all Black Texans to boldly display their Texas Pride:

> The Lone Star flag is a proud symbol because people have equal rights in the state now despite their race. Texas righted its wrongs, whereas the Confederacy never did. That's a big difference......Speaking for myself, I may have some concerns over what triggered the war and the fact that it did not free my ancestors, but I celebrate Texas Independence Day for what Texas is today and the promise it holds for tomorrow for all Texans (Stanley

2000: B5).

Bledsoe's degree of strategic denial is monumental, but all too common. If race relations in Texas are now so wonderful, why is his organization still needed? The sad truth—which Bledsoe knows but is not outspoken about—is that Texas is in many ways the most racist and unreconstructed state in the country. Its appalling and unapologetic environmental[176] racism toward minorities has been amply documented (see Bullard 1987, Bullard 1992, and Feagin 1988), its level of social spending for pressing needs such as homelessness, poverty, housing, and equitable education is pathetic for such a large state, its regressive taxation system (no income tax, heavy reliance on sales and property taxes) is unfair and places a disproportionate burden on the poor, and its undeniably racist

---

[176] "Texas has very dirty air. According to the North American Commission on Environmental Cooperation set up by NAFTA, we pollute more than any other state or Canadian province. According to the Environmental Protection Agency, Texas is No. 1 in overall toxic releases, recognized carcinogens in the air, developmental toxins in the air, cancer risk and 10 other equally depressing categories" (Ivins 2000: 22). Many of the petrochemical complexes along the Texas gulf coast are located in predominantly minority neighborhoods (Corpus Christi is a good example).

and classist criminal justice system is an appalling disgrace.[177] It is unacceptable and unfortunate that the Black leadership of Texas is letting the power structure of the state get away with using an over-optimistic and romanticized notion of Texas Pride in order to perpetuate injustice; the interests of Black Texans at large (and not just an elite clique) are not well served by such a retrograde political strategy.

My critique of Barbara Jordan in the introduction of this dissertation and of Gary Bledsoe and the African-American leadership of Texas in this chapter is not meant to impugn them and their accomplishments personally; the point I wish to make is to suggest that their brand of neo-plantation

---

[177] "When George W. Bush, presidential candidate and Governor of Texas began his tenure in Texas, 41,000 [persons] were in prison there. Now there are 150,000" (*Z Magazine* 2000: 4). A significant proportion of Texas's Black male population is disenfranchised due to laws that prevent "criminals" from voting. This is a national problem:

> In Florida, for example, one in three African-American male voters is barred from voting. In Texas, 21 percent of the black population is disenfranchised. In five other states, more than one-fourth of all black men are permanently stripped of the vote. In 1996, 4.6 million African-American men voted; 1.4 million were legally disenfranchised. Given current rates of incarceration, 30 percent of black men will be disenfranchised at some point in their life. This Jim Crow law is now more than decimating the black male vote (Jackson 2000: 19).

politicking is not suitable for the twenty-first century and is in need of some significant progressive invigoration. Their Black variant of Texas Pride elitism represents a specific brand of regional political accommodation to the white male power structure.[178] The price Black Texans have paid and continue to pay for the fact that their leadership has bought into the sanctioned narrative of Texas history is that the recently increasing ranks of the Black working poor and jobless are politically marginalized and economically exploited. The solution to these structural inequalities, so the master narrative goes, is not systemic change; rather, "proud" Texans, individualistic and strong, dust themselves off and pull themselves up by the bootstraps like their revolutionary forefathers and foremothers. The employment of this sort of doleful rhetoric continues to justify ongoing Texas-sized

---

[178] It also represents a peculiarly Texas-based need to build memorials. Rep. Al Edwards' (D-Houston) recently formed Juneteenth Commission, for example, instead of launching educational and outreach inititiatives about the real history of Black Texas that could challenge the master narrative, instead intends to build statues and monuments around the state (and the country), all of which, of course, have to have Rep. Edwards' name on them. These sorts of cult of personality politics are another negative aspect of Black Texas accommodationism.

lectures on "personal responsibility" to former welfare recipients, public housing residents and youth offenders, among others. When was the last time that "personal initiative," "deferral of gratification" or similar personal traits produced a living wage job? The end effect is that on questions such as this, the Texas Myth individualizes complicated social problems, excuses gross social and economic exploitation by an arrogant and stupid elite, and diminishes awareness of what actually occurred in Texas history.

"Means Testing" Historical Significance

The point that Texas history is misused to perpetuate injustice is not merely a theoretical one. There are many case studies one could use to make the point that history and historic preservation in Texas are woefully racist and corrupt. The fiascos surrounding the destruction and gentrification of Black communities throughout Texas (and minority communities generally), in order to facilitate speedy and greedy development are illustrative of how historical significance is always a politically contested phenomenon, and how unequal power relations are constitutive of what becomes understood as historical "fact." The material remains of history (sites, buildings, neighborhoods, etc.) symbolize what a power structure considers to be historically significant. To paraphrase George Orwell (Loewen 1999: 197): "Who controls the present controls the landscape. Who controls the landscape controls the future." In Texas, "history" and historical commemoration are defined as "Anglo history." Mexican-American, Native American, and African-American history are considered historically relevant only to the degree that they contribute to the master narrative; and minority history that challenges the master narrative certainly will never be included in tourist brochures.[179] The politics of National Register inclusion or

---

[179] A recently produced Texas Historical Commission brochure on African-American historical sites in Texas (brochure title: "African Americans in Texas: Historical & Cultural Legacies), for instance, leaves out Allen Parkway Village in Houston and the Old Bear Creek Cemetery in Arlington, two highly significant, yet controversial and contested, African-American historical sites. The last section of the brochure, the visitor information section, contains a listing of Chambers of Commerce for the respective cities cited in the document. This is logical; history, like culture is a commodity.

exclusion are a good example of how these sorts of conceptions play themselves out.

The state agency that probably plays the leading role in the process of Texas Myth making is the Texas Historical Commission, which oversees a state historical marker program that contains more historical markers than the rest of the United States combined,[180] and commemorates everything from the mundane to the bizarre—if it exalts the "right" things. A majority of the current board members of "the state agency for historic preservation" are George W. Bush appointees.

A recent and ongoing controversy in Houston, for example, concerns itself with the Freedmen's Town section of Fourth Ward, the cultural and historical heart of Black Houston.

---

[180] "Texas has nearly 12,000 historical markers—more than the rest of the United States combined. When I remarked about this to various Texas officials, they shrugged as if to say, 'Well, we've had more history!' But Texas hasn't. Moreover, like other states, Texas refrains from recognizing events that might embarrass or offend local communities" (Loewen 1999: 195). I would disagree with Loewen somewhat; while it certainly is true that Texas refrains from recognizing controversial historical sites, it is not braggadocio to recognize that Texas does have more history than many places in the United States. Furthermore, after years of propaganda it is undeniable that the Alamo and the "story of Texas" hold a powerful place in the American imagination. Rightly or wrongly, people believe that Texas is a powerful historical place. This belief operates squarely at the convergence of Trouillot's (1995) convergence of two historicities; it is a combination of historical fact and the power of myth.

More specifically, the conflict is about Allen Parkway Village, formerly a 1,000 unit public housing complex built in the early 1940's for returning white war veterans. Fourth Ward and Allen Parkway Village sit in the western edge of Houston's central business district and occupy some of the most coveted real estate in Houston.[181] The neighborhood, which is boxed in on all sides by more affluent surroundings, is inhabited by predominantly minority renters, and the houses in the neighborhood are some of the most representative examples of

---

[181] Fourth Ward is Houston's oldest and most historically significant black neighborhood. It began to be settled by African Americans shortly after Texas emancipation on June 19, 1865 (commonly referred to as "Juneteenth") when former slaves from plantations in the Brazos river valley emigrated to Houston in search of jobs. They named the area "Freedmantown" and established a thriving community of black businesses and churches and developed a tightly-knit network of cultural and social institutions. By the 1880's most of the land in Freedmantown was owned by black settlers into the area, whereas adjacent Fourth Ward neighborhoods were principally occupied by renters. But the depression of the 1920's and 30's hit the area hard, and by 1980 less than 5 percent of the housing in the area was owner occupied (Bullard 1987: 15). After 1930, due to discrimination and other factors, the neighborhood began to deteriorate and much of the housing stock and neighborhood amenities declined significantly in quality. Allen Parkway Village, a public housing project built in the early 1940's as an all white development for returning war veterans, sits atop what used to be the original Freedmantown settlement. Before San Felipe Courts (the original name of Allen Parkway Village) could be built, the land had to first be cleared of all inhabitants. Utilizing newly enacted eminent domain laws, the city's public housing authority acquired the land in the late 1930's, evicted the mostly Black tenants from their homes, and built a fence around the property to separate it from the nearly all-Black surrounding neighborhood. The historical significance of that property was not considered relevant then. Over sixty years later, it still isn't; the property is not considered historically "significant" for the right reasons. Chapter 8 of Williams' *Bricks Without Straw* (Maxwell 1997: 125-152) contains a good general historical overview of Freedmantown.

turn-of-the-century vernacular urban and semi-urban architecture in the south. In the mid 1970's the city of Houston and then mayor Fred Hofheinz, citing "inevitable economic progress," decided that Allen Parkway Village was "urban blight" and should be demolished. There was resistance on the part of the tenants, most notably Lenwood Johnson of the Allen Parkway Village residents' council, who sued the housing authority, exposed their corrupt and illegal strong-arming tactics, and prevented demolition of the property. Until 1994; that is when the "Republican revolution" took place in Washington and the remaining compassion for the poor was expunged from national governance. House majority Whip Tom Delay—who does not represent Fourth Ward in Congress—decided to take a more active interest in ensuring the destruction of the neighborhood (many of the developers in line to develop the site were contributors to his campaign), and along with an acquiescent Congresswoman Sheila Jackson-Lee saw to it that statutory and other safeguards that prevented the destruction of APV were either repealed or bypassed. The Housing Authority of the City of Houston received a demolition permit from HUD in 1995 and after forcibly evicting the last few remaining families at the site, promptly began demolition using funds from a HOPE VI grant it had received the year before.

Certain Cultural Resource Management firms specialize in cultivating "mutually beneficial" relationships with developers, as observers of the destruction of Techwood Homes in Atlanta or of Cabrini Extension in Chicago know all too well. In Texas, where there is no shortage of such firms, one of the better examples is Espey Huston & Associates, which was awarded the Section 106 mitigation contract for APV in 1995, with Steven Hoyt, now the state Marine Archaeologist, as lead investigator.

Residents of APV and Fourth Ward, some of whom had worked on the construction of Allen Parkway Village when it was first built, repeatedly notified officials that there was a cemetery located somewhere in the northwest portion of the site. They were ignored. Espey Huston and its employer released repeated press releases—faithfully reported almost word for word by the local ministry of truth, the Houston Chronicle—claiming that "extensive" test trenching had revealed the presence of no burials on the site. Until January of 1998. That is when construction workers installing plumbing began to unearth body parts. As per the programmatic agreement signed by the Advisory Council for Historic Preservation, the Texas Historical Commission, HUD, and the Housing Authority (the residents were excluded from meaningfully participating in the Section 106 process and refused to sign the agreement), construction stopped and a more thorough assessment of the site was undertaken. This did not result in a major modification of the excavation strategy, since investors had placed all the contractors under considerable pressure to start construction right away. The end result is that more smoothbladed backhoes and grade-alls were used on this

National Register site.[182]

The story of the destruction and gentrification of Allen Parkway Village and Fourth Ward is long and complex but not that unusual. Underlying the justifications put forth for the easy dismissal of the inconvenient history represented by the neighborhood, and the necessary speedy "renaissance" of the area are a particular and peculiar conception of historical significance. In the contemporary political economy of urban Texas, history—especially minority history—is viewed as a special sort of commodity that can be employed quite profitably by real estate speculators. Texas history is a sort of carte blanche that can be strategically invoked whenever deemed necessary. Smart Texas real estate developers, who like their Negro speculating forebears generally value money

---

[182] The major reason why EH&A and Mark Denton of the THC felt comfortable with such a crude excavation strategy for such a sensitive site is that the "historical study" of the area performed by Janet K. Wagner, a landscape architect, indicated that nothing of significance would be found there. Ms. Wagner's racist historical "study" was fatally flawed and was deliberately designed to understate 19th century African American presence in the area. But it did provide "legal" justification for the destruction and "renaissance" of the neighborhood, which was the point all along anyway.

more than history, nonetheless have a thorough understanding of historic tax credit procedure as part of their investment toolkits.[183] What could be better than an opportunity to "do good" and make money at the same time?

Military Sites and What Else?

One of the best—perhaps the best—guides to dominant/elite sentiment concerning history and historic preservation in Texas is a publication titled *On Sacred Soil: Preserving Texas Military Sites of the Nineteenth Century*, which contains the proceedings of the Nineteenth Century Texas Military Sites Conference. There are many things of interest in the document, but most notable are the statements of historical significance made by the Texas' historic preservation establishment and their benefactors in the Texas

---

[183] A good beginning guide to the structure and use of historic tax credits is the Department of the Interior publication *Affordable Housing Through Historic Preservation*.

legislature.[184] In reiterating his political support for preserving Texas heritage, House speaker Pete Laney, for instance proclaimed that

> those of you who are from other states may have heard that Texans tend to be somewhat proud of their state. Well, that's putting it very mildly. We're very proud, and a big part of that Texas pride is probably based on our fascinating history, including our struggle to settle this frontier—and my part of the state was a frontier not very many years ago—our legacy as an independent nation, and our determination, of all people, to develop Texas into a thriving state (Graves et. al. 1997: 9).

Most revealing, however, were the comments of Frances Kennedy of the Arlington, VA based Conservation Fund. In her speech, Dr. Kennedy described what sets her organization apart:

> We believe that economic and environmental returns can be compatible. The Fund is the first national conservation organization whose charter includes economic development and conservation as primary goals.

She went on to note that historic preservation and economic

---

[184] Although there are some notable exceptions, many members of the Texas legislature are utterly incompetent and ignorant about Texas history (the same, probably more, applies to the governor's appointees to the Texas Historical Commission board), albeit when the occasion demands it they act as if they were geniuses of Texana. Their superficial understanding of Texas history, especially multicultural history, is another example of Texas white supremacy.

"development" can (should) go hand-in-hand:

> Protected historic land functions as a basic industry for a community: it creates jobs, buys services, and brings money into the community. And it is an industry that will never move away. It also draws another industry to the community—heritage tourism—that creates more jobs, new businesses, brings in more money, and generates tax revenue through sales taxes on goods and services. And, it never moves away (Graves et. al. 1997: 33).

How exactly does one arrive at consensus for what constitutes historical significance? What sort of sites should get preserved? Who should reap the benefits (economic, social, and otherwise) of land and property protection? Kennedy's answer is that

> Successful heritage tourism grows out of a community's planning together. By working together—such as through this conference—to build community, we can get to know each other and our individual and mutual needs. The process of building community involves listening to others, making plans, setting goals, fashioning a vision, and remaining true. Sounds like what goes into a good marriage or a happy family......A state or a town can preserve its character if the citizens have agreed upon a vision that incorporates its heritage in its comprehensive plan for the future.

It would seem that Kennedy's rather Clintonesque[185] understanding of the urban American political economy is somewhat naive and unrealistic. To those making such a criticism she admonishes that "Greed and expediency have no place in a functioning, loving family or a functioning, effective community" (Graves et. al. 1997: 36).

The notion that historic preservation and economic development are in fact compatible is not new; many adherents

---

[185] Much of her language sounds like one of the historic preservation stump speeches given by former HUD secretary Henry Cisneros. In the sixth installment of a series of essays dealing with urban America, Cisneros (1996) hypocritically declared that:

> I believe that more emphasis needs to be given to history, linked to culture, in asset-oriented strategies to strengthen older urban neighborhoods. Historic preservation, in the sense of preserving and renovating valuable structures in ways that they remain affordable to current residents, is certainly an important component. But traditional preservation should be seen as one part of a program that brings out the history of the community more broadly in ways suggested by Dolores Hayden: heightening awareness of key political and social, as well as architectural, themes, all in the context of place. Hayden also stressed the value of community public histories as giving "power to communities to define their own collective pasts." Consistent with the tenets of the asset-based approach, the benefits will not be gained unless community residents do it for themselves--unless they own the process--but there is ample room for historic preservation professionals to provide guidance and assistance along the way.

The question follows: what about Allen Parkway Village? And the scores of other developments like it around the country? Cisneros's lofty rhetoric rings hollow and is utterly unprincipled; there are many examples where as HUD secretary he acted to deliberately destroy community self-determination when it was politically necessary or expedient to do so. Cisneros' anti-union leadership of Univision since leaving HUD only reaffirms what community advocates have known about him for a long time: he is a businessman and bureaucrat, not a historic preservationist.

of such a view are also under the similarly liberal notion that "development" and environmental protection are not necessarily at odds with one another. The solution in many forward thinking urban locales has been the embracement of various "smart growth" initiatives that seek to maintain a high quality of life with aggressive economic development and growth. It goes without saying, of course, that the primary consideration in these schemes goes to capital, not community. That is, when civic concerns clash with economic ones, there is almost never a consideration that the business entity must shut down or submit to community control; the community is expected to modify its position so as to accommodate the "jobs," "growth," and "progress" that are as immutable as Newton's laws and constitute the lifeblood of American consumer capitalism. Another problem with such notions is that not only are affected communities, especially minority communities and the poor, not allowed to meaningfully participate in the "redevelopment" schemes cooked up for their benefit by city hall and the developers in their rolodexes, but the historical foundations or justifications of such efforts are based on parochial and Eurocentric notions of significance. "Military sites" or "ships of the explorers" are worthy of commemoration, not to mention millions of dollars of taxpayer expenditure, but public housing developments must be carefully watched, lest commemorating them cuts too closely to uncomfortable truths such as historical and ongoing institutional racism (i.e. segregation), for example. When community residents vocally and repeatedly reject the attempted "renaissances" of their neighborhoods in favor of something more locally and communally planned, for instance, the usual response—in Texas at least—is to accuse the community members of being "naive," "stupid," "emotional," "obstructionary," engaged in "NIMBY-ism" (Not In My Back Yard), or worse. Still, these heroic and downtrodden citizens fight and persevere. The awesome courage displayed by concerned Texas citizens determined to prevent the exploitation, commodification, and gentrification of their communities is the kind of fortitude and "Texas Pride" that really matters but is all too often ignored or buried.

Although to some I might have engaged in an extended "bashing" of Texas in this study, I do not wish to be misunderstood; my view is that the Texas Myth and the ideology of Texas Pride are not <u>all</u> rubbish. Modern Texas did emerge from a powerful convergence of historical forces and Texans should be justifiably proud of their unique and exciting history. But one of the most important forces—ultimately <u>the</u> most important force in my opinion—shaping this history was slavery. Slavery—or rather the "freedom" to engage in slavery—was the primary cause of the Texas Revolution, affected debates regarding the annexation of Texas to the United States, played a considerable role during the Mexican-American War and in Manifest Destiny generally, and, of course, was the reason why Texas joined the Confederacy at the start of the Civil War. The eradication of slavery in America has not terminated racism, and it most definitely has not ended racism in Texas. The legacies of slavery and slave trading have left deep emotional, spiritual, and psychological wounds in our collective consciousness, and the healing cannot begin until we begin to acknowledge and address the sources of this hurt with candor and with vigor.

APPENDIX A: A NEW DIRECTION FOR HISTORY AND ARCHAEOLOGY IN TEXAS (AND ELSEWHERE)

Museums, landmarks, and commemmorations should not simply be cavalier displays and flourishes exalting the achievements or whatever group happens to wield power at a moment in time. And archaeologists and historians—most of whom at least claim to be performing objective analysis and not propaganda—should not be engaged in the process of literally writing out of existence the stories of the colonized and dispossessed.

How, then, should historical and archaeological narratives be written? Is consultation with descendant communities enough? Are outreach and teaching sufficient correctives to the conflicting "historicities" mentioned by Trouillot? (1995). According to Trouillot (1995: 150), a key factor in the production of morally acceptable historical narratives is "authenticity." For Trouillot authenticity

> implies a relation with what is known that duplicates the two sides of historicity; it engages us both as actors and

> narrators. Thus, authenticity cannot reside in attitudes toward a discrete past kept alive through narratives. Whether it invokes, claims, or rejects The Past, authenticity obtains only in regard to current practices that engage us as witnesses, actors, and commentators—including practices of historical narration....only in the present can we be true or false to the past we choose to acknowledge.

Trouillot's recommendation requires a change of perspective. Historical sites (and all historical representations), therefore, should engage visitors as active participants and should actively encourage them to presentize and personalize history. In other words, "history" should not be conceived of as an abstract "thing" based on a "fetishism of the facts premised on an antiquated model of the natural sciences" (p. 151), but as a dynamic instrument whose meaning is constantly shifting and contingent. This sort of "authentic" approach not only can serve to empower a deeper sense of historical appreciation, but can also hopefully address some of the historically constituted power imbalances that go into the writing of historical narratives. The key point to re-emphasize here is to recognize that the past—or rather pastness itself—is a position. Only by embracing the situatedness of state retrospection and the other present circumstances that give rise to our selective appreciation of history, will we fully learn and take responsibility for the fact that too often "history" and propaganda are interchangeable.[186]

How does one place such understanding into practice? Practical advice is available. Appendix B of James W. Loewen's *Lies Across America* (1999: 459), for example, contains "ten questions to ask at a historic site" and I strongly recommend that the Texas historic preservation establishment read and heed Loewen's comments. Because these questions are a good "how-to" for people to follow, I reproduce them here:

> 1. When did this location become a historic site? (When was the marker or monument put up? Or the house "interpreted"?) How did that time differ from ours? From

---

[186] One of the best essays ever written on the subject of history and historization is Mark Twain's 1914 essay "How to Make History Dates Stick" (Twain 1963[1914]: 495-516. In this satiric and funny essay Twain provides a "valuable hint" for notetakers: "When a man is making a speech and you are to follow him don't jot down notes to speak from, jot down *pictures*."

the time of the event or person commemorated?
2. Who sponsored it? Representing which participant group's point of view? What was their position in social structure when the event occurred? When the site went "up?"
3. What were the sponsors' motives? What were their ideological needs and social purposes? What were their values?
4. Who is the intended audience for the site? What values were they trying to leave for us, today? What does the site ask us to go and do or think about?
5. Did the sponsors have government support? At what level? Who was ruling the government at the time? What ideological arguments were used to get the government to acquiesce?
6. Who is left out? What points of view go largely unheard? How would the story differ if a different group told it? Another political party? Race? Sex? Class? Religious group?
7. Are there problematic (insulting, degrading) words or symbols that would not be used today, or by other groups?
8. How is the site used today? Do traditional rituals continue to connect today's public to it? Or is it ignored? Why?
9. Is the presentation accurate? What actually happened? What historical sources tell of the event, people, or period commemorated at the site?
10. How does this site fit in with others that treat the same era? Or subject? What other people lived and events happened then but are not commemorated? Why?

If the perspectives outlined by Loewen begin to be placed into practice, then hopefully heretorore ommitted histories and archaeologies will begin to be conducted and the pertinent stories they tell will start to be commemmorated.[187] Texas has had a bloody race relations history; but wishful thinking, blithe optimism, and bland and colorless storytelling will not make that past go away. There are many opportunities to conduct African American archaeology and history in Texas. Some suggestions include:

1.) Given the history outlined in this dissertation, it is likely that there are (perhaps) dozens of slave shipwrecks lying off the Texas coast and along inland riverbanks. Because the maritime history of Texas has been woefully misconceived, many of these wrecks are not thought of as "slave ships." They should be.

---

[187] This, of course, means that there needs to be much more archaeology conducted and run by minorities themselves. At the museum end of things, I believe that "experimental" museum design and other types of techniques should be used to draw visitors in as participants as much as possible. "Living museums" should not just act out an imagined (and largely white) fantasy of the past, but should also allow visitors to draw conclusions about the relevance of that history for today. This is especially true with museums that in some way concern themselves with race.

2.) Plantation sites in Texas and elsewhere should not be talking about masters' clothing and silverware during their tours. Most of the inhabitants of antebellum plantations were enslaved African Americans. What were their lives like? There needs to be far more investigative work into this area in Texas. The excavations that have been carried out at the Levi Jordan Plantation site in Brazoria county over the years are a good example of the sort of participatory archaeology that can serve as a model for future work.

3.) Because Texas thought of itself as unconquered after the Civil War, there was a significant amount of reconstruction violence in the state. More research needs to be conducted into this aspect of Texas race relations and its lingering effects into the present.

One could produce many other examples. My hope is that Texas history stops being so pale, male, and stale, and starts becoming more pigmented, multicultural, and energized.

REFERENCES

Abernethy, Francis E., Patrick B. Mullen, and Alan B. Govenar (Eds.)
1996 *Juneteenth Texas*. Denton, TX: University of North Texas Press.

Adams, Ephraim D. (Ed.)
1917 *British Diplomatic Correspondence Concerning the Republic of Texas, 1838-1946*. Austin: Texas State Historical Association.

Addington, Wendell G.
1950 Slave Insurrections in Texas. *Journal of Negro History*, XXXV (Oct.1950).

Ailey, Alvin with Peter A. Bailey
1995 *Revelations: The Autobiography of Alvin Ailey*. New York: Birch Lane Press.

Affleck, Thomas
1855 The Duties of an Overseer, taken from Affleck's Cotton Plantation Record and Account Book. *De Bow's Review*, XXIII (March 1855): 339-345.

Amin, Samir
1989 *Eurocentrism*. New York: Monthly Review Press.

Andrews, William L. (Ed.)
1996 *The Oxford Frederick Douglass Reader*. New York: Oxford University Press.

Aptheker, Herbert
1971 *Afro-American History: The Modern Era*. New York:

Citadel Press.
1963 *American Negro Slave Revolts.* New York: International Publishers. (originally published 1943).

Arnold III, J. Barto
1998 The Denbigh Project. Available online at: http://nautarch.tamu.edu/projects/denbigh/denbigh.html.
1987 Marine magnetometer Survey of Archaeological Materials Found Near Galveston, Texas. *Texas Antiquities Committee Publication No. 10.*

Bailey, Ronald.
1997 "Out of Sight Out of Mind": The Struggle of African American Intellectuals Against the Invisibility of the Slave[ry] Trade in World Economic History. In Thomas D. Boston (Ed.) *A Different Vision: Race and Public Policy, Vol. Two.* pp. 253-279. New York: Routledge.
1992 The Slave(ry) Trade and the Development of Capitalism in the United States: The Textile Industry in New England. In Joseph E. Inikori and Stanley L. Engerman (Eds.) *The Atlantic Slave Trade: Effects on Economies, Societies, and Peoples in Africa, the Americas, and Europe.* pp. 205-246. Durham: Duke University Press.

Baker, T. Lindsay
1999 Review of *The Slave Narratives of Texas* edited by Ron Tyler and Lawrence R. Murphy. *Southwestern Historical Quarterly* Vol. CII, No. 1, July 1999: 120-121.

Baker, T. Lindsay and Julie P. Baker (Eds.)
1997 *Till Freedom Cried Out: Memories of Texas Slave Life.* College Station: Texas A&M University Press.

Barber, Russell J. And Frances F. Berdan
1998 *The Emperor's Mirror: Understanding Cultures Through Primary Sources.* Tucson: The University of Arizona Press.

Barker, Eugene Campbell
1926 (As editor). *The Papers of Stephen F. Austin.* 3 vols. Washington, DC, 1924, 1928. Austin, 1926.
1925 *The Life of Stephen F. Austin, Founder of Texas, 1793-1836.* Nashville: Cokesbury Press.
1924 *The Influence of Slavery in the Colonization of Texas.* Austin, TX: Texas State Historical Association.
1902 The African Slave Trade in Texas. *The Quarterly of the Texas State Historical Association,* Volume VI: 145-158.

Barr, Alwyn
1996 *Black Texans: A History of African-Americans in Texas, 1528-1995.* (2d ed.). Norman: University of Oklahoma Press.
1961 Texas Coastal Defense, 1861-1865. *Southwestern Historical Quarterly,* LXV, 1-31.

Barrera, Mario
1979 *Race and Class in the Southwest.* Notre Dame: University of Notre Dame Press.

Barsky, Robert
1997 *Noam Chomsky: A Life of Dissent.* Cambridge, MA: MIT Press.

Bass, George F.
1996 Ships and Shipwrecks in the Americas. (Ed.). London: Thames and Hudson.
1975 Archaeology Beneath the Sea. New York: Walker and Co.

Baughman, James P.
1972 *The Mallorys of Mystic: Six Generations in American Maritime Enterprise.* Middletown, CT: Wesleyan University Press.
1968 *Charles Morgan and the Development of Southern Transportation.* Nashville: Vanderbilt University Press.

Beeth, Howard and Cary D. Wintz (Eds.)
1992 *Black Dixie: Afro-Texan History and Culture in Houston.* College Station: Texas A&M University Press.

Bergad, Laird W., Fe Iglesias García, and María del Carmen Barcia
1995 *The Cuban Slave Market, 1790-1880.* Cambridge and New York: Cambridge University Press.

Betts, Edwin Morris (Ed.)
1953 *Thomas Jefferson's Farm Book: With Commentary and Relevant Extracts from Other Writings.* Princeton: Princeton University Press.

Binkley, William C. (Ed.)
1936 *Official Correspondence of the Texas Revolution, 1835-1836.* 2 vols. New York.

Blaut, J.M.
1993 *The Colonizer's Model of The World.* New York: Guilford Press.

Bolster, W. Jeffrey
1997 *Black Jacks: African-American Seamen in the Age of Sail.* Cambridge, MA: Harvard University Press.

Bornholst, Jacquelyn Wooley
1971   *Plantation Settlement in the Brazos River Valley, 1820-1860*. M.A. Thesis, Texas A&M University.

Boyd, Eva Jolene
1995   *Noble Brutes: Camels on the American Frontier*. Plano: Republic of Texas Press.

Brack, Gene
1975   *Mexico Views Manifest Destiny*. Albuquerque: University of New Mexico Press.
1974   The Diplomacy of Racism: Manifest Destiny and Mexico, 1821-1848. *The Forum Series*. St. Charles, MO: Forum Press.

Braudel, Fernand
1972   The Mediterranean and the Mediterranean World in the Age of Philip II, Vol. I. Originally published 1949, revised 1966. Translated from the French by Siân Reynolds.

Breitman, George (Ed.)
1990   *Malcolm X Speaks: Selected Speeches and Statements*. New York: Grove Weidenfeld.

Brewer, J. Mason
1968   *American Negro Folklore*. Chicago: Quadrangle Books.
1953   *The Word on the Brazos*. Austin: University of Texas Press.

Brill, Harry
1999   Partners in Deceit: The Bureau of Labor Statistics (BLS) and the Census Bureau. *Z Magazine* September 1999: 39-44.

British Consulate Papers
Var. *Annual Reports of the British Consulate, Galveston, Texas, on Shipping, Navigation, Trade, Commerce, Agriculture, and Industry to the British Foreign Office, 1950-1861.* Center for American History, University of Texas at Austin.

Bullard, Robert D.
1992 Housing Problems and Prospects in Contemporary Houston. In *Black Dixie: Afro-Texan History and Culture in Houston*, edited by Howard Beeth and Cary D. Wintz, pp.236-252. Texas A&M University Press, College Station.
1987 *Invisible Houston: The Black Experience in Boom and Bust.* Texas A&M University Press, College Station.

Campbell, Randolph B.
1993 *Sam Houston and the American Southwest.* New York: Harper Collins College Publishers.
1989 *An Empire for Slavery: The Peculiar Institution in Texas, 1821-1865.* Baton Rouge: Louisiana State University Press.

Cantrell, Gregg
1999 *Stephen F. Austin, Empresario of Texas.* New Haven: Yale University Press.

Caren, Eric C. (Ed.)
1999 *Texas Extra: A Newspaper History of the Lone Star State, 1835-1935.* Edison, NJ: Castle Books.

Carr, J.T., Jr.
1967 *Climate and Physiography of Texas.* Report 53. Austin:

Texas Development Board.

Cartwright, Gary
1991　*Galveston: A History of the Island.* Forth Worth: Texas Christian University Press.

Chalberg, John C. (Ed.)
1992　*Slavery: Opposing Viewpoints.* San Diego: Greenhaven Press.

Chapa, Juan Bautista
1997　*Texas and Northeastern Mexico, 1630-1690* (edited by William C. Foster). Austin: University of Texas Press.

Chávez Leyva, Yolanda
2000　Crossing Bridges/Burning Bridges: Tejas and the Loss of the Mexican North. *La Voz de Esperanza* 13(1), Feb. 2000, pp. 3-6.

Chipman, Donald E.
1992　*Spanish Texas 1519-1821.* Austin: University of Texas Press.

Chomsky, Noam
1996　*Power and Prospects: Reflections on Human Nature and the Social Order.* Boston: South End Press.
1993　*Year 501: The Conquest Continues.* Boston: South End Press.
1993　*Language and Thought.* Wakefield, RI: Moyer Bell.
1989　*Necessary Illusions: Thought Control in Democratic Societies.* Boston: South End Press.
1987　The Manufacture of Consent. In James Peck (Ed.) *The Chomsky Reader.* New York: Pantheon. (speech originally delivered December 9, 1984).

1987 The Responsibility of Intellectuals. In James Peck (Ed.) *The Chomsky Reader.* New York: Pantheon. (orig. published 1966).

Christian, Charles M.
1995 *Black Saga.* Boston: Houghton Mifflin.

Cisneros, Henry
1996 Preserving Everybody's History. Sixth in a series of essays. Online at: http://www.huduser.org/publications/hsgpolicy/secessays/essay6.txt. Washington, D.C. December 1996

Cochran, Hamilton
1958 *Blockade Runners of the Confederacy.* Indianapolis: Bobbs-Merrill.

Cohn, Michael and Michael K.H. Platzer
1978 *Black Men of the Sea.* New York: Dodd, Mead & Company.

Cogswell, David
1996 *Chomsky for Beginners.* New York: Writers and Readers Publishing, Inc.

Cotham, Edward T. Jr.
1998 *Battle on the Bay: The Civil War Struggle for Galveston.* Austin: University of Texas Press.

Cowling, Anne
1926 *The Civil War Trade of the Lower Rio Grande Valley.* Unpublished Masters Thesis, The University of Texas at Austin.

Crossley-Holland, Kevin
1985 *Folktales of the British Isles.* New York: Pantheon Books.

Crow, John Burchell
1957 *Confederate Military Operations in Texas, 1861-1865.* M.A. Thesis, North Texas State College.

Cumberland, Charles C.
1947 The Confederate Loss and Recapture of Galveston, 1862-1863. *Southwestern Historical Quarterly,* LI, 109-30.

Curlee, Abigail
1932 *A Study of Texas Slave Plantations, 1822 to 1865.* Unpublished Ph.D. Thesis, University of Texas at Austin.

Delvac, William F., Susan Escherich, and Bridget Hartman
1995 *Affordable Housing Through Historic Preservation: A Case Study Guide to Combining the Tax Credits.* Co-produced by the U.S. Department of the Interior, National Park Service, and the National Trust for Historic Preservation. Washington D.C.: Government Printing Office.

Du Bois, W.E.B.
1969 *The Suppression of the African Slave Trade to the United States of America, 1638-1870.* New York: Schocken Books (reprint of the 1896 edition).
1935 *Black Reconstruction in America.* New York: 1935
1903 *The Souls of Black Folk.* New York: Dover Publications.

Ellenberger, Matthew
1985 Illuminating the Lesser Lights: Notes on the Life of

Albert Clinton Horton. *Southwestern Historical Quarterly* 88, 363-386 (April 1985).

Ellis, L. Tuffy
1973   Maritime Commerce on the Far Western Gulf, 1861-1865. *Southwestern Historical Quarterly*, 77 no. 2 (Oct. 1973).

Escott, Paul
1979   *Slavery Remembered: A Record of Twentieth-Century Slave Narratives.* Chapel Hill: University of North Carolina Press.

Fabre, Geneviéve and Robert O'Meally (Eds.)
1994   *History and Memory In African-American Culture.* New York: Oxford University Press.

Fannin Jr., James W.
1904   J.W. Fannin, Jr. to Major Francis Belton, August 27, 1835. Fannin Correspondence. *Southwestern Historical Quarterly VII,* April 1904, pp. 320.

Favata Martin, A. and Jose B. Fernandez (Eds.)
1993   *The Account: Alvar Nunez Cabeza de Vaca's Relacion.* Houston: Publico Press.

Feagin, Joe
1988   *Free Enterprise City: Houston in Political-Economic Perspective.* New Brunswick: Rutgers University Press.

Featherstonhaugh, George W.
1844   *Excursion Through the Slave States: From Washington on the Potomac to the Frontier of Mexico, with Sketches*

of Popular Manners and Geological Notices. New York.

Foner, Eric
1988 *Reconstruction: America's Unfinished Revolution 1863-1877.* New York: Harper and Row.

Francaviglia, Richard V.
1998 *From Sail to Steam.* Austin: University of Texas Press.

Franklin, John Hope and Alfred A. Moss, Jr.
1988 *From Slavery to Freedom* (6th ed.). New York: Alfred A. Knopf.

Frazier, Thomas R. (Ed.)
1970 *Afro-American History: Primary Sources.* New York: Harcourt, Brace & World.

Frederickson, George M.
1988 *The Arrogance of Race.* Hanover, NH: Wesleyan University Press.

Gallaway, B.P. (Ed.)
1994 *Texas, the Dark Corner of the Confederacy.* (third edition). Austin: University of Texas Press.

Gamble, Clive
1997 Review of Geoffrey Irwin's The Prehistoric Exploration and Colonisation of the Pacific. *Pacific Studies,* Vol. 20, No. 2—June 1997.

Gaspar, David Barry and Darlene Clark Hine (Eds.)
1996 *More Than Chattel.* Bloomington: Indiana University Press.

Genovese, Eugene D.
1974   *Roll, Jordan Roll: The World the Slaves Made.* New York: Vintage.

Giggal, Kenneth
1988   *Classic Sailing Ships.* Stamford, CT: Longmeadow Press.

Gilroy, Paul
1993   *The Black Atlantic: Modernity and Double Consciousness.* Cambridge: Harvard University Press.
1992   Cultural Studies and Ethnic Absolutism. In Grossberg et. al. *Cultural Studies* pp. 187-198. New York: Routledge.

Gordon, Edmund T.
1998   *Disparate Diasporas: Identity and Politics in an African-Nicaraguan Community.* Austin: University of Texas Press.

Graham, Don
2000   Wayne's World. *Texas Monthly,* March, 2000.

Graves, Stanley O., Lisa A. Harvell, and Dan K. Utley (Eds.)
1997   *On Sacred Soil: Preserving Military Sites of the Nineteenth Century.* Proceedings of the Nineteenth Century Texas Military Sites Conference. Austin: Texas Historical Commission.

Gray, William F.
1965   *From Virginia to Texas, 1835: Diary of Col. Wm. F. Gray, Giving Details of His Journeys to Texas and Return in 1835-1836 and Second Journey to Texas in 1837.* Houston: Fletcher Young, 1965. Originally published by Gray, Dillaye & Co., Printers, 1909.

Grimshaw, Anna (Ed.).
1992   *The C.LR. James Reader.* Oxford: Blackwell.

Gutman, Herbert G.
1976   *The Black Family in Slavery and Freedom, 1750-1925.* New York: Pantheon Books.
1975   *Slavery and the Numbers Game.* Urbana: University of Illinois Press.

The Handbook of Texas (Walter Prescott Webb, Editor-in-Chief)
1952   Austin: Texas State Historical Association.

The Handbook of Texas Online
1998   http://www.tsha.utexas.edu

Harrison, Ira E. and Faye V. Harrison (Eds.)
1999   *African-American Pioneers in Anthropology.* Urbana and Chicago: University of Illinois Press.

Haygood, Tamara
1992   Use and Distribution of Slave Labor in Harris County, Texas, 1836-60. In Howard Beeth and Cary D. Wintz (Eds.) *Black Dixie: Afro-Texan History and Culture in Houston,* pp. 32-53.

Hedrick, Layne
1999   The Caney Creek Steamboat Wreck. Online at: http://aleister.home.texas.net/title_page.html

Henson, Margaret Swett and Deolece Parmelee
1993   *The Cartwrights of San Augustine: Three Generations of Agrarian Entrepreneurs in Nineteenth-Century Texas.* Austin: Texas State Historical Association.

Hobsbawm, Eric and Terence Ranger (Eds.)
1983　*The Invention of Tradition*. Cambridge: Cambridge University Press.

Holmes, Steven A.
2000　Census blamed in internment of Japanese: Scholars Study Wartime Bureau. *The New York Times*, March 17, 2000 (online version).

Howard, Warren
1963　*American Slavers and the Federal Law 1837-1862*. Berkeley: University of California Press.

Hoyt, Steven D., Eugene R. Foster, and James S. Schmidt
1998　*Intensive Archival Research, Close-Order Magnetometer Survey, Dating, and Offshore Diving, Houston-Galveston Navigation Channels, Texas Project, Galveston, Harris, Liberty, and Chambers Counties, Texas Offshore, Galveston Bay, and Houston Ship Channel*. Prepared by Espey Huston & Associates, Inc. Submitted to United States Army, Corps of Engineers, Galveston District.

Hoyt, Steven D. and James S. Schmidt
1997　*Diving Assessments for Twenty-Six Localities Sabine Pass Channel Jefferson County, Texas Cameron Parish, Louisiana*. Prepared by Espey Huston & Associates, Inc. Submitted to United States Army, Corps of Engineers, Galveston District.

Hyman, Harold M.
1984　William Marsh Rice's Credit Ratings, 1846-1866. *Houston Review*, 6 (1984): 91-96.

Inikori, Joseph E. and Stanley L. Engerman (Eds.)

1992 *The Atlantic Slave Trade: Effects on Economies, Societies, and Peoples in Africa, the Americas, and Europe.* pp. 205-246. Durham: Duke University Press.

Institute of Texan Cultures
1975 *The Afro-American Texans.* Principal Researcher: Melvin M. Sance, Jr.

Ivins, Molly
2000 Lies, Half Lies and Pioneers. *The Progressive Populist,* 1 April: 22. Storm Lake, IA.

Jackson, Donald
1985 *Voyages of the Steamboat Yellowstone.* New York: Ticknor and Fields.

Jackson, Jesse
2000 Stripped of the Right to Vote. *The Progressive Populist* April 15, 2000: 19.

James, C.L.R.
1963 *The Black Jacobins.* New York: Vintage.

Jay, William
1835 *Slavery in America or an Inquiry into the Character and Tendency of the American Colonization and American Anti-Slavery Societies.* New York, Leavitt, Lord; Boston, Crocker & Brewster.

Jenkins, John H. (Ed.)
1973 *The Papers of the Texas Revolution, 1835-1836.* Austin: Presidial Press.

Johnson, Lenwood

1998 Personal Interview, 25 March 1998.

Jordan, Terry G.
1989 Germans and Blacks in Texas. *States of Progress: Germans and Blacks in America over 300 Years. Lectures from the Tricentennial of the Germantown Protest Against Slavery*, edited by Randall M. Miller. Philadelphia: The German Society of Pennsylvania.
1966 *German Seed in Texas Soil: Immigrant Farmers in Nineteenth Century Texas.* Austin: University of Texas Press.

Jordan, Terry G., J.L. Bean, and William M. Holmes
1984 *Texas: A Geography.* Boulder: Westview Press.

Katz, William Loren
1996 *The Black West.* New York: Touchstone.

Lowe, Richard and Randolph B. Campbell
1976 The Slave-Breeding Hypothesis: A Demographic Comment on the Buying and Selling States. *Journal of Southern History*, XLII (August 1976), 401-412.

Martin, Peter
1985 Das rebellische Eigentum: Vom Kampf der Afroamerikaner gegen ihre Versklavung. Hamburg: Junius Verlag.

Maxwell, Louise Passey
1997 Freedmantown: The Origins of a Black Neighborhood in Houston, 1865-1880. In Williams, David A. (Ed) *Bricks Without Straw: A Comprehensive History of African Americans in Texas*, pp. 125-152.

McColley, Robert
1973 *Slavery and Jeffersonian Virginia.* Urbana: University of Illinois Press.

McCown, Leonard Joe
1974 *Indianola Scrap Book.* Austin: Jenkins Publishing.

McDavid, Carol and David W. Babson (Eds.)
1997 In the Realm of Politics: Prospects for Public Participation in African-American and Plantation Archaeology. *Historical Archaeology* 31(3).

McGhee, Fred L.
1999 How Archaeology is Helping to Destroy a Historic Houston Neighborhood. Paper presented at the American Anthropological Association Conference, Chicago, IL.
1997 *Toward a Postcolonial Nautical Archaeology.* Unpublished Master's Thesis, Department of Anthropology, University of Texas at Austin.

McNutt, Jim (Ed.)
1986 *These Kind of Times: Afro-American Communities in Houston.* San Antonio: Institute of Texan Cultures.

Meiners, Fredericka
1982 A History of Rice University: The Institute Years, 1907-1963. *Rice University Studies Special Publication.* Houston: Rice University.

Mel Fisher Maritime Historical Society
1995 *A Slave Ship Speaks: The Wreck of the Henrietta Marie.* Museum Exhibition Booklet. Mel Fisher Maritime Historical Society, Key West.

Merk, Frederick
1972 *Slavery and the Annexation of Texas.* New York: Alfred A. Knopf.

Mintz, Sidney W.
1985 *Sweetness and Power.* New York: Viking Penguin.
1984 *Caribbean Transformations.* New York: Columbia University Press.

Mintz, Sidney W. And Richard Price
1992 *The Birth of African-American Culture: An Anthropological Perspective.* Beacon Press, Boston.

Montejano, David
1987 *Anglos and Mexicans in the Making of Texas, 1836-1986.* Austin: University of Texas Press.

Morris, Thomas D.
1996 *Southern Slavery and the Law 1619-1860.* Chapel Hill: University of North Carolina Press.

Muir, Andrew Forest
1972 William Marsh Rice and His Institute. Edited by Sylvia Stallings Morris. *Rice University Studies,* 58: 2 (Spring 1972).
1964 William Marsh Rice, Houstonian. *East Texas Historical Journal* II (February 1964), 32-39.

Mullin, Michael
1992 *Africa in America: Slave Acculturation and Resistance in the American South and the British Caribbean 1736-1831.* University of Illinois Press, Urbana.

Murry, Ellen N.
1991   *Notes on the Republic*. Washington, Texas: Star of the Republic Museum.

Nevin, David.
1975   *Time-Life Books: The Texans*. New York: Time-Life Books.

Northrup, David (Ed.)
1994   *The Atlantic Slave Trade*. Lexington, MA: D.C. Heath and Company.

Notes and Fragments
1906   Immigration to Texas and the Domestic Slave Trade. *Southwestern Historical Quarterly*, IX (April 1906), 282-291.
1904   Some Fannin Correspondence. *Texas Historical Association Quarterly*, VII (April 1904), 318-325.

O' Connor, Robert F. (Ed.)
1986   *Texas Myths*. College Station: Texas A&M University Press.

Official Records of the Union and Confederate Navies in the War of the Rebellion
1894   Edited by LCDR Richard Rush, USN and Robert H. Woods. Washington: Government Printing Office.

Olmstead, Frederick Law
1857   *A Journey Through Texas: Or, A Saddle-Trip on the Southwestern Frontier, With a Statistical Appendix*. New York.

Orser Jr., Charles E.

1996 *A Historical Archaeology of the Modern World.* Plenum Press, New York.

Oliver, Melvin L. and Thomas M. Shapiro
1995 *Black Wealth/White Wealth: A New Perspective on Racial Inequality.* New York: Routledge.

Parmet, Herbert S.
1997 *George Bush: The Life of a Lone Star Yankee.* New York: Scribner.

Pinker, Steven
1994 *The Language Instinct: How the Mind Creates Language.* New York: William Morrow.

Porter, Kenneth Wiggins
1956 Negroes and Indians on the Texas Frontier, 1831-1876. *Journal of Negro History,* XLI (July and Oct. 1956).

Potts, Howard E.
1997 *A Comprehensive Name Index for The American Slave.* Westport, CT: Greenwood Press.

Ramos, Mary G. (Ed.)
1997 *The 1998-1999 Texas Almanac.* Dallas: Dallas Morning News.

Rawick, George P. (Ed.)
1979 *The American Slave: A Composite Autobiography.* Supplement, Series 2: 10 vols.
1977 *The American Slave: A Composite Autobiography.* Supplement, Series 1: 12 vols.
1972 *The American Slave: A Composite Autobiography.* Series 1: 7 vols. Westport, CT: Greenwood Press.

Reichstein, Andreas
1984   Der texanische Unabhängigkeistkrieg 1835/36: Ursachen und Wirkung. Berlin: Dietrich Reimer Verlag.

Ricklis, Robert A.
1996   *The Karankawa Indians of Texas.* Austin: University of Texas Press.

Robbins, Fred
1972   *The Origins and Development of the African Slave Trade Into Texas, 1816-1860.* Unpublished Master's Thesis, University of Houston.
1971   The Origin and Development of the African Slave Trade in Galveston, Texas, and Surrounding Areas. *East Texas Historical Journal* IX (October 1971), 153-162.

Robertson, Claire
1996   Africa Into the Americas? Slavery and Women, The Family, and the Gender Division of Labor. In Gaspar, David Barry and Darlene Clark Hine (Eds.) *More Than Chattel,* pp. 3-40. Bloomington: Indiana University Press.

Robinson, William Morrison
1990   *The Confederate Privateers.* Columbia: University of South Carolina Press. (originally published 1928).

Roemer, Ferdinand
1935   *Texas.* San Antonio: Standard Printing Company.

Rozek, Barbara J.
1993   Galveston Slavery. *Houston Review: History and Culture of the Gulf Coast.* 15, no. 2 (1993).

Said, Edward W.
1994 *The Pen and the Sword.* Monroe, ME: Common Courage Press.
1993 *Culture and Imperialism.* New York: Alfred A. Knopf.
1978 *Orientalism.* New York: Vintage.

Sale, Maggie Montesinos
1997 *The Slumbering Volcano: American Slave Ship Revolts and the Production of Rebellious Masculinity.* Durham: Duke University Press.

Schoen, Harold
1936 The Free Negro in the Republic of Texas. *Southwestern Historical Quarterly 39,* (April, 1936), 292-301.

Shohat, Ella and Robert Stam
1994 *Unthinking Eurocentrism:* New York: Routledge.

Silverthorne, Elizabeth
1986 *Plantation Life in Texas.* College Station: Texas A&M University Press.

Singleton, Theresa A.
1996 The Archaeology of Slave Life. In *Images of the Recent Past: Readings in Historical Archaeology,* edited by Charles E. Orser, Jr. pp. 141-165. Originally published in 1991. Altamira Press, Walnut Creek.

Singleton, Theresa A. and Mark D. Bograd
1995 *The Archaeology of the African Diaspora in the Americas.* Guides to the Archaeological Literature of the Immigrant Experience 2. The Society for Historical Archaeology.

Smith, D. Ryan, Sherry B. Humphreys, Joann V. Pappas, and Ellen N. Murry
1983   *Commerce.* Washington, TX: Star of the Republic Museum.

Solow, Barbara L. (Ed.)
1991   *Slavery and the Rise of the Atlantic System.* New York: Cambridge University Press.

Spaw, Patsy McDonald (Ed.)
1990   *The Texas Senate, Vol. I, Republic to Civil War, 1836-1861.* College Station: Texas A&M University Press.

Steffy, J.R
1994   *Wooden Shipbuilding and the Interpretation of Shipwrecks.* College Station: Texas A&M University Press.

Stephens, A. Ray and William M. Holmes
1989   *Historical Atlas of Texas.* Norman: University of Oklahoma Press.

Stephanson, Anders
1995   *Manifest Destiny: American Expansion and the Empire of Right.* New York: Hill and Wang.

Stenberg, Richard Rollin
1932   *American Imperialism in the Southwest, 1880-1837.* Unpublished Ph.D. dissertation, University of Texas.

Strasburg, Jenny
1998   The Northside: A Place in History. Forgotten Neighborhood. *Corpus Christi Caller-Times,* 8 February:

A8-A9.

Strom, Steven
1986   Cotton and Profits Across the Border: William Marsh Rice in Mexico, 1863-1865. *Houston Review* 8 (1986): 89-96.

Tadman, Michael
1999   Letter to the author dated 16 April 1999.
1996   The Hidden History of Slave Trading in Antebellum South Carolina: John Springs III and Other 'Gentlemen Dealing in Slaves." *South Carolina Historical Magazine* 97 No. 1 (January 1996): 6-29.
1996a *Speculators and Slaves: Masters, Traders, and Slaves in the Old South.* Madison: University of Wisconsin Press (originally published 1989).
1993   Slave Traders. In *Encyclopedia of the Confederacy* edited by Richard N. Current (Ed. in chief) pp. 1451-1453. New York: Simon & Schuster.

Takaki, Ronald
1993   *A Different Mirror: A History of Multicultural America.* Boston: Back Bay Books.
1990   *Iron Cages.* New York: Oxford University Press.

The Texas Slavery Project at the University of Houston
2000   Online at: http://www.texasslaveryproject.uh.edu/

Thomas, Hugh
1997   *The Slave Trade.* New York: Simon and Schuster.

Thomas, Lorenzo
1996   The African-American Folktale and J. Mason Brewer. In Abernethy, Francis E., Patrick B. Mullen, and Alan B.

Govenar (Eds.) *Juneteenth Texas*, pp. 223-234. Denton, TX: University of North Texas Press.

Throckmorton, P. (Ed.)
1987 *The Sea Remembers*. New York: Weidenfeld & Nicolson.

Trouillot, Michel-Rolph
1995 *Silencing the Past: Power in the Production of History*. Boston: Beacon Press.

Turner, Frederick
1992 *Beyond Geography: The Western Spirit Against the Wilderness*. New Brunswick: Rutgers University Press.

Twain, Mark
1963 How to Make History Stick. In Charles Neider (Ed.) *The Complete Essays of Mark Twain*. Originally published 1914. Garden City, NY: Doubleday.

Tyler, Ron, and Murphy, Lawrence R. (eds).
1974 *The Slave Narratives of Texas*. Austin: State House Press.

Tyler, Ronnie C.
1972 Fugitive Slaves in Mexico. *Journal of Negro History*, LVII (1972), 2-5
1970 Cotton on the Border, 1861-1865. *Southwestern Historical Quarterly* 73 (April, 1970), pp. 456-477.

United States Congress
Var. *Congressional Records*, 15, 16, 31, 35, 35 Congresses. Washington D.C., 1817-1860. (Printed in *Niles Weekly Register*, Baltimore).
Var. American State Papers. 14-17 Congress. Washington

D.C., 1815-1822.

Ward, William A.
1983 The Saga of the Will O' The Wisp: The Story of a Confederate Blockade Runner. *In Between* 164 (Nov. 1983): 1.

Williams, Amelia W. and Eugene C. Barker (Eds.)
1938 *The Writings of Sam Houston.* (8 vols.). Austin: University of Texas Press. (1938-1943).

Williams, David A. (Ed.)
1997 *Bricks Without Straw: A Comprehensive History of African Americans in Texas.* Austin: Eakin Press.

Williams, Patrick and Laura Chrisman (Eds.)
1994 *Colonial Discourse and Post-Colonial Theory.* New York: Columbia University Press.

Williams, Raymond
1977 *Marxism and Literature.* Oxford: Oxford University Press.

Willis Jr., William S.
1970 Anthropology and Negroes on the Southern Colonial Frontier. In *The Black Experience in America: Selected Essays.* Ed. James C. Curtis and Lewis L. Gould, 33-50. Austin: University of Texas Press.

Wilson, Gary E. (Ed.)
1985 The Ordeal of William H. Cowdin and the Officers of the Forty-Second Massachusetts Regiment: Union Prisoners in Texas. *East Texas Historical Journal* 23 (Spring 1985), 16-26.

1984   Diary of a Union Prisoner. *Southern Studies* 23 (Spring 1984), 103-119.

Wise, Stephen R.
1988   *Lifeline of the Confederacy.* Columbia: University of South Carolina Press.

Wolf, Eric R.
1982   *Europe and the People Without History.* Berkeley: University of California Press.

Wolff, Linda
1999   *Indianola and Matagorda Island, 1837-1887.* Austin: Eakin Press.

Z Magazine
2000   For Justice and Against Prison. Commentary. *Z Magazine* March, 2000, 4).

Zinn, Howard
1991   *Declarations of Independence.* New York: Harper Perennial.
1980   *A People's History of the United States.* New York: Harper Perennial.

www.ingramcontent.com/pod-product-compliance
Lightning Source LLC
Chambersburg PA
CBHW050424170426
43201CB00008B/538